D0890230

METAPHORS DEAD AND ALIVE,
SLEEPING AND WAKING

METAPHORS DEAD AND ALIVE, SLEEPING AND WAKING

A Dynamic View

CORNELIA MÜLLER

UNIVERSITY OF CHICAGO PRESS

CHICAGO AND LONDON

CORNELIA MÜLLER is professor of applied linguistics at European University
Viadrina in Frankfurt (Oder). She is coeditor of several books, the journal *Gesture*
and its accompanying book series, and is the author of *Co-verbal Gestures: Cultural
History—Theory—Cross-linguistic Comparison.*

The University of Chicago Press, Chicago 60637
The University of Chicago Press, Ltd., London
© 2008 by The University of Chicago
All rights reserved. Published 2008
Printed in the United States of America

17 16 15 14 13 12 11 10 09 08   1 2 3 4 5

ISBN-13: 978-0-226-54825-8   (cloth)
ISBN-10: 0-226-54825-2   (cloth)

Library of Congress Cataloging-in-Publication Data

Müller, Cornelia, 1960–
    Metaphors dead and alive, sleeping and waking : a dynamic view / Cornelia Müller.
        p. cm.
    Includes bibliographical references and index.
    ISBN-13: 978-0-226-54825-8   (cloth : alk. paper)
    ISBN-10: 0-226-54825-2   (cloth : alk. paper)   1. Metaphor.   I. Title.
    PN228.M4M87   2008
    808–dc22

                                                                    2008025297

⊗ The paper used in this publication meets the minimum requirements of the
American National Standard for Information Sciences—Permanence of Paper for
Printed Library Materials, ANSI z39.48-1992.

FOR CHRISTIAN

CONTENTS

☙

ILLUSTRATIONS

Figures

Examples

Tables

ACKNOWLEDGMENTS

This book is a product of many years of public and private reflections concerning metaphors, mental imagery, iconicity in language, and how they relate and bear upon processes and products of thought. This issue has fascinated me for a long time because it challenges one of the taken-for-granted tenets of linguistics, namely, that imagery and iconicity are not relevant features of language. Arbitrariness of signs is what makes language the system it is. Iconicity, imagery, and metaphors are traditionally seen as random facets of language. I believe the book is a further proof that imagery of supposedly dead metaphors is still alive. In an earlier version this book was submitted and accepted as a Habilitation Thesis to the Freie Universität, Berlin, in July 2004.

I am especially grateful to Sakis Kyratzis, David McNeill, and Wallace Chafe for sharing their thoughts both in personal communications as well as through their writings. My own view on metaphors is highly sympathetic to the idea of a single dynamic category as proposed by Kyratzis. McNeill's reflections upon the static and dynamic properties of language in the context of a unified theory of language and gesture have provided important theoretical support for the position I hold. Similarly, Chafe's focus on the dynamic aspects of cognitive organization during speaking has significantly enhanced my own reflections. The pioneering work of Lynne Cameron on the dynamic aspects of metaphors in use has provided inspiration and support for my research approach. And last but not least, I wish to mention the work of Wilhelm Stählin, who wrote an empirical dissertation in 1914 on the psychology of metaphor that determined grades of metaphoricity. Stählin was the first confirmation of my then still tentative reflections on the dynamic nature of metaphor.

During the work on the book I profited from a tremendous range of support from various sides. In the first place, I wish to thank the students who participated in the classes I taught over the past years and who with their fresh minds often hit the critical points right on target. In a similar way I profited from supportive and critical comments on talks that presented earlier stages of my thinking on the vitality of dead metaphors. Without them, the argument proposed in this book would have been significantly less clear cut. The discussions with them helped me greatly in understanding the problems of metaphor theories: they cleared my mind and my argument. I am especially grateful to Alan Cienki for helping me to find the "straight" paths through the wild forests of cognitive linguistic approaches to metaphor. Without his guidance, this book would not only have taken at least one more year, it would have presumably been much less focused and attached to current lines of debate. Special thanks go also to Ray Gibbs and Gerard Steen for encouragement, for providing immediate online and snail mail support and for their inspiring and lucid publications, which seek to bind metaphor research to larger scholarly fields such as cognitive linguistics, stylistics, and psychology. I am extremely grateful to Gerard Steen for sharing and discussing his thoughts on the issues on system and use and language and thought as well as their evolution into a new approach, which distinguishes grammar and usage, language and thought, and symbolic structure and behavior. The dynamic view on metaphor in language use presented in this book is highly sympathetic with these meticulous methodological and theoretical distinctions. I owe a huge amount of debt to David McNeill for discussing my ideas on imagery in language and on a dynamic concept of metaphor as they evolved over the past years and for his always positive and encouraging stance and his ease in giving me company and support on the way to this book. I have also profited greatly from Wallace Chafe's comments on earlier versions of some chapters of this book and from the discussions we conducted on his idea of the flow of consciousness and on the history of American linguistics. Eve Sweetser's vivid and prompt responses to some of my ideas were invaluable because they significantly enhanced my understanding of conceptual metaphor and blending theory and because they greatly helped me to clarify my own assumptions. As always, Adam Kendon helped me shape my thoughts through extended and pleasant conversations; this time I am especially grateful for his company and encouragement along the way as I wrote this book.

I owe a great many thanks to my advisors and former colleagues at the Freie Universität Berlin in the institute of German Philology and especially in German and general linguistics. They have provided institutional and personal support for writing this book. Gisela Klann-Delius and Helmut Richter have been most supportive and generous advisors for many years by now. Their intellectual and personal advice guided me throughout the sometimes difficult process of writing this book. Hans-Heinrich Lieb and Harald Haferland were an important source of inspiration; their critical minds have helped me clarify much of what otherwise would have remained terminological and conceptual haze. Many thanks go to Harald Haferland for sharing his ingenious gift of discovering even the remotest publications, for making them available for me, and for the challenging discussions in the spirit of Ockham's razor. I am very grateful to Ulrike Bohle and Ellen Fricke for their meticulous reading of earlier drafts of the manuscript and to Ellen Fricke for sharing her clear mind and her expertise in formal semantics and cognitive science. I thank Mary Copple for her passionate and fine-grained work on my English expression and for her patience and will to spend sunny weekends on finishing my manuscript. Her meticulous approach to language has helped me to clarify all core concepts that I have been using in this book.

My greatest thanks go to my group of gesture students of the Berlin Gesture Project (now working in our Grammar of Gesture Project at the European University Viadrina in Frankfurt [Oder]). They offered their spare time to get this manuscript ready even on Sundays and until late at night. My thanks go to Janina Beins, Jana Bressem, Gudrun Borgschulte, Silva Ladewig, and Sedinha Teßendorf. Most of all I thank Karin Becker. She did all the drawings, most of the diagrams, and tables; made the layout of the manuscript; and was a constant aid in preventing me from getting lost in piles of books, notes, and papers. Special thanks go to Stefan Rook, who, despite other urgent obligations, redid all the diagrams for publication and found solutions for all technical problems with the manifold types of figures that are included in the book. I am also extremely grateful for the care of Bertolt Fessen who prepared the manuscript for the publisher. Last but not least I would like to thank the crew at the University of Chicago Press for meticulous copyediting.

I dedicate this book to Christian, who throughout the years of thinking about dead metaphors kept reminding me of their aliveness.

TYPOGRAPHICAL CONVENTIONS

FOR TRANSCRIPTS

The following transcription conventions have been used:

Gesture Description

rh	right hand
lh	left hand
bh	both hands
PU	palm oriented upward
PD	palm oriemted downward
PA	palm oriented away from the body
OH	open hand
[text]	square brackets in the verbal line indicate beginning and end of the gesture phrase
text	bold faces indicate the gesture stroke
‖	vertical lines indicate change of configuration within one gesture phrase

Speech transcription

tExt	capitals indicate emphasis
=	cutting off an utterance and beginning of an interruption
/	rising intonation
\	falling intonation
.h	audible inhalation
(.)	micropause
(--)	longer pause (each dash for about 0.25 second pause)
a::	lengthening of vowels
(? 4sec ?)	unintelligible speech with lenght
(...)	ellipsis in the transcript

A basic and commonly held assumption of theories of metaphor is that verbal metaphors may be either dead or alive. The following quote from one of the most influential twentieth-century scholars of metaphor—Max Black—may serve as a representative illustration: "For the only entrenched classification is grounded in the trite opposition (itself expressed metaphorically) between 'dead' and 'live' metaphors" (Black 1993, 25).

Black's polemic statement demonstrates how commonplace the idea of attributing the properties of dead or alive to metaphors is among scholars of metaphor. This well-established classification of metaphors is explicitly challenged by George Lakoff and Mark Turner's claim that a huge amount of so-called dead metaphors (that is, conventional metaphoric expressions) are in fact alive: "Determining whether a given metaphor is dead or just unconsciously conventional is not always an easy matter. . . . However, there are plenty of clear cases of basic conventional metaphors that are alive—hundreds of them—certainly enough to show that what is conventional and fixed need not be dead" (Lakoff and Turner 1989, 130).

Clearly, this claim—first formulated by Lakoff and Mark Johnson in their 1980 monograph *Metaphors We Live By*—implies that the category of "live" metaphors is much larger than generally assumed and encompasses the conventional metaphoric expressions of ordinary language. This conception stands in sharp contrast to traditional views holding that only novel and poetic metaphors are to be considered as vital or alive.

I wish to challenge this commonly shared but empirically unverified view by providing theoretical arguments and empirical evidence in support of the Lakoffian position, namely, that conventional verbal metaphors are for the most part dead *and* alive. Moreover, I shall suggest that this is not only because they supposedly draw upon active conceptual metaphors, as Lakoff, Johnson,

and Turner argue, but also because their metaphoricity is empirically doc-
umentable. Verbal, pictorial, and gestural contexts of conventional verbal
metaphors clearly show that the source domains of conventionalized verbal
metaphors may be active for a given speaker/writer at a given moment in time
and may be not active for another speaker/writer at another moment in time.
This observation has important theoretical consequences for a theory of metaphor since it suggests that metaphoricity is not merely a property of a linguistic item but the cognitive achievement of a speaker/writer or listener/reader.

Furthermore, adopting a cognitive and a usage-based approach to the problem of dead versus live metaphors reveals that metaphoricity is by nature
gradable; it may be more active in one context and less active in another one,
which turns the question of a fixed property—dead versus alive—into a question of the activation of metaphoricity. Note that this implies a shift toward
the production side of metaphors, which contrasts with the more common
focus of metaphor theory and research on the reception side.

In sum, I hold that departing from a cognitive approach to metaphors in
language use reveals that metaphors are a cognitive activity of speakers/writ-
ers and that as such they are inherently dynamic. This dynamic view has fundamental consequences for a theory of metaphor and—as I shall suggest—is
an unfilled gap in contemporary and traditional Western reflections on metaphor.

0.1 Dead and Live Metaphors: Two Examples

Take the following lines as if they were the initial sentences of a newspaper article reporting on the relationship between the leader of the German
Christian Democratic Party, Angela Merkel, and her general secretary, Laurenz Meyer.

Example 1: "In den Schatten stellen" *(to put in the shade)*
In den Schatten stellen will Laurenz Meyer CDU-Chefin Angela
Merkel sicher nicht, aber ein eigenes Profil gewinnen schon.

[Laurenz Meyer certainly does not want to put the leader of the
CDU, Angela Merkel, in the shade, but he does want to create a
distinctive image of himself.] (*Der Tagesspiegel*, October 25,
2000).[1]

Typically, the idiomatic expression "in den Schatten stellen" (to put in
the shade) would be considered a dead metaphor. Traditional theories of

metaphor would assume that its imagistic or source dimension has faded and, therefore, that it would not be consciously perceived by an average reader. Instead, only its figurative meaning should be activated. The standard *Dictionary of German Idiomatic Expressions* paraphrases this figurative meaning as follows: "Shade or shadow: to put something, someone in the shade [Schatten: etwas, jemanden in den Schatten stellen]: make something... appear small, surpass a person in his/her achievements, diminish him/her in the eyes of others" (Röhrich 1994, 1304). Hence, "in den Schatten stellen" (to put in the shade) is a dead metaphor because its concrete, sensory dimension is no longer consciously perceived. In an instructive overview of metaphor theories, Gerhard Kurz summarizes this commonplace understanding of vital metaphors: "Nur eine Metapher, die als solche bewußt ist, ist eine 'lebendige' Metapher." [Only a metaphor which is conscious as such is a "vital" metaphor] (Kurz 1976, 60).

Of course, Paul Ricœur's (1986) famous work entitled "La métaphore vive" is based on the very same line of argument. For him, a metaphor is the creation of a novel sense in the context of a given sentence. Metaphors are per se not accountable on the level of the lexicon; there is no purely lexical criterion to account for the vitality of metaphor. This is, Ricœur holds, because metaphors are not phenomena of lexemes but of sentences or, more precisely, of what he calls "impertinente Prädikation" (impertinent predication). Ricœur 1986, vi).[2]

> To generate a *new* metaphor, at least a sentence is necessary. To put it more precisely, the metaphorical process is to be sought in the main process whose framework is the sentence, namely, the predication. Now, this thesis holds that the semantic extension that takes place within the word is based on a peculiar, unusual use of a predication. The metaphor is an "impertinent predication," that is, one which does not comply with the usual criteria of appropriateness or pertinence that are applicable to predicates.[3]

A metaphor is a function of language use; it emerges in the creation of a novel sentence in which two distant semantic fields clash and provoke a novel metaphoric sense: a vital metaphor. Therefore, a vocabulary must be considered to be full of dead metaphors—to be a cemetery of dead metaphors.

> It is certain that vocabulary is a cemetery of extinguished, obsolete, "dead" metaphors; however, this fact only confirms the thesis that there is no lexical criterion for determining whether or not a metaphor is alive

or dead. Only in the generation of a new sentence, in an act of outrageous predication is a new metaphor created like a spark that flashes when two semantic fields that were hitherto distant from each other collide. In this sense, a metaphor only exists in the instant in which reading lends new life to the collision of the semantic fields and generates the impertinent predication.[4]

Put another way, the fact that "shade" (*Schatten*) in our example above may literally refer to light and shade is supposed to be no longer actively processed by a given reader. Note that Ricœur only regards the process of metaphor comprehension. The process of metaphor production, the process of employing metaphors, is disregarded. Note, furthermore, that the dead metaphor theory (to use a term coined by Lakoff and Turner 1989, 128) has hitherto not made significant efforts to prove that these everyday metaphors are in fact used as dead metaphors; it has merely been taken for granted that nonpoetic language is full of formerly vital or live metaphors.

Yet if we take into consideration the context surrounding the sentence quoted above, things look different. It turns out that the sentence is a caption accompanying two pictures, one of which depicts the leader of the German Christian Democratic Party as a shadow, and the other of which shows the general secretary looking in the direction of his superior's shadow.

The pictures indicate that for the journalist, while working on this article and looking for pictures to accompany it, the formerly dead metaphor was in fact alive. In other words, the pictures depict the source domain of the dead metaphor, and in doing so—and this is my point—they display that its metaphoricity was activated at the moment of composing this ensemble of words and pictures. This specific form of text-picture combination may also be interpreted as a device for activating metaphoricity in the comprehension process of the readers, but this is not what I want to stress initially. Rather, I shall focus on the disregarded side of the metaphorical process: the production side of using seemingly dead metaphors in written and spoken language.

We have just seen that pictures may indicate the activation of dead metaphors by depicting their source domain. Now as such this is not a new observation; activations of metaphoricity are known as revitalizations, or re-motivations of dead metaphors (cf. Stöckl 2004). It is a widespread form of text-picture interaction that has been widely exploited in caricature. See, for instance, the caricature below that depicts someone who is able to jump over his own shadow:

Since the use of the prefix "re-" presupposes that under normal circumstances this metaphor would not be vital or motivated, I will not use it.

IN DEN SCHATTEN STELLEN will Laurenz Meyer CDU-Chefin Angela Merkel sicher nicht, aber ein eigenes Profil gewinnen schon.   Fotos: dpa/imo

Fig. 1. "In den Schatten stellen" (to put in the shade). A dead metaphor comes to life. Text-picture ensemble as an indicator of activated metaphoricity during metaphor production. *Der Tagesspiegel*, October 25, 2000.

Fig. 2. "Über seinen eigenen Schatten springen können" (somebody who is able to jump over his own shadow). Röhrich (1994, 1304).

Instead, I propose the expression "activation of metaphoricity," which implies that the product metaphor is always a result of the procedure for establishing metaphoricity. I am, in this regard, in line with Ricœur's procedural view.

Although this phenomenon may seem hardly surprising as such and has not escaped the attention of metaphor scholars, I consider it to be a first step toward a refutation of the dichotomy dead versus alive because, and this is crucial for the argument I develop, characterizing text-picture combinations of the above kind as revitalizations implies that under normal circumstances this metaphor is dead. In other words, explaining the text-picture combination in terms of revitalization or re-motivation presupposes the dichotomous dead versus alive distinction. It is this dichotomous and static view of verbal metaphors that I am challenging and seeking to replace (that is, supersede) with a dynamic view. This captures the fact that seemingly dead metaphors may potentially be activated during language use, and hence, they must be considered as either sleeping (when showing a low or no degree of activation) or waking (when showing a high degree of activation). We will return to this distinction in more detail later in this chapter.

For now, let us note that the dynamic view does not just rename the well-known role of the verbal context of metaphors. On the contrary, speaking of a dynamic view highlights the assertion that a core element of metaphor is the cognitive activity of individual speakers/hearers; context in this view is not a disembodied entity that determines the metaphoricity of a given verbal item. Rather, this view suggests that context is always provided by a given writer or speaker. As such, it indicates whether the metaphoricity of a lexical item was active for her or him at a given moment in time. Moreover, the context is provided for a reader or listener, and this means that what is salient for a speaker is made salient for a listener too. Thus, we may methodologically exploit the context and use it as a window onto the cognitive processes underlying metaphor production.

But is the metaphoricity of verbal metaphors indeed gradable? One could quite convincingly argue that the example presented above could also be described in terms of the revitalization of a dead metaphor. So far, we have only seen that a seemingly dead metaphor may be active enough to stimulate the pictorial representation of its source domain. Further argumentative support is needed to strengthen the gradability claim. Another example of the same expression, "im Schatten stehen," will provide further support. Consider the verbal expression first:

Example 2: "Aus dem Schatten treten" *(to step out of the shadows)*

Aus dem Schatten will Likud Chef Ariel Scharon heute ins Rampenlicht treten und neuer israelischer Ministerpräsident werden. Seine Chancen dafür stehen gut.

[Today, the leader of the Likud Party, Ariel Scharon, wants to step out of the shadows and into the limelight, and become the

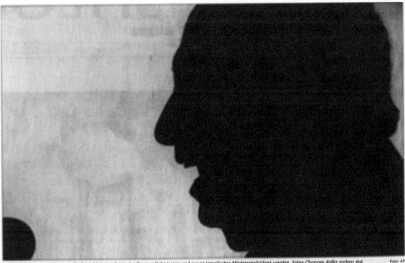

AUS DEM SCHATTEN will Likud-Chef Ariel Scharon heute ins Rampenlicht treten und neuer israelischer Ministerpräsident werden. Seine Chancen dafür stehen gut.　Foto: AP

Fig. 3. "Aus dem Schatten... ins Rampenlicht treten" (to step out of the shadows and into the limelight). Metaphoricity is dynamic and gradable. *Der Tagesspiegel*, February 6, 2001.

new Israeli Prime Minister. His chances are good.] (*Der Tages-spiegel*, June 2, 2001)

In contrast to example 1 above, in example 2 the activation of the source domain of "to step out of the shadows" (aus dem Schatten treten) stimulates verbal elaboration of a specific kind. Here the writer employs an expression that is semantically opposed to the verbal metaphor; more specifically, this opposition functions on the level of the literal meaning of the verbal metaphor, or on the source-domain level. He or she combines "to step out of the shadows" with "into the limelight" (ins Rampenlicht treten), which indicates that the source domain (light and shade as physical states) of the metaphoric expression must have been cognitively activated when this sentence was being written.

Again, this is not a truly new discovery. Recent research on metaphorical discourse, as well as more traditional stylistic research, has documented the same phenomenon and a fairly broad range of similar contextual cues (Heckhausen 1968; Kurz and Pelster 1976; Kyratzis 2003; Stibbe 1996).[5] If, however, we take the pictorial context of the above lines into consideration as well, it turns out that it also depicts the source domain of the dead metaphor. Why? Because Sharon is depicted in the form of a shadow.

Put another way, the source domain of the metaphoric expression is symbolized twice (verbally and pictorially) in addition to the verbal metaphor. This clustering of contextual cues (verbal and pictorial) that I am suggesting[6] indicates a higher degree of activation of metaphoricity in its producer. This proposal is based on a straightforward iconic argument: the more cues point to the source domain, the more active the source domain is at a given moment in time for the language user. In this sense, contextual cues may serve as indicators that allow different degrees of activation in a metaphor to be distinguished. But for the time being, the crucial point is that they indicate that metaphoricity is not only dynamic (that is, a matter of activation) but also gradable (that is, a matter of degrees of activation). In chapters 3 and 5, more evidence for the claimed dynamics will be offered, and chapter 6 presents more evidence in favor of the gradability claim.

Let me conclude the presentation of the two examples given above with a further methodological remark. How can we systematically and reliably decide whether or not metaphoricity is activated in a given speaker at a given moment in time, and if it is, to what degree? My line of argument is rather simple: it takes what is *inter*personally salient to be salient *intra*personally. Thus, if a given speaker foregrounds a metaphor by using contextual cues, such as semantic opposition, that is, verbal or pictorial elaboration of the source domain, then these are empirically observable cues that allow the listener/reader to uncover foregrounded, meaningful elements in a given speaker's/writer's stretch of discourse.

In other words, those aspects of meaning that are perceivably foregrounded are regarded as cognitively active for a given speaker/writer during language production. A metaphor then would show a high degree of activation in a given writer at a given moment in time when it is foregrounded in discourse. Why? Because the seemingly dead metaphor was capable of stimulating elaborations of its source domain—be they verbal or pictorial. This observation is the critical point of departure of the argument unfolded in this book. As I intend to show, it has rather far-reaching consequences for a theory of metaphor.

0.2 Consequences: Sleeping and Waking Metaphors

One seemingly minor consequence of the activation potential inherent in dead metaphors is that it directs our attention to the necessity of inspecting this common set of categories more closely. It is remarkable how little attention has been paid to this fundamental distinction between dead and live, or dead and vital, metaphors. It strikes us as very much taken for granted and as a merely random aspect of what metaphor scholars should be concerned with. As chapter 6 documents in detail, this holds for both the rhetorical and the philosophical traditions as well as for cognitive linguistic accounts of metaphor. Max Black (1993, 25–26) discusses it briefly and only as a preliminary to introducing his notions of emphasis and resonance. George Lakoff and Mark Turner (1989, 128–31) devote some attention to it in their critical evaluation of what they call the dead metaphor theory. In both cases, it merely serves as a foil to the presentation of a specific kind of argument and as a framework for identifying the particular forms of metaphors that are considered to be the core of the respective theoretical accounts. Hence, whereas for Lakoff and Turner the dead metaphors are of major interest, for Black the live or vital ones are of utmost concern. As Black states, "I shall be concerned hereafter only with metaphors needing no artificial respiration, recognized by speaker and hearer as authentically 'vital' or 'active'" (Black 1993, 25). This is a quite notable fact, especially because Black recognizes the coarseness of the established bipolar distinction and introduces a more finely grained tripartite classification, which distinguishes extinct, dormant, and active metaphors. Yet his comments on this new classificatory variant are rather discouraging: "But not much is to be expected of this schema or any more finely tuned substitute" (Black 1993, 25). Clearly, such an evaluation deters one from reflecting more closely upon the nature and range of phenomena that this classification struggles with.

With a different goal but with almost similar consequences, Lakoff and Turner discuss the dead versus alive distinction. Their intention is to show that what traditional metaphor theories (including Black's ground-breaking interaction theory) have considered to be dead metaphors are actually the most vital and active ones because these dead verbal metaphors rest upon highly vital and active conceptual metaphors:

> One reason that some theorists have not come to grips with the fact that ordinary everyday language is inescapably metaphoric is that they hold the belief that all metaphors that are conventional are "dead"—they are not metaphors any longer, though they once might have been. This position which fails to distinguish between conventional metaphors, which are part of our live conceptual system, and historical metaphors that have long since died out, constitutes the Dead Metaphor Theory. (Lakoff and Turner 1989, 128–29)

In a provocative stance, Lakoff and Turner turn the traditional argument upside down: what has hitherto been considered dead is now considered to be the most alive. Hence, instead of taking novel, poetic, and vital metaphors as *the* topic of a metaphor theory, they regard conventionalized, everyday, and only seemingly dead metaphors as *the* core of a theory of metaphor (and even of a neural theory of language in which dead metaphors are mediated through the concept of embodiment).[7] The grounds they give deserve consideration: "The mistake derives from a basic confusion: it assumes that those things in our cognition that are most alive and most active are those that are conscious. On the contrary, those that are most alive and most deeply entrenched, efficient, and powerful are those that are so automatic as to be unconscious and effortless" (Lakoff and Turner 1989, 129).

What is most entrenched is most powerful. Lakoff and Turner use the term "entrenched" verbal metaphors instead of the established terms "dead" or "conventionalized" verbal metaphors. This alternative term reflects the shift in focus regarding the characteristics of the concept of vitality. They are right to emphasize that vitality has traditionally been equated with consciousness of metaphoricity. Now they invert this criterion and introduce a typically cognitive linguistic argument: precisely those linguistic structures that are highly conventionalized provide basic structural frames for the organization of thought. In this context, they implicitly introduce a tripartite classification similar to the one that Black provided a decade before. Here they distinguish among conventional and dead, conventional and alive, and novel metaphors. Unfortunately, the range of phenomena and the problems related to this variation are only discussed insofar as they concern either refutations of the dead metaphor theory or confirmations of Lakoff and Johnson's conceptual metaphor theory (1980, 1999; Lakoff 1993).[8] Nevertheless, they touch upon further interesting facets of the dead versus alive distinction, which will be taken up in detail later in chapter 6.

For the introductory purposes that we are concerned with at the moment, it is sufficient to bear in mind that the distinction between dead and live metaphors is indeed at the core of traditional as well as of cognitive metaphor theories and, moreover, that it has not received the profound attention of metaphor scholars, resulting in the lack of its systematic integration into theories of metaphor. This is the gap that this book intends to bridge. Instead of taking the dead versus alive classification for granted or as a relatively random issue, I will first of all argue that a systematic reflection upon the dead versus alive distinction is a relevant issue for any theory of metaphor and, second, that a close consideration of the phenomenological grounds of this distinction directly bears upon metaphor theories, be they linguistic or cognitive.

An initial consequence of this change in perspective is the distinction between two sets of categories that replace the dead versus alive distinction.

Until now, the systems perspective and the perspective of use of verbal metaphors have figured as implicit frames of reference for the criteria that have informed this one single classification. The criteria are conventionalization, novelty, transparency, and consciousness. Conventionalization and novelty are properties of lexemes in relation to a linguistic system, and consciousness of metaphoricity is clearly a matter of individual activation, not a property of a lexeme as such. Transparency may figure on both levels. I, however, suggest that it is primarily a property related to the linguistic system. Note that one of the major characteristics of language change is loss of transparency, and what is relevant here is not that a metaphor becomes opaque for a specific person at the specific moment when he or she is speaking or writing but that it ceases to be transparent for a community of speakers.[9] In other words, processes of conventionalization in verbal metaphors are often, if not mostly, accompanied by a loss of transparency. A systematic way of accounting for the loss of transparency is to check whether the verbal metaphor continues to figure as a literal expression in the language. If it does, then transparency is ensured for an average speaker. If not, then transparency can be reestablished through etymological reconstruction, that is, the identification of a historical, literal meaning.[10]

On the basis of a similar (but not the same) set of criteria, two classifications that are intended to replace the dead versus alive distinction shall be proposed: a tripartite one that relates to the system and a bipolar one that relates to use. The first one is a close elaboration of the classifications proposed by Black and by Lakoff and Turner. It distinguishes dead, entrenched, and novel verbal metaphors, and it is based on the criteria of conventionalization, novelty, and transparency. Dead metaphors are highly conventionalized and opaque, entrenched metaphors are conventionalized and transparent, and novel metaphors are not conventionalized and transparent. The second classification already sketched above only applies to metaphors that are transparent (entrenched and novel ones) and rests upon the criterion of cognitive activation in a given speaker/writer (listener/reader) at a given moment in time. Sleeping metaphors show a low degree of activation, while waking metaphors show a high or higher degree of activated metaphoricity. Thus, the examples presented in section 0.1 would be considered to be entrenched metaphors with respect to the linguistic system, and they would be considered to be waking ones with respect to the activation of metaphoricity in language use. The bipolar classification is conceived of as a scale that allows for various degrees of metaphoricity and not as a set of two rigid categories. These two classifications will be presented and discussed in detail in chapter 6. To conclude this issue for now, I shall only make one further pertinent remark.

In the two distinct classifications, the criterion of consciousness of metaphoricity was replaced with activation of metaphoricity. There are several reasons for doing this: first of all, what it means to be conscious of something is a highly controversial and complex topic of contemporary debate. It depends on the philosophical, neuropsychological, and/or psychological theories of the architecture and processes of consciousness. Consequently, deciding whether a metaphor is conscious for a given speaker at a given moment in time presupposes nothing less than a theory of consciousness. Yet, to my knowledge, there is no such thing as a single comprehensive theory of consciousness available at the moment (cf. Bartsch 2002; Chafe 1994, 1996; Edelmann and Tononi 2000; Farthing 1992; Flanagan 1998; Frey 1980; Jackendoff 1996a; Metzinger 1996; Ornstein 1977; Pauen and Roth 2001; Pöppel 2000; Pylkkänen and Vadén 2001). Hence, every account of the consciousness of metaphors would have to be built on theoretical and empirical grounds that are still pretty much under discussion.

Instead of reapplying a range of problematic presuppositions in order to analyze metaphors from a perspective of use, I choose to rely on a facet of cognitive processes that is empirically accessible through microanalyses of language use: activation of metaphoricity. Activation does not presuppose consciousness, but it can be related to consciousness. Activation of metaphoricity simply means that the metaphoricity of a given linguistic expression or conceptual metaphor has had some empirically observable consequences, be it in speech or writing (semantic opposition) or in pictures (depiction of source domain) or, as we will see later on, in cospeech gestures (depiction of source domain).

How the activation of metaphoricity in a speaker may be related to models of consciousness would deserve a further in-depth treatment beyond the scope of this book. I shall, however, in a concluding chapter, offer one way of conceiving of this relation between activation and consciousness, a way that may figure as a point of departure for further reflection. But before this is possible, many more aspects of metaphor use and what they reveal about underlying cognitive processes need to be clarified. The next step will be to determine what exactly is activated when metaphoricity is activated, or what are the cognitive realms of metaphors?

0.3 Bridging Gaps: Realms of Metaphors in Language Use

The two classifications introduced above rest upon a distinction that metaphor theories tend not to reflect upon systematically: the distinction between the collective level of linguistic and/or conceptual systems and the individual level of representation and actualization of those systems. As Gerard Steen (2006, 2007) points out, these distinctions have played a minor role in cognitive linguistics as well as in other cognitive approaches to language. However, while speech-production models, such as those proposed by Levelt (1989) and Levelt, Roelofs, and Meyer (1999),[11] do aim at describing the flow of information online, the models are based mostly on experimentally induced situations of language production (slips of the tongue figure as an exception). Psycholinguistic models of speech production do not ground their theories on spontaneous forms of language use. Here lies an implicit assumption that language use is the defective realization of the competence of an idealized speaker. Thus, the relation between the level of the system and the level of individual use is conceived of as relatively unproblematic and merely a question of how to model the facets of the linguistic system so that they are all accessed and processed in a plausible order. Use is the instantiation of a linguistic system, not a possible point of theoretical or empirical departure. Take the following quote from Ray Jackendoff as a representative example of this kind of stance[12]: "In *speaking* a sentence, a brain must translate the initial thought, in the form of a conceptual structure, through the intermediate levels of syntactic and phonological structure into information in the form of motor instructions to the vocal tract" (Jackendoff 1992, 9, emphasis in the original). In this concept of speaking, even the speaker has disappeared, and it is only the brain that computes information so that the vocal tract receives the necessary instructions to begin to work. The relation between a collective system and its individual realization in language use is a matter of computation only. Language use is the mere product of this computational process.

Cognitive linguistics handles the relation between the collective and the individual level in a basically similar manner. Despite adopting fundamentally distinct viewpoints regarding the nature and structure of human cognition, the two frameworks share the same lack of concern for this cardinal issue.

Let us consider in some detail how Lakoff and Johnson's conceptual metaphor theory[13] deals with this problem because it has informed a pervasive amount of subsequent studies, all in the same spirit. Conceptual metaphor theory, in a characteristic move, treats the relation between the collective level of conceptual metaphors (embodied in a language system) and the private or individual ways of understanding the world (thinking, speaking, acting) simply as unproblematic. Lakoff and Johnson's claims formulated in the first paragraph of their famous little monograph *Metaphors We Live By* are a good example: "We have found, on the contrary, that metaphor is pervasive in everyday life, not just in language but in thought and action. Our ordinary conceptual system, in terms of which we both think and act, is fundamentally metaphorical in nature" (Lakoff and Johnson 1980, 3). Two decades later, Lakoff has not changed his view: individuals draw upon the collective level of conceptual metaphor to structure their everyday experiences. How these two levels relate or whether they are different is not a focal point of interest. So, for instance, in his book *Moral Politics: How Liberals and Conservatives Think*, he continues to base his argument about the ways in which morality is conceptualized in politics on the study of linguistic expressions, while at the same time assuming that those expressions reflect forms of conceptualizing politics, which in turn influence the thoughts and actions of individual people (Lakoff 2002):

> That is what I study: what, exactly, our unconscious system of concepts is and how we think and talk using that system of concepts. . . . For example, many people may not be aware that we commonly conceptualize morality in terms of financial transactions and accounting. If you do me a big favor, I will be *indebted* to you, I will *owe* you one, and I will be concerned about *repaying* the favor. We not only talk about morality in terms of paying debts, but we also think about morality that way. (Lakoff 2002, 5; emphasis in the original)

Thus, Lakoff's conceptual metaphor theory and theories of speech production are unconcerned with the issue of how a collective system of linguistic structures relates to what we actually observe when people use language. Conceptual metaphor theory and psycholinguistic theories of speech production regard spontaneous speech as the partial or, at worst, as the defective instantiation of the conceptual system or the language faculty of an idealized speaker. Yet I shall argue that, in fact, it is in itself an important point of theoretical departure with inherent properties—which, as we have seen above, may give rise to usage-specific categories.

This is not to say that the perspective of individual use should replace the systems perspective or that with regard to metaphors it should replace semantics with pragmatics. Rather, individual use must be considered as a noteworthy dimension of language with its coherent structures and organizational principles and not just as a defective instantiation of whatever system. Reconsider the distinction introduced in the preceding section: metaphors are classified differently depending on whether we regard them on the level of the linguistic system or on the level of individual use. On the systems level, we distinguish dead, entrenched, and novel metaphors, whereas we differentiate sleeping from waking metaphors on the individual level. Now the change in perspective bears directly upon what are taken to be relevant criteria: conventionalization, novelty, and transparency on the collective dimension and availability for cognitive activation on the individual dimension. The two dimensions relate so that only those categories on the systems level that are transparent (entrenched and novel) can be activated.

All this implies that the dead versus alive distinction is problematic *because* it uncritically projects categories of the collective system into the minds of individual speakers/listeners and writers/readers. In other words, the level of use has characteristics that are not relevant to the systems level and vice versa. This is one of the gaps in current research on metaphor that the present book seeks to bridge: the gap between system and use. Careful consideration of the specific properties of metaphors in language use and of how they relate to the categories and structures that metaphor theories have postulated on the level of a collective system is therefore a major tenet of this book.

This perspective gains support from recent developments in cognitive linguistics. Over the past few years, Raymond Gibbs and Gerard Steen have taken quite a few initiatives to direct the attention of students of metaphor and thought to the methodological and theoretical problems arising from a lack of disentangling these two facets of metaphor (Gibbs 1998; Steen 2006, 2007; Steen and Gibbs 1999).[14]

The usage-based approach advocated in this book is generally sympathetic to locating metaphor primarily on the level of utterance meaning, but it will be suggested that speakers and writers activate different cognitive realms of metaphors selectively, such as conceptual metaphors, which point to a level of general cognition, and lexical metaphors, which indicate a specific level of linguistic cognition. Furthermore, it is proposed that lexical metaphors are not reducible to conceptual metaphors, even if the one is an instantiation of the other, and, on the other hand, that systems of conceptual metaphors are not activated each and every time a metaphor is produced. Steen and Gibbs's (1999) warning not to assume that conceptual metaphors uncovered through linguistic analysis are part of each individual's repertoire of metaphors addresses the same critical point: "Cognitive linguists should be careful not to immediately assume that the results of their systematic examination of language necessarily implies that each individual person must have all the full-blown conceptual metaphors uncovered by linguistic analysis" (Steen and Gibbs 1999, 4). I believe that the kind of usage-based approach proposed in this book fills an important gap in current metaphor discussions because it indicates an empirically grounded access to the different realms of metaphor that may be activated online during speaking.

In a nutshell, this view complements the concept of conceptual metaphor with a level of verbal metaphor and complements the concept of metaphor as a uniquely verbal phenomenon with a level of metaphor that is subject to general cognitive principles. Hence, it provides support for the general claims of conceptual metaphor theory, while at the same time pointing out the necessity of postulating a linguistic level of metaphoric structure. Conversely, it provides support for the claim of linguistic metaphor theories that a specific linguistic level of metaphoric structure may be assumed, while at the same time pointing out the necessity of postulating a general conceptual level of metaphoric structure.

Note, however, that in assuming these two levels based on the analysis of metaphors in language use, we are still trapped in the vicious circle that cognitive linguists have been (correctly) blamed for: using, on the one hand, the study of language to gain insights into the nature of nonlinguistic cognitive structures while claiming, on the other hand, that language is fundamentally structured according to general cognitive principles. Cognitive linguists, psycholinguists, and gesture scholars (Cienki 1998, 2003; Gibbs 1998; Gibbs and Colston 1995; Steen and Gibbs 1999) have critically addressed this issue: "In fact, this issue is a significant source of tension in the contemporary study of metaphor in cognitive science. Many cognitive psychologists are skeptical about trying to infer much about human conceptual systems from an analysis of systematic patterns in language ... " (Steen and Gibbs 1999, 4). Furthermore, Steen and Gibbs have pointed out that extralinguistic evidence is needed to substantiate the claim that a conceptual metaphor exists as a form of general cognitive structure that in turn informs the cognitive processing of language: "An important claim of this psycholinguistic research is that very different methods must be employed to assess the potential role that conceptual metaphors may have in different aspects of language production and understanding" (Steen and Gibbs 1999, 4). Studying metaphors in various modalities, not just in language, is one way of breaking out of this circle (cf. Cienki 1998, 2003, Cienki and Müller, forthcoming a, forthcoming b, 2003, 2007, in preparation).

Hence, I propose that the multimodal nature of metaphor offers important insights into the realms of metaphor during language use. It provides empirical support that forms the material for the bridge between the facets of metaphor addressed by conceptual metaphor theory and by linguistic metaphor theories: it indicates that metaphor is subject to a general cognitive principle with modality-specific characteristics. By doing this, further evidence is provided that breaks the vicious circle that cognitive linguists have been criticized for. So far, cognitive properties of metaphor use have not served as a major source of inspiration for the construction of metaphor theories. The existing metaphor theories so far are theories of products, not of processes. If they are interested in processes, they focus on recognition, interpretation, or appreciation but not on comprehension. And different aspects of the process of understanding figurative language are often conflated. Consider Gibbs:

> One reason many scholars believe figurative language violates communicative maxims is that they confuse the processes and products of linguistic understanding. All language interpretation takes place in real time ranging from the first milliseconds of processing to long-term reflective analysis. This temporal continuum may be roughly divided into moments corresponding to linguistic comprehension, recognition, interpretation, and appreciation.... Philosophers, linguists, and literary theorists focus on trope understanding as a product and generally study recognition, interpretation, and interpretation. From an examination of the various products of trope recognition and interpretation, these scholars try to infer something about figurative language comprehension. (Gibbs 1993a, 255–56)

The dynamic view proposed in this book seeks to incorporate the characteristics of metaphor as a cognitive process of establishing or activating metaphoricity into a theory of metaphor. Hence it focuses on two hitherto widely neglected aspects of the psychology of metaphor: the production rather than the comprehension of verbal metaphors and their dynamic properties.

We shall see that by studying metaphor as it is used and in terms of cognitive organization it becomes clear that we need to assume different realms of metaphor that are activated online during speaking and writing. Distinguishing between realms of metaphors will allow us to work out a much more precise answer to the question of dead versus live metaphors; it will allow us to specify in which sense verbal metaphors that are supposedly dead are alive and in which sense sleeping metaphors may turn into waking ones. And it will systematically address the question of how structures of general and of modality-specific cognition are activated online during the process of language production, be it written or spoken. In other words, it addresses the relation between a collective system of both conceptual and linguistic metaphors and its forms of activation during language production.

0.4 Objective, Scope, and Structure of the Book

The major theoretical point of this book is the proposal of a dynamic view on metaphors; a dynamic view that takes language use and cognitive activity as points of reference for theoretical reflection. By taking metaphors to be not just instantiations of a linguistic system, it accords with Steen's proposal to systematically distinguish four approaches to the study of metaphor (cf. Steen 2006, 2007)[15] :

- Metaphor in language as system,
- Metaphor in thought as system,
- Metaphor in language as use, and
- Metaphor in thought as use.

My focus is on the two latter approaches. More specifically, it is on verbal metaphors and their cognitive activation during speaking or writing. The cognitive activation of metaphoricity is related to empirically observable "metaphoricity cues" in language, picture, sculpture, and gesture, and it leads in a straightforward way to a refutation of the dead versus alive distinction prevalent in theories of metaphor. The observations lead to two important consequences: first, the distinction of two sets of categories: one regarding the level of the linguistic system and the other regarding the level of use; second, they lead to a dynamic concept of metaphoricity—"dynamic" in the sense that the metaphoricity of verbal metaphors in language use is also active in so-called dead metaphors, that it may be activated selectively and then motivate semantic productivity; and, finally, in the sense that the metaphoricity inherent in dead metaphors is gradable, that is, it may be more or less activated.

A fundamental concern of this book is transparency or, to put it another way, accessibility. It seeks to be as explicit as possible and does not presuppose familiarity with any of the currently available metaphor theories. Therefore, some sections may feel repetitive or unnecessarily explicit for readers who are already initiated in metaphor theories, but for novices they may serve as a useful condensed introduction. I chose this approach for several reasons, one of which is the tendency in current metaphor research to focus on one kind of theory while reducing the accounts of competing metaphor theories, at best, to the discussion of a few controversial points. This holds for both the major trends: conceptual metaphor theory and linguistic metaphor theories (cf., for instance, Kövecses 2002; Lakoff 1993; White 1996).[16] But I believe that even for readers more familiar with this topic, the explicit description of some of the core assumptions may recall some problematic or especially insightful facets that are otherwise merely taken for granted.

Needless to say, such an objective presupposes a big reduction in the possible approaches one could consider taking. Metaphor continues to be a hot topic, and the number of the publications dealing with it has exploded over the past thirty years (Shibles 1971, 1972; van Noppen 1985; van Noppen and Hols 1990). In other words, the account offered here is reductive in that it only takes into consideration the more prominent approaches—prominent in the sense that they are currently controversial. Still, I think that the scope is such that it provides a valuable basis and a starting point both for novices and for the initiated who are interested in an unbiased discussion of pertinent aspects of the phenomenon of verbal metaphors from a cognitive perspective.

A further criterion for choosing the theories included in this book concerns the fact that some important German treatments of metaphor have not received the attention they deserve in contemporary discussions. This is mainly because German as a language of international research tends nowadays to be inaccessible to Anglophone scholars of metaphor (cf. Jäkel 1999). The present book intends to give a wide Anglophone readership access to at least some important and basic lines of argument that have come from German scholars.

Note, however, that the different approaches to metaphor are not in toto and separately presented; rather their presentation follows the development of the leading argument. This means that the book does not simply summarize distinct approaches as such but rather discusses selected aspects of the phenomenon of metaphor that turn out to be relevant and fundamental to a systematic study of the dead versus alive distinction. The chapters summarize the ways in which different theories approach these issues and offer support, criticism, and/or alternatives from a dynamic point of view.

Adopting a strictly cognitive and usage-based perspective provides new insights into some of the basic issues of metaphor theories, such as the nature of metaphors (cognitive and linguistic), the vital realms of metaphors (conceptual, verbal, verbo-pictorial, and verbo-gestural), the structure of metaphor or of metaphoricity (triadic), and the vitality of the metaphoricity inherent in dead metaphors (active realms, selective activation of metaphoricity, and gradability of metaphoricity). Taken as a whole, these observations constitute the puzzle pieces of the refutation of the dead versus alive distinction. This in turn documents that the dynamic view, which regards language use from the point of view of cognition, may have an influence on metaphor theory and provide empirical and theoretical grounds for a re-formulation of the concepts underlying metaphor theories.

Each chapter may be read as an unbiased introduction to the phe-nomenon or aspect under discussion. The chapters constitute autonomous arguments and hence may be read independently. Taken together, they are pieces of one fundamental line of argument, namely, that adopting a cog-nitive approach to metaphors in language use leads to a dynamic view of metaphors and to a refutation of the mutually exclusive dichotomy of dead versus live metaphors.

Chapter 1 presents the four basic assumptions of the dynamic view in a nutshell: metaphors are a cognitive activity, depend on use, have a triadic meaning structure, and are modality independent.

Chapter 2 discusses the epistemological discrepancies underlying the-ories of metaphor and uncovers their diverging lines. It sketches their as-sumptions on the nature of metaphor (cognitive or linguistic) and provides a comprehensive overview of the competing linguistic and cognitive theo-ries of metaphor. It concludes that the establishment of metaphoricity is a cognitive process with multimodal products.

Chapter 3 describes realms of metaphors that are activated in language use: conceptual, verbal, pictorial, and gestural. It provides sketches of dif-ferent kinds of theoretically assumed realms of verbal metaphors in terms of Lakoff and Johnson's conceptual metaphor theory and Weinrich's Bild-feldtheorie (theory of image field) and confronts these with examples of multimodal forms of language use. It poses the following questions: are dead metaphors activated online, how are systems of conceptual metaphors acti-vated online, do verbal metaphors reside in a general conceptual structure or in a language-specific conceptual structure, and what are the implications of multimodal metaphors? It concludes that dead metaphors are alive in instances of language use.

Chapter 4 offers a detailed treatment of what I shall regard as the core of metaphor: a triadic structure. The activation of metaphoricity critically depends on the activation of this triadic structure, which is highly abstract and ontologically neutral. It is argued that this abstract structure is the common ground of historical and contemporary concepts of metaphor. The chapter offers an overview of major accounts of the structure of metaphor from classical times to the present. It concludes that at the core of concepts of metaphor and metaphoricity there is a shared assumption that activated metaphors establish a triadic structure.

Chapter 5 offers an in-depth analysis of so-called mixed metaphors and shows why they do and do not make sense at the same time. The analyses are carried out from three different methodological perspectives provided by traditional linguistics, conceptual metaphor theory, and blending theory. Thereby, they provide a critical and comparative account of three different methodological and theoretical frameworks. The analysis of mixed metaphors is just as revealing as slips of the tongue for investigating the online cognitive processes underlying language production. The chapter reveals that metaphoricity may be activated selectively and that it may motivate semantic productivity. Or, to conclude in terms of blending theory, the analysis of mixed metaphors shows that dead metaphors are available for conceptual integration.

In chapter 6, the dead versus alive distinction is reviewed and critically evaluated on theoretical as well as on empirical grounds. It proposes two distinct categories: one pertinent to the systems level that differentiates dead, entrenched, and novel metaphors and is based on the criteria of transparency and conventionalization and another one addressing the level of use that differentiates sleeping and waking metaphors and is based on the criterion of activated metaphoricity. It is concluded that dead metaphors that are conventionalized and transparent or metaphors that are novel (and transparent) may be more or less sleeping or more or less waking when they are used. Hence a subset of the traditional category of dead metaphors may vary in activation and salience.

Chapter 7 unites the arguments put forward in each chapter to argue for a refutation of the dead versus alive distinction of verbal metaphors and discusses them in the light of their relevance to theories of metaphor in general. More specifically, it is argued that a dynamic view on language and cognition throws a great deal of light onto a range of pertinent issues in contemporary research, not only furthering inquiry into metaphor and thought, but also more generally into language and thought.

Metaphors and Cognitive Activity:
A Dynamic View

Characterizing metaphors as cognitive activity does not create an altogether new understanding of metaphor. Rather it foregrounds a facet of verbal metaphor that has been at least implicitly present since the dawn of scholarly reflections upon metaphor in the classical rhetorical tradition. There are even passages in Aristotle's *Poetics* where it seems that he connects metaphors with a specific kind of cognitive activity: "It is important to use aptly each of the features mentioned, including double nouns and loan words; but much the greatest asset is a capacity for metaphor. This alone cannot be acquired from another, and is a sign of natural gifts: because to use metaphor well is to discern similarities" (Aristotle 1995, 1459a).

It is clear that this passage has mainly been understood as an expression of the extraordinary capacity that the process of finding metaphors presupposes, a kind of capacity that some people are supposed to dispose of while others do not. Probably one of the most prominent and influential of those endowed with it was Ivor Armstrong Richards (cf. 1936, 89–90). Yet I do not think that this fully captures what Aristotle says in this passage. I believe that the essence of this passage is that using metaphor "well" cannot be learned from another person: it is a sign of talent. Not everybody has the same capacity for discerning similarities in the external world. Put another way, it is not that finding metaphors is generally a matter of talent or of natural gift, but that finding good ones is. What is implied in this description is that finding metaphors is a kind of general cognitive activity, while finding good metaphors presupposes a specific cognitive capacity (talent) for discovering similarities in the external world.[1] Aristotle does not suggest that finding metaphors is a constructive process (an assumption of contemporary metaphor theories), yet what this passage does imply is that using metaphors is a natural cognitive activity: the capacity for discerning analogies.[2]

In his *Philosophy of Rhetoric*, Richards (1936) characterizes the cognitive and procedural dimension of using metaphors in a particularly clear and straightforward way, and his cognitive stance regarding metaphor has been a major source of inspiration for Lakoff and Johnson's conceptual metaphor theory (Lakoff and Johnson 1980, 1999; Lakoff 1993, 2002; Johnson 1987): "In the simplest formulation, when we use a metaphor we have two thoughts of different things active together and supported by a single word, or phrase, whose meaning is a resultant of their interaction" (Richards 1936, 93). The point I wish to draw attention to is that the procedural and cognitive property of metaphors has hitherto not received sufficient attention, and, therefore, it still lacks the place it deserves in theories of metaphor. Although many theories do mention it, or even regard metaphor as primarily conceptual, what they do not do is systematically account for the cognitive and procedural character of metaphors when they are used.

The dynamic view advocated in this book takes these characteristics of metaphors seriously and as a point of departure. It regards four properties of metaphors as essential: metaphors are a specific form of cognitive activity, they have a triadic structure, they are modality independent, and they critically depend on the procedural character of language use. This chapter offers a sketch of these basic assumptions.

1.1 Metaphors Are Based on a Cognitive Activity

The dynamic view departs from the assumption that, at their core, metaphors are products of a cognitive activity. More specifically, they are conceived of as materialized products of the process of establishing metaphoricity. This may seem trivial at first sight, but as I shall seek to demonstrate throughout the book, it has important consequences for a theory of metaphor.

First of all, and as pointed out in the introduction, it implies a shift from the systems perspective on metaphor to the perspective of use, because the cognitive activation of metaphoricity is, of course, and by default, a phenomenon of use. Second, it necessitates a reconsideration of the nature of metaphoricity, which has so far been treated primarily as a static property of words, expressions, or sentences, rather than as a dynamic property, which critically depends on cognitive activation in an individual person. Metaphors, be they verbal or conceptual, have been primarily regarded as conventionalized products of collective practices. The dead versus alive distinction and the assumption of the existence of conceptual metaphors (and systems of conceptual metaphors) clearly presuppose such a view. Hence, approaching metaphors from the point of view of an implied cognitive activity opens the path to recognizing that metaphoricity is variable, and when activation is taking place, it may occur selectively and to varying degrees. More specifically, this means that metaphoricity need not be activated each and every time a verbal metaphor is used. The same holds for systems of conceptual metaphors: the entire system need not be activated when language is being used metaphorically (cf. Lakoff 1993; Gibbs 1998; Steen and Gibbs 1999). It also means that activation may differ in focus and in degree.

Furthermore, regarding metaphors as a form of cognitive activity implies a shift from considering the semantic or pragmatic structure of words, sentences, and utterances to inquiring into the constructive processes involved in conceiving and perceiving metaphors. It assumes metaphor to be related to the process of "seeing-as" in Ludwig Wittgenstein's terminology. Wittgenstein illustrates his concept of seeing-as with reference to two examples: the illustration of a cube of glass and the famous duck-rabbit from Jastrow (1900). In both cases, it is the orientation of our perceptive processes that turns the object into the one thing or the other: "But we can also see the illustration [of a glass cube] now as one thing now as another.—So we interpret it, and see it as we interpret it" (Wittgenstein 1958, 194). With respect to the duck-rabbit, Wittgenstein says, "It can be seen as a rabbit's head or as a duck's" (Wittgenstein, 1958, 194). Consider the figure of the Necker cube and duck-rabbit. This means that we can deliberately choose to see the duck or the rabbit in the head and the cube from one perspective or the other (cf. also Mitchell 1994). In this sense, seeing-as is interpretation, is constructing a meaningful object. This cognitive process is metaphoric when a duality of meaning is a core part of the process. Duality of meaning refers to the simultaneous activation of two aspects. Thus, the duck-rabbit head would turn into a metaphor in which the duck would be taken for the rabbit but not cease to be the duck. The process of seeing-as that Wittgenstein describes is nothing other than the familiar principle of variable figure-ground perception as described in gestalt psychology (Köhler 1947; Metzger 1954; Wertheimer 1923). (Recall the famous example of a picture that oscillates between an old lady's head and a young lady in an elegant robe.) The process of establishing metaphoricity clearly involves a process akin to seeing-as, but a specific form of it, a form that will heuristically be paraphrased as "seeing one thing in terms of another."[3] Specifically, seeing (one thing) in terms of (another) implies that two concepts or two conceptual domains are active at the same time, with one concept or domain providing specific elements of meaning that are mapped onto another concept or domain.

In other words, when speakers use metaphors, such as "to put in the shade" (in den Schatten stellen), they conceive of an abstract procedure for

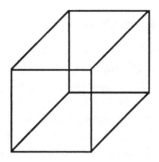

Fig. 4. The Necker cube and the duck-rabbit. Mitchell (1994, 47); Jastrow (1900);
cf. Wittgenstein (1984, 519–20; 1958, 194).

downgrading or surpassing somebody via a concrete, visual situation in
which somebody who is standing in the shade is less visible than somebody
standing in full sunlight. It is a specific form of seeing, of constructing reality
in terms of something else. This account of metaphor as "seeing in terms of"
is informed by Virgil Aldrich's (1996) concept of visual metaphor, to which
we will return in more detail later in chapter 3 and in the section on pictorial
metaphor.

To sum up, binding metaphors to some kind of cognitive procedure for establishing metaphoricity is not a new discovery but one that deserves closer
consideration than it has received so far.

1.2 Metaphors Are Based on a Triadic Structure

As introduced above, the dynamic view characterizes metaphors as the outcome of the process of establishing metaphoricity. Yet what exactly *is* metaphoricity? Typically, the answer to this question is that metaphors rest upon
some kind of awareness of a duality of meaning or reference that is based on
a transfer or mapping between concepts or domains (cf. Black 1962; Closs-
Traugott 1985; Lakoff and Johnson 1980; Lakoff 1993; Richards 1936; Stählin
1914). Instead, I assume a triadic structure to be at the core of metaphor.

Note that the duality of meaning also plays a central role—in many theories without overt reflection—in distinguishing dead from live metaphors.
We will return to this in detail in chapter 6. For the moment, let me just mention that awareness of metaphoricity (as a criterion for live metaphors) rests
upon the assumption that two concepts or domains are activated in parallel.
In other words, one of the criteria that applies to the vitality or "aliveness"
of metaphors is the activation of a duality of meaning. For the most part,
these two elements show up in the form of a pair of categories, such as literal
and figurative or source and target, or they show up as double reference.
Without the activation of these two elements, there is no metaphor.

Dualistic conceptualizations reduce the structure of metaphor to a transfer or mapping between two entities, B and C (e.g., "love is seen as a journey,"
or "love is seen as a rose"), without systematically including the role of the
mediating or connecting entity or process. Now, from the point of view of
cognition in language use, as advocated in this book, the third mediating element is of central importance. For without such a mediating force, without
the process of seeing one thing in terms of another, there is no establishment
of metaphoricity. Without it, no metaphor can be motivated or activated.
Establishing metaphoricity then is activating a triadic structure in which B is
seen in terms of C, where the third factor is the process of seeing-in-terms-
of. On the level of a collective system, this process of seeing-in-terms-of
may be fixed and branded as a verbal expression. And in the case of a conventionalized verbal metaphor, the third element (the process of seeing-in-
terms-of) is replaced by convention (the product of a conventionalized verbal
metaphor).

Seeing-in-terms-of as a property of metaphor is not a new discovery in
metaphor research. As we have seen above, Lakoff and Johnson have argued
along similar lines in their characterization of conceptual metaphors (Lakoff
and Johnson 1980), and Lynne Cameron (1999a) also speaks of seeing-in-
terms-of when she discusses "how the topic is seen in terms of the vehicle"
(Cameron 1999a, 23). A triadic structure for verbal metaphors has been a

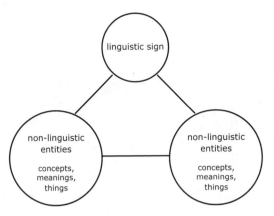

Fig. 5. The wide relational concept of metaphor (type 1rw). Cf. Lieb (1996).

well-documented facet of metaphor since the classical period, as Hans-Heinrich Lieb (1996) has meticulously reconstructed. Since Aristotle, metaphor has been conceived of as a three-place relation: a relation in which an entity A refers to a concept or class or domain B, whereby it denotes a concept or class or domain C. This tripartite relation is nothing less than Aristotle's wide concept of metaphor. Consider what is probably the most famous Aristotelian passage on metaphor[4]: "Metaphor is the application of a word that does not belong: either from the genus to the species, or from the species to the genus, or from the species to the species, or according to what is analogous" (Aristotle, 1995, *Poetics* XXI, 1457b, trans. H.-H. Lieb; cf. Lieb 1996).[5] In other words, the differentiation among metaphor, synecdoche, and metonymy has not yet been made. Metaphor refers to all kinds of uncommon uses of words that show this tripartite relation. Lieb characterizes this relational structure as follows: "Generally, and slightly simplified, a term of type '1rw' denotes a class of ordered triples (consisting) of linguistic signs, and two non-linguistic entities specified either as 'concepts', or as 'meanings', or as 'things', or the like" (Lieb 1996, 346). A metaphor (of the type "1rw")[6] would consist of three elements: a linguistic sign and two non-linguistic entities (concepts, meanings, or things). Among these elements, there exists a specific form of relation such that the linguistic sign means the first but not the second concept, meaning, or thing. More specifically, the linguistic sign establishes a relation of uncommon use between the two nonlinguistic entities. See the diagram in figure 5 for an illustration.

This three-place relation is clearly a more appropriate characterization of what, historically, has been conceived of as the core structure of metaphor

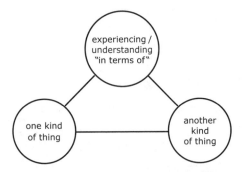

Fig. 6. Lakoff and Johnson's triadic structure of conceptual metaphors.

than the concept of a duality of meaning because it systematically integrates the linguistic sign, which mediates between and connects two nonlinguistic entities. Lieb's reconstructions have documented how this schema relates to historical concepts of metaphor; beginning with Greek and Roman philosophy and rhetoric, he traces variants within these traditions up to the early 1960s.

I shall put forward the argument that a triadic structure is implied not only in historical concepts of metaphor, as documented by Lieb, but also in contemporary theories of metaphor, for instance, in Lakoff and Johnson's conceptual metaphor theory (1980, 1999; Lakoff 1993), in Harald Weinrich's Bildfeldtheorie (1958, 1963, 1964, 1967, 1976), and in John Searle's pragmatic theory of metaphor (Searle 1993).[7] Thus, when Lakoff and Johnson write, "The essence of metaphor is understanding and experiencing one kind of thing in terms of another" (1980, 5), they implicitly assume such a triadic structure, except that the ontology of the three entities is comparatively different from the historical concept of metaphor. Instead of a word mediating between two nonlinguistic entities, Lakoff and Johnson propose that it is experience and understanding that mediate between two other kinds of entities or, expressed in terms of conceptual metaphor theory, that motivates the mapping between two conceptual domains. See figure 6 for an illustration.

In other words, "another kind of thing" is used to experience "one kind of thing"; journeys are used to understand love relationships in the conceptual metaphor LOVE IS A JOURNEY.[8] This too is a triadic structure, albeit a fundamentally different one.

We find a similar structure in Weinrich's characterization of the processes underlying the production of a verbal metaphor: "In the case of the actual and apparently punctual metaphor, what really happens is the coupling of two verbal domains of sense. . . . It is only decisive that two verbal domains of sense are coupled and established as analogies through a verbal act."

Weinrich suggests that in performing a verbal act (sprachlicher Akt), two verbal domains of sense (Sinnbereiche) are coupled (Koppelung sprachlicher Sinnbezirke) and analogies between the two verbal domains are established. Consider the diagram in figure 7 for a summary.

The philosopher of art Virgil Aldrich has formulated a concept of visual metaphor that is closely related to the one suggested in this book. As mentioned above, he uses Wittgenstein's concept of seeing-as to explain the perceptual processes involved in metaphoric seeing. He argues that, for instance, conceiving of clouds as the head of a woman implies the establishment of a triadic structure between a specific material (M, the clouds), a specific subject matter (A, the prototypical head of a woman), and, as a result of the process of seeing-as, a mental image (B, clouds seen as the head of a woman):

> In this relation, we have (1) something arbitrary that is seen in any kind of way. We call this M. Then, we have (2) the thing that M is seen as. We call this A. M is seen as A. The third factor, that is difficult to grasp and not easy to contrast with M and A, is constituted by perceiving M as A. . . . It (the third factor B) is a kind of image of A (that M is seen as), an image that is 'embodied' or takes shape through M.[9]

Consider the diagram in figure 8 below for an illustration of Aldrich's concept of pictorial metaphors. The process of seeing-as results in the production of a new "embodied" mental image, which Aldrich conceives of as the third element in this triadic structure. The clouds are really seen in terms

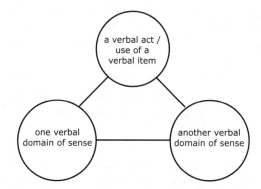

Fig. 7. Weinrich's triadic structure of verbal metaphors.

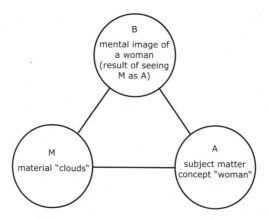

Fig. 8. Aldrich's triadic structure of pictorial metaphors.

of a woman—since they do not cease to be simultaneously conceived of as clouds; the result of this mapping is a specific embodied mental image.[10] Put differently, establishing metaphoricity in pictorial metaphors would amount to the activation of a triadic structure in which seeing M (clouds) in terms of A (woman's head) creates a new mental image B (woman's head) materialized in clouds. Notably, the process described by Aldrich does not appear to be very different from the principles underlying human creativity that are accounted for in blending theory.

The identification of such a triadic meaning structure in the above-mentioned cases clearly operates on a rather strong abstraction. Since it constitutes a minimal point of convergence in existing theories, it is not only an attractive point of departure for a critical evaluation of metaphor theories—which will be done in chapter 4—but it is also a theoretically highly interesting fact. In spite of important discrepancies regarding the nature of the relata and the assumed relations between them, the intuition of metaphor scholars would seem to correspond in this respect. Therefore, I shall risk suggesting that an abstract triadic structure, without a specified ontology of the relata, is at the core of historical and contemporary concepts of metaphors. This triadic structure could be paraphrased as follows: there is an entity or process A, which relates two entities B and C, such that C is seen in terms of B.

Again, we need to distinguish between the systems perspective and the use perspective. On the level of the system, the third element is a verbal item; on the level of use, the third element is the cognitive process that establishes the relation between B and C. It is this process on which the establishment of metaphoricity depends. The role of a conventionalized verbal or conceptual metaphor adds a preconfiguration or a certain prefigured route to this process.

Clearly this triadic structure is exceptionally simplistic in terms of its underlying concept of meaning. Hence, even if we assume that metaphor theories implicitly assume a triadic rather than a dualistic structure of metaphorical meaning, this rests upon a very simple concept of meaning. Issues of sense or reference or type and token are not taken up in most theories of metaphor.

It appears that this neglect correlates with the prevailing stance of conceptualizing metaphor primarily on the level of the linguistic system. As argued before, judging metaphors as dead or alive on the grounds of conventionalization relates to a linguistic system, not to language in use. But if we regard metaphor primarily on the level of the linguistic system, we do not have to worry about something like the meaning of an utterance or the process involved in establishing metaphoricity. Therefore, the triadic structures documented in historical and contemporary concepts of metaphor are ultimately a reconstruction of the products of collective ways of seeing-in-terms-of or of collective ways of establishing metaphoricity. In contrast, when metaphors are used, another kind of triadic structure needs to be activated by the process of seeing-in-terms-of. This activation takes place as they are being used, and it is not only observable in language but also in other modalities, such as pictures and gestures.

Bearing this in mind, the term "triadic structure" of metaphor will be used to refer to the abstract structural relation, which is independent of the ontology of the relata that it entails and which is at the core of both historical and contemporary concepts of metaphor. I shall refer to the core of establishing metaphoricity in language use as the activation of the triadic structure of seeing C as B.

Taking up the line of argument of the introduction to this book, this means that a dead metaphor is dead because the triadic structure cannot possibly be established (by an average speaker). A metaphor is sleeping because

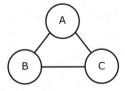

Fig. 9. The core triadic structure of metaphors.

the activation of it is low; it is waking when the activation is high, and it is something in between when the activation takes place on an intermediate level.

With respect to the analysis of the shadow examples given in the introduction, this means that at the moment of writing and of looking for accompanying pictures, there were not just "two thoughts active together" (to use Richards's 1936 formulation) or an "awareness of double meaning" (in Stählin's 1914 terms) but that the two activated thoughts were mediated by the process of seeing one thing in terms of another.

To sum up, it shall be argued that instead of there being a duality of meaning at the core of metaphor in language use, there is a triadic structure that critically depends upon a third mediating element or process. On the level of a collective system, this is a word or conceptual domain; on the level of use, it is the process of seeing-in-terms-of.

1.3 Metaphors Are Modality-Independent

The establishment of metaphoricity does not depend upon the medium of language. The process of seeing C in terms of B (e.g., a love relationship as journey, a hero as a lion, or a cloud as a woman) is a general cognitive process that may materialize in different modalities. Consequently, the product of this process is independent of a specific modality. Pushing this line of argument one step further, I shall propose that metaphors are, in principle, modality independent.

We have already seen above that pictures may not only accompany verbal metaphors and depict their source domain but that pictorial and verbal expressions may merge and form one multimodal metaphor. But is this sufficient to claim that metaphors are, in principle, modality independent? Certainly not. Therefore, let me introduce a third kind of modality, which shows a similar kind of interplay with verbal metaphor, namely, gesture. It is evident that coverbal gestures may enact or depict elements of the source domain of verbal metaphors in a form akin to pictures in almost any kind of conversational interaction (cf. Cienki 1998, 2000, 2003; Cienki and Müller forthcoming a, forthcoming b, Müller and Cienki forthcoming). We just need to focus on how verbal metaphors in conversation may be accompanied by spontaneous gestures, and we will often see that the gestures embody aspects of the source domains of the verbal metaphors. Consider example 3 as a first illustration.

This short sequence is taken from a conversation about the experience of falling in love for the first time. The woman on the left, Alina, is describing

Fig. 10. Metaphors are modality-independent: the case of verbogestural metaphors.

the first cautious advances between her and her first boyfriend. This happened during a long bus ride on a school trip. As they were sitting side by side on the bus, she felt that there was a kind of electric spark that passed between them ("daß es zwischen uns irgendwie gefunkt hat"). In German, the expression "es hat gefunkt" (literally, "it sparked") is a colloquial expression for falling in love. This colloquial expression uses the image of an electric spark that discharges when two electrically loaded entities touch. In the metaphoric expression, the two electrically loaded entities are the future lovers, and the electric spark is their moment of falling in love. Yet traditionally this expression would be considered a dead metaphor, that is, a metaphor that is conventional and no longer perceived as a metaphor by the speaker.

Example 3: "Falling in love" or "something 'sparked' between us"

1   auf der Hinfahrt (---) irgendwie in Omnibus
       (.) ehm (--)
       it was during the outward journey somehow in the bus

                          rh, moves to RING inwards
2   hat hat es angefangen dass es [zwischen uns
       that it began   [between us

                   quick outward turn of RING
3   irgendwie ge**funk**t hat]\
       somehow it **sparked** (lit.)]\
       (something **clicked** between us)

Alina's gesture tells a different story. Let us, therefore, take a closer look at it. Just as she is uttering the word "gefunkt" (sparked), she performs the brief, accentuated outward movement of a ring gesture. In this gesture, the index finger and the thumb touch each other at the fingertips as if they were picking up a tiny little object and form the shape of a ring. Her right hand moves into the ring configuration as she begins to talk about what happened between them (zwischen uns) on this bus ride. Initially, the ring gesture is performed in a somewhat unusual position, namely, with the fingertips directed toward the speaker. As soon as she utters the word "gefunkt," she quickly turns it outward, holds it for a short moment (now it is in a standard orientation with the fingers directed away from speaker), and as the metaphorical lexeme ends, she releases the ring configuration, and moves her hand downward into a resting position.

What does this little gesture tell us about the metaphoricity of the lexeme "gefunkt"? First of all, I suggest that the gesture represents two semantic elements of the co-occurring lexical item: the dynamics of the movement and the properties of the moving object. Sparks are tiny objects that move fast; the ring gesture is known to be derived from the activity of picking up tiny objects and to be widely used via semantic extension and conventionalization to express precision (cf. Kendon 1995, 2004; Morris 1977, 1994; Morris et al. 1979; Müller n.d.; Neumann 2004). In other words, I would argue that the ring configuration represents the tiny object mentioned verbally (a spark), whereas the fast outward movement represents the fast movements that characterize the motion pattern of sparks.

Yet if the metaphor is dead, how could the speaker have accessed the mental image or the idea of exploding sparks? In light of conceptual metaphor theory findings, one could argue that this is because she has activated the underlying conceptual metaphor LOVE IS A PHYSICAL FORCE (Lakoff and Johnson 1980, 49).[11] This is possible, although this example does not give us empirical hints that would support the existence of a conceptual metaphor rather than just the mental concept of a one-shot verbal metaphor. What the example does show is that two semantic elements of the lexeme "gefunkt" were active at the moment of speaking. Moreover, if the metaphor were dead and the gesture were derived from the conceptual metaphor only, then it would be difficult to explain why the kinetic part of the gesture was synchronized exactly with the lexeme that verbally encodes the very same property. For these reasons and on these empirical grounds, we may come to the following tentative conclusion: the gesture reveals that somehow the speaker must have activated the image of a spark at the same time she was producing the seemingly dead metaphor "gefunkt".

Now how does all this relate to the idea that metaphors are independent of the modalities in which they materialize? I am suggesting that, instead of only regarding gesture as a window onto online thought processes, it is adequate to conceive of the verbal expression and the coproduced gesture as one multimodal metaphor in which the gesture represents the elements of the source domain of the verbal metaphor. We will return to these issues in detail in chapter 3. The basic assumption that was illustrated in this section is that metaphoricity may crosscut modalities and that it therefore makes sense to speak of multimodal metaphors.

The examples of dead metaphors presented so far have documented that metaphor is a phenomenon that is not restricted to language. We have seen that pictures as well as coverbal gestures may represent elements of the source domain of the verbal metaphor. These examples are intended to illustrate the view suggested in this book, namely, that the establishment of metaphoricity is a general cognitive process based on a triadic structure. Traditionally, metaphor has been taken to be primarily a matter of language; others have argued that there are pictorial, sculptural (Aldrich 1996; Forceville 1996), and gestural metaphors (Cienki 1998, 2000, 2003; Cienki and Müller forthcoming a, forthcoming b; McNeill 1992; Mittelberg 2003, 2006; Müller 1998a, 2003, 2007; Müller and Cienki forthcoming; Sweetser 1999), thereby implying that metaphors may materialize in different sign systems or in different modalities (cf. Lakoff and Johnson 1999). What I wish to suggest here is that metaphors may not only materialize in different modalities, but they may also conflate to multimodal metaphors, in the above cases, verbo-gestural or verbo-pictorial. Note that the order of the compound is significant and relates to the point of departure in this book: verbal metaphors, or more specifically, supposedly dead ones. Moreover, because the pictures and gestures we have analyzed so far have represented aspects of the source domain of a copresent verbal metaphor, the order verbal first and gestural or pictorial second expresses an implied semantic dependency. Thus, I propose a view that regards metaphors as potentially multimodal and that at the same time indicates that the establishment of metaphoricity is modality independent.

Such a view finds support in Umberto Eco's semiotic approach to the philosophy of language (1984). Eco argues that the "scandal" of metaphor arises because it is fundamentally not a linguistic phenomenon but a semiotic one; as such it not only exists in other modalities, but verbal metaphor may also directly relate to visual, acoustic, tactile, and olfactory experiences.

> When closely studied in connection with verbal language, the metaphor becomes a source of scandal in a merely linguistic framework, because it is in fact a semiotic phenomenon permitted by almost all semiotic

systems. The inner nature of metaphors produces a shifting of the linguistic explanation onto semiotic mechanisms that are not peculiar to
spoken languages; one need only think of the frequently metaphorical
nature of oneiric images. However, it is not a matter of saying that visual
metaphors *also* exist, or that there perhaps *also* exist olfactory or musical
metaphors. The problem is that the verbal metaphor itself often elicits
references to visual, aural, and olfactory experiences. (Eco 1984, 88–89)

1.4 Metaphors Are a Matter of Use

The activation of a metaphor critically depends on the context in which
it is used, and this holds for poetic as well as for ordinary language. The
dynamic view regards the procedural dimension of language use as essential
for the establishment of metaphoricity. Not only does the metaphoricity of a
spoken or written metaphor depend on the cognitive process represented by
the triadic structure, but this activity is also embedded in the flow of speech,
writing, and, in Wallace Chafe's terms, in the flow of consciousness (Chafe
1994, 1996). In other words, the activation of metaphoricity only depends
on the specific and immediate contexts in which these verbal metaphors
are used, and these immediate contexts crosscut poetic and everyday uses
of language—to reject a more than common assumption of stylistic and
rhetorical metaphor theories.

Poetic and everyday uses of language as two general contexts in which
metaphors are used have played a fundamental role in metaphor theories
since classical times. Typically, dead metaphors have been considered a
characteristic of ordinary language, and live metaphors a crucial trait of
poetic language. There is little doubt that everyday language is full of so-
called dead metaphors, but it is also obvious that novel metaphors are not
excluded from ordinary language, in which they may figure as vital motors
of language change (cf. Blank 1997; Blank and Koch 1999; Bréal 1899; Closs-
Traugott 1985; Dornseiff 1966; Paul 1937; Stern 1931; Ullman 1967). Dead
metaphors, on the other hand, are not restricted to instances of ordinary
language use.

It seems important, therefore, to emphasize that a significant portion of
what have traditionally been termed dead metaphors may be sleeping in one
context and waking in another. The same holds for novel metaphors. They
may go unnoticed in one context and receive focused attention in another;
hence they may be sleeping in one context and waking in another. Note
that this property is a question of use, which again crosscuts the distinction
between poetic and ordinary language.

The fact that dead metaphors play an important role in poetic language has not gone unnoticed in the long history of metaphor research. Consider, for instance, the early romantic scholar August Wilhelm Schlegel. For him, it was an obvious matter of fact that in poetry metaphors cannot fade:

> In poetry, "images and metaphors" cannot "become old and jaded... Only truly beautiful images are immortal, and even if they are used often, they are rejuvenated over and over again through the hand of a genuine poet. They are born where they are placed, and so one does not think that one already knows them. Therefore, one sees that, also in this respect, checking the poem for individual occurrences does not get us anywhere: how easy would it be, then, out of the most divine work to extract images which in themselves could be called trivial?" (August Wilhelm Schlegel 1963, 252)

Schlegel says that in poetry, images and metaphors may not become outdated or wear out. A great poet may rejuvenate a metaphor again and again by integrating it into a new context. Accordingly, one can only observe and judge this if the metaphor is considered within its larger context of use; a metaphor of divine beauty may appear trivial when deprived of its context.[12] Hence, dead metaphors may be activated in poetic contexts of language use, but live or novel metaphors exist in ordinary everyday language too. Thus, the dead versus alive distinction is not a matter of whether a context is poetic or ordinary, but it depends on the immediate textual context of a verbal metaphor.

Furthermore, the point that metaphorical uses of language are not solely a matter of vital metaphors in poetic texts but constitute a general principle of language has been mentioned from the classical period to the present day, and especially since the emergence of historical linguistics and historical semantics in the nineteenth century, it figures as a major principle of language change. Once again, this is an aspect that Aristotle has at least also mentioned as a property of metaphor. Notably, only a few paragraphs after the famous passages on metaphor in the *Poetics*, Aristotle characterizes metaphor as a natural form of ordinary language, a form that is especially suitable for a specific type of poetic text: iambic verse. The explanation he gives is straightforward: iambic verse is most closely related to ordinary speech, and suitable expressions contain words that one would use in prose; prose, in turn, is a poetic kind of text that is close to ordinary speech, and the words that are used in prose are standard terms as well as metaphors and ornaments: "[I]n iambic verse, because of the very close relation to ordinary speech, suitable words are those one would also use in prose—namely, standard terms, metaphors, ornaments" (Aristotle 1995, XXIII, 1459a). I think that in this passage Aristotle at least comes close to recognizing metaphor not only as a purely poetic device of language. Rather, it seems that he makes the points that some forms of poetic language may use a form of language that is typically associated with ordinary language and that among the instruments of ordinary language are standard terms, metaphors, and ornaments.[13]

Ever since Aristotle's treatment, the idea that ordinary language is full of dead metaphors has survived. However, this fact has not been treated as a fundamental dimension of metaphors, at least not until the emergence of historical linguistics, presumably because of the sweeping inference insinuated by the metaphor "dead" itself, namely, that a dead metaphor is not a metaphor at all and therefore cannot be regarded as a valuable starting point for any theory of metaphor. Looking more closely at the ways in which dead metaphors are used uncovers that this assumption is, in fact, misleading.

Lakoff and Johnson's theory of conceptual metaphors has made the reorientation of metaphor theories toward ordinary language popular. Yet this reorientation also implies a shift toward the conceptual foundations of verbal metaphors. It has not so much inspired the close consideration of verbal metaphors themselves, that is, their forms, functions, or roles within language; rather, Lakoff and Johnson's conceptual metaphor theory takes the pervasiveness of metaphoric expressions in ordinary language as the empirical grounds for assuming that human understanding is ultimately based on metaphoric thinking. This groundbreaking change in perspective—to which we will return in more detail later—has somehow obscured the necessity of studying verbal metaphors in depth. Only relatively recently have there been attempts to systematize the empirical grounds of these claims. Until now, deciding whether or not a certain verbal element should be considered a metaphor has been a matter of linguistic intuition. In other words, the claim that metaphors are pervasive in everyday language is a claim that is not empirically verified, at least not by quantitative studies of metaphors in ordinary language. Corpus linguistic studies are needed here, and fortunately the interest of cognitive linguistic metaphor scholars in the verbal foundations of their claims is receiving increasing attention.[14]

Still, it remains a striking fact that only since Lakoff and Johnson's provoking 1980 monograph *Metaphors We Live By* has the role of metaphors in ordinary language begun to receive the deserved and appropriate degree of attention of scholars of linguistics at all. Notably, this shift toward ordinary language has inspired reflections about metaphors in use primarily in applied linguistics (Cameron 1999a, 1999b, 2003; Cameron and Low 1999; Deignan 2005; Gibbs 1999b; Kyratzis 2003; PragglejazzGroup 2007; Steen 2007a, 2007b; Stibbe 1996) but also in psycholinguistics (Gibbs 1993a, 1993b, 1994, 1999a, forthcoming; Giora 2003, 2007; Glucksberg and Keysar 1990, 1993; Glucksberg 2001; Keysar and Bly 1995; Paivio and Walsh 1993).[15] Lakoff and Johnson's conceptual metaphor theory takes a systems—not a use—perspective, and in this sense it is in harmony with the traditional approaches to metaphor that have established the dead versus alive distinction.

To sum up, in spite of the important shift from poetic to ordinary language in metaphor theories, which was stimulated by Lakoff and Johnson's work, theoretical as well as empirical research has mostly retained its focus on metaphors as elements of a collective system, be it linguistic, conceptual, or both.

1.5 Summary: The Dynamic View

The perspective advocated in this book both harmonizes with and fills an important gap in contemporary metaphor research. In regarding metaphors as a fundamental principle of language grounded in a general cognitive activity, it is in harmony with current and older approaches; in adopting a strictly use-oriented perspective, it is in line with applied research on metaphors and helps to fill a gap in mainstream metaphor research and theory that for the most part has either conflated the systems and the use perspectives or has been biased toward a systems view.[16] In a nutshell, the dynamic view as presented in this book focuses on the following processes and products:

- The process of establishing metaphoricity as cognitive activation,
- The process of activating a triadic structure, that is, seeing C in terms of B,
- The process of speaking and writing, and
- The product of multimodal metaphors.

CHAPTER TWO

Metaphors in Thought and Language: Fundamental Issues

> Metaphor is our most striking evidence of *abstractive seeing*, of the power of human minds to use presentational symbols. Every new experience, or new idea about things, evokes first of all some metaphorical expression.
>
> —*Susanne K. Langer (1957, 141; emphasis in the original)*

> A formal semantics specifies the conditions under which such metaphorical sentences may be said to have a truth value.
>
> —*Teun van Dijk (1975, 173)*

Metaphor is viewed in these quotes, on the one hand, as a form of abstractive seeing, as the capacity of the human mind to use presentational symbols and as an aberration of the declarative sentences of formal logic, requiring a specific modeling in a truth-conditional semantics on the other hand. Both authors put metaphor into some kind of relation to understanding—albeit fundamentally different ones. Whereas Langer takes metaphor to be a fundamental, intellectual process suited to the expansion of our understanding of the world,[1] Van Dijk takes metaphorical sentences to be a violation of "normal" declarative sentences, which in their propositional structure objectively reflect reality and may be said to have one of two truth values: true or false. In the view of logical positivism, the study of language reveals the nature and structure of the world by virtue of declaring states of affairs to be true or false. In this light, metaphors are nonsense sentences because they make statements that are plainly false. Although van Dijk seeks to overcome this narrow analysis, his proposal for a "formal semantics of metaphorical discourse" does not depart from the inherent epistemological claim of formal logic. He solves the problem by introducing context to the analysis of sentence meaning, but the meaning of a sentence is still defined relative to its truth values: "The idea is not, as usual, to assign the value 'false' or a neutral value, e.g. 'non-sense', to all metaphorical sentences, but to reconstruct formally the idea that metaphorical sentences may be true in a given context" (van Dijk 1975, 173). The positions of Langer and van Dijk reflect two fundamentally distinct conceptions of the relationship between language (or symbols in general) and thought. According to the latter, thought is a specific form of language, and language may mirror an objective positive world; the former position holds that language is a form of thought and that the use of symbols in general is a way of conceptualizing sensory experiences and hence is a form of constructing the world.[2] These two positions illustrate the poles of two major lines of philosophical thought, which continue to characterize more or less explicitly linguistic and cognitive approaches to metaphor. As such, however, they represent extreme positions on a scale of theories of metaphor. For the most part, approaches to metaphor do not clearly adopt either the one position or the other. Rather, they tend to be inclined more toward one end of the scale or the other;[3] and often, the positions taken are not really internally consistent, for example, they may not follow one, and only one, line of argument with regard to the different aspects of metaphor under discussion. Therefore, I shall not primarily discuss theories of metaphors as such, but I shall present different and competing viewpoints with regard to two fundamental issues that inquiry into this highly complex phenomenon have raised: the epistemological role and the nature of metaphor.

2.1 Metaphor, Reason, and Understanding?
Epistemological Discrepancies

Metaphor has been, and continues to be, a controversial topic in philosophy. This holds especially for theories of human understanding and imagination (cf. de Man 1978; Fauconnier and Turner 2002; Goodman 1981; Johnson 1987; Lakoff and Johnson 1980, 1999; Lakoff and Núñez 2000; Langer 1957)[4] and in contemporary theories of the evolution of the modern mind and of the evolution of language (cf. Deacon 1997; Jaynes 1976; Mithen 1996). Many of the linguistically relevant controversies regarding metaphor reside in fundamentally different philosophical stances toward the relationship between language and thought. Given that the philosophical underpinnings of the current "fight over metaphor in thought and language" (to use a formulation coined by Gibbs 1998) remain mostly implicit assumptions, which nevertheless provide the argumentative fundament of many of the contemporary controversies in metaphor theory, a brief but explicit treatment appears worthwhile.

The contemporary fight over metaphor in thought and language is first and foremost a fight between cognitive scientists, on the one hand, who adhere to the belief that the mind is a machine modeled according to the processing properties of computers (which is why most cognitive science programs are, in fact, artificial intelligence programs), and cognitive linguists, on the other hand, who advocate the view that the fundamental principle of mind is not the computation of arbitrary symbols, but the construction of meaning, or that the mind is a meaning-producing organism. Psycholinguists, cognitive psychologists, and linguists split into the same two groups (cf. Katz 1998; Gibbs 1998). In a nutshell, in cognitive science the "mind as a computer" view competes with a "mind as meaning-producing organism" view.

The foremost question under discussion is, What is metaphor? A misuse of language, a proposition that is false because it violates truth values, or a fundamental, conceptual structure? Metaphor's fate as a valuable object of scientific interest highly depends on the epistemological role philosophers have attributed to language. As we have already seen above, when language is considered to objectively mirror an equally objective world, metaphor can only be conceived of as misuse of language or as a false proposition. Why? Because metaphors are typically part of a contradictory predication/proposition. Thus, John Searle's (1993, 83) example, "Sally is a block of ice," contains a predication that is plainly false, because, of course, Sally is not really a block of ice; she just shares some properties with one. Hence, the proposition would receive the truth value "false" in a formal semantic account, "because a statement is defined as being true if, and only if, the state of affairs described by the statement holds" (Cann 1993, 15). This formal semantic analysis is rooted in the "correspondence theory of truth" (Cann 1993, 15–19) developed by the logician Alfred Tarski (1935) in the first half of the twentieth century. This formal semantic approach to language was characteristic of logical positivism and became very influential in Europe and the Anglo-Saxon world, especially through the work of Donald Davidson (1967, 1975).[5] Logical positivism put forward the idea that the study of language would reveal the nature of the world because of its capacity to objectively reflect reality. Philosophers such as Rudolf Carnap, Betrand Russell, Hans Reichenbach, and the young Ludwig Wittgenstein believed that reality was in principle objectively describable, that is, directly accessible to sensory experience, and that the ultimate form of description was made up of declarative sentences containing literal expressions.[6] Truth-conditional semantics maintains these views and equates the meaning of a sentence with the conditions under which it could be true: "To know the core meaning of a sentence uttered as a statement is to understand the conditions under which it could be true" (Cann 1993, 15). Following this line of argument, the sentence "Sally is a dancer" would be true if and only if Sally were in fact a dancer. In the same vein, the following lines from a German rock singer would all be false:

> You are a dancer in the storm
> You are a child on thin ice
> You throw love around recklessly
> And you are always hitting me.[7]

These lines would be false because the woman is not literally dancing in a storm, nor is she literally a child, nor does she literally throw love around (this is an impossible statement, because "love" is not a tangible entity), nor could she literally hit the singer with her love.

An epistemology that takes a highly specific form of language as reflecting the objective world must take these forms of language use to be false statements, as violations of the correct, literal use. Possible-world semantics has sought to overcome these shortcomings; yet formal semantics is firmly rooted in the mathematical understanding of language as a kind of calculus (to use Lyons's 1977 term) and would always view figurative language as defective, deviant, and parasitic on literal language (and literal language as defective with respect to mathematical logic). In this view, metaphor as the prototype of figurative language would be regarded—at best—as an exception that is useful and adequate in poetic language and a motor of language change.

A radically opposing view to metaphor and its role in human understanding has been advocated by George Lakoff and Mark Johnson (1980, 1999) over the past two decades. It is more than just a notable historical aside that Lakoff himself, in his early days, while adopting a formal linguistic view of language, was already extending it to what at that time he termed "natural logic" (Lakoff 1970), although this was still firmly rooted in what he likes to call the "objectivist" tradition in Western philosophy, that is, logical positivism and its epigones (Lakoff 1987). He changed his mind when he began to study metaphor, as he realized that, apart from the logical problems connected with a linguistic account of metaphor, metaphor appeared not to be as random a phenomenon in language as traditional accounts suggested. In shifting his perspective from the philosophical and semantic disputes over metaphor to the ways in which metaphor is used in everyday language, he found that metaphor seemed to be a ubiquitous and highly organized form of conceptualizing experiences.[8] Thus, expressions like the following are common:

> This relationship is a *dead-end street.*
> It's been a *long, bumpy road.*
> I'm *crazy* about her.
> She *drives me out of my mind.*
> Is that the *foundation* for your theory?
> He *attacked every weak point* in my argument.[9]

Far from being dead and therefore not metaphorically conceived those kinds of metaphoric expressions seem to directly reflect the ways in which speakers experience the love relationships, theories, and argumentative points they are talking about. Thus, metaphor appears to provide people with a device for conceptualizing abstract realms in particular, such as the nature of love relationships, scientific theories, and arguments. Instead of being violations of literal statements, or aberrations of the truth, the metaphors in these sentences seem to work as a productive device for the linguistic conceptualization of a new meaning. Once the attention had been drawn to these everyday uses of metaphor, Lakoff discovered—as Weinrich had a few years before him—that these expressions were not random, isolated forms of conceptualized experience, but that they clustered into groups according to a common principle, a principle that seemed to underlie all these expressions (cf. Weinrich 1958, 1963, 1964, 1967, 1976). The linguist Lakoff joined forces with the philosopher Mark Johnson, and in their small monograph, *Metaphors We Live By* (1980), they described this general principle and coined the term "conceptual metaphor" for it. Since then, the term and the theory of conceptual metaphors have generated a tremendous amount of interest worldwide, and conceptual metaphor theory has been a major stimulating force in the formation of the field of cognitive linguistics.[10]

Lakoff and Johnson observed that verbal expressions for love relationships could be grouped into at least two homogenous sets: one conceptualizing love as journey, and another one conceptualizing it as madness:

This relationship is a *dead-end street.*	He has gone *mad* over her.
It's been a *long, bumpy road.*	I'm *crazy* about her.
We'll just have to *go our separate ways.*	She drives *me out of my mind.*

I don't think this relationship is *going anywhere*.	He constantly *raves* about her.
We're *at a crossroads*.	I'm just *wild* about Harry.
	I'm *insane* about her.

→ LOVE IS A JOURNEY   → LOVE IS MADNESS

Lakoff and Johnson took these kinds of clusters as indications of the existence of an underlying general principle of conceptual organization, which they termed conceptual metaphor. Thus, in American English, love experiences were said to be instantiations of at least two conceptual metaphors: LOVE IS A JOURNEY and LOVE IS MADNESS.

The same holds for the other examples mentioned above: the verbal expressions for theories and arguments. They too follow more general principles, or conceptual metaphors, which are called THEORIES ARE BUILDINGS, and ARGUMENT IS WAR.[11]

Is that the *foundation* for your theory?	You disagree? OK, *shoot*!
The theory needs more *support*.	His criticisms were *right on target*.
The theory will *stand* or *fall* on the *strength* of that argument.	He *attacked every weak* point in my argument.
So far we have only put together the *framework* of the theory.	Your claims are *indefensible*.

→ THEORIES ARE BUILDINGS   → ARGUMENT IS WAR

Lakoff and Johnson (1980) brought together the observations we have documented above: the fact that ordinary language seemed to provide a powerful device for conceptualizing experience and that these linguistic conceptualizations followed some higher-level, structural principle that they called conceptual metaphors. Situating this structuring principle on the level of concepts, or more specifically on the level of conceptualizations of experience, has once again turned the study of language into a study of thought and understanding. In other words, Lakoff has adopted a new position toward an old epistemological problem, a problem with which he was already concerned when he outlined a framework of "linguistics and natural logics": language, thought, and human understanding (Lakoff 1970).

Notice, however, that whereas the discovery procedure for conceptual metaphors was bottom-up, that is, from the linguistic to the conceptual level, the hypothesized relationship between linguistic and conceptual meta-phors is claimed to be top-down, that is, from the conceptual to the linguistic level. In other words, conceptual metaphors are held to generate or give rise to these seemingly homogenous sets of linguistic expressions or, as I prefer to call them, "groups of verbal metaphors."[12]

On the basis of these observations, Lakoff and Johnson formulate their most radical claims, namely, that the conceptual system is "fundamentally metaphorical" and that it governs "the way we think, what we experience, and what we do every day" (Lakoff and Johnson 1980, 3). With these claims, they position themselves at the margins of linguistics and philosophy. The goal of ultimately formulating an empirical theory of understanding has con-tinued to inform the works of both authors since then (Lakoff 1987; Lakoff and Johnson 1999; Johnson 1987). It is important to bear this in mind, be-cause the fact that they push their enterprise toward a theory of human un-derstanding strongly influences the way they conceive of verbal metaphors.

In his 1987 book, Lakoff extends the treatment of metaphor to an analysis of categorization. He challenges the formal notion of categories (defined as a set of shared properties with clear-cut boundaries) and proposes an empirically based concept of category that follows the logic of prototypes and fuzzy sets. Lakoff explicitly connects his enterprise with the objectivist conception of understanding but seeks to present a new and alternative view:

> I will refer to the new view as *experiential realism* or alternatively as *ex-perientialism*. The term *experiential realism* emphasizes what experien-tialism shares with objectivism: (a) a commitment to the existence of the real world, (b) a recognition that reality places constraints on concepts, (c) a conception of truth that goes beyond mere internal coherence, and (d) a commitment to the existence of a stable knowledge of the world. Both names reflect the idea that thought fundamentally grows out of embodi-ment. "Experience" here is taken in a broad rather than a narrow sense. It includes everything that goes to make up actual or potential experi-ences of either individual organisms or communities of organisms—not merely perception, motor movement, etc., but *especially* the internal genetically acquired makeup of the organism and the nature of its inter-actions in both its physical and its social environments. (Lakoff 1987a, xv, emphasis in the original)

In the same year, Johnson (1987) published a philosophical treatment with the subtitle *Bodily Basis of Meaning, Imagination, and Reason*, which argues for the constitutive role of the imagination in a concept of mind and understanding.

He bases his account on the psychological concept of gestalt and the Kantian notion of schema (which he terms "image-schema") and holds that fundamental experiences are organized in image-schemata, such as CONTAINMENT, PATH, IN-OUT, FORCE, SCALE, BALANCE, CYCLE, CENTER-PERIPHERY. These image-schemata may then be projected metaphorically, providing a means of organizing abstract concepts of all kinds. In their most recent book, *Philosophy in the Flesh* (1999), Lakoff and Johnson explicitly intend to challenge some of the tenets of (what they conceive of as) traditional Western philosophy with the proposal for a cognitive science of basic philosophical ideas, a cognitive science of philosophy, which leads to an "embodied philosophy" or a "philosophy in the flesh."

Remember that the ultimate goal of Lakoff and Johnson's enterprise is, at its core, an experiential theory of human understanding that is based on processes of figurative thinking or, in Gibbs's words, that is based on "the poetics of mind" (Gibbs 1994). Thus, language is primarily of interest insofar as it provides insights into the functioning of the mind and more specifically into general cognitive mechanisms. These are then projected back to explain verbal metaphorical expressions in terms of conceptual metaphors. This procedure, important as it is, necessarily ignores linguistic variation. Its focus is on the common principles that underlie language and language use and not on variation, be it caused by differences in interindividual usage or in the conditions under which language is used. In contrast, this latter stance is the one advocated in this book. The assumed conceptual metaphors may well be plausible on the level of a language community and probably also on the level of a collective mind. Yet the extent to which they guide the understanding and actions of individuals is a fundamentally different question that hitherto has been primarily addressed by means of psychological experiments designed to elucidate metaphor comprehension.[13] The production side of metaphors has not received comparable interest, probably because it is notoriously more difficult to investigate experimentally. In this book, I intend to demonstrate that the microanalysis of instances of spontaneous metaphor use may provide important insights into the individual processes of metaphor production and that, as such, microanalyses add one more piece to the theoretical puzzle of whether, and how, metaphorical concepts may govern online processes of thinking for speaking (Slobin 1987, 1991).

Another important consequence of focusing on the identification of conceptual metaphors and systems of conceptual metaphors, which are ultimately derived from bodily experience, is a lack of close reflection upon the possibility of a purely linguistic organization of metaphorical concepts. Yet this is a concept that, at least since Wilhelm von Humboldt's formulation

of a "sprachliche Weltsicht" (linguistic worldview; cf. Humboldt 1985, 1839;
Trabant 1985a, 1985b), has informed European as well as Anglo-Saxon discussions of the relationship between language and thought. The assumption
of a linguistic relativism rooted in the works of Edward Sapir (1949) and
Benjamin Lee Whorf (1956) continues to inspire contemporary research in
cognitive and linguistic anthropology (Gumperz and Levinson 1996; Levinson 2003; Lucy 1992a, 1992b). Having recently undergone a reformulation
as "thinking for speaking" by Dan Slobin (1987, 1991), the idea that patterns of linguistic structure, be they grammaticalized or lexicalized, orient
online cognitive processes is not only prominent, but, to some extent, it has
also been empirically validated.[14] In his monographic analysis of systems
of morality informing American politics, Lakoff (2002) uses the language of
politicians to reconstruct hidden conceptual systems. And although he uses
language as a primary source of evidence, he does not talk about a linguistic
worldview, but about worldview in general: "As a student of the mind and of
language, I think we can make much better sense than has been made of the
worldviews and forms of discourse of conservatives and liberals. . . . The sub-
field [of cognitive science—CM] most concerned with issues of worldview,
that is, with everyday conceptualization, reasoning, and language, is cognitive linguistics" (Lakoff 2002, 3). Language is conceived of as a window into
general non-language-specific conceptual structures, which are presumed
largely unconscious: "That is what I study: what, exactly, our unconscious
system of concepts is and how we think and talk using that system of concepts" (Lakoff 2002, 4). Thus, a level of purely verbal organization is not hypothesized and, accordingly, does not receive much attention. Yet I shall argue that it has to be taken into consideration, at least as a possible realm of
cognitive organization. Throughout the book, I shall collate indications that
provide support for assuming a differentiation between structures of general
conceptualizations and language-specific conceptual structures.

An important contribution to such a view was offered by the eminent
linguist Harald Weinrich. Educated in Romance philology, his work is primarily linguistic but firmly rooted in the criticism of European literature.
He has become widely known for his analysis of *tempus* in the French language (1964), for his text grammar of French (1982), and for his work on
the semantics of metaphor (1958, 1963, 1964, 1967, 1976). It is astonishing,
however, that his foundations for a general theory of metaphor ("allgemeine
Metaphernlehre") have not received much attention, in Europe or in the
Anglo-Saxon world.[15]

Weinrich departs from observations that are similar to those of Lakoff
and Johnson. He shows that verbal metaphors are not isolated occurrences

but fall into semantically homogenic groups, which he terms "Bildfeld" (image field) in accordance with Jost Trier's (1931, 1934a, 1934b, 1938, 1968) concept of "Wortfeld" (lexical field). Weinrich bases his account on examples taken from European literature, from ancient Greek to modern French texts, to illustrate his point. One pertinent group he identifies is what he calls "metaphora memoriae," the metaphors for memory (Weinrich 1976, 291–94). He finds that two image fields for memory have existed since Plato: "Gedächtnis-Magazin" (memory as a storehouse) and "Gedächtnis als Wachstafel" (memory as a wax tablet). He gives the following list of quotes from European philosophers from antiquity to the eighteenth century as examples:

MEMORY AS A STOREHOUSE

1. Memory as palace, receptacle, a general's headquarters, a place for safekeeping treasure, cellar or storehouse, room or space, hiding-place for memories (Augustine, 8, 12–15).

2. Memory as a place for safekeeping treasure; a place for storing images, views, or aspects (Aquinas, 2, q. 49, a.1).

3. "A head stocked up with lots of disparate things is quite similar to a library of incomplete volumes . . . It is one of those storerooms filled with analyses of and judgments on works that analysis has not understood" (Diderot 1875, 370).

Note that Weinrich provides these examples to illustrate the idea that image fields function as mental models; he conceives of them as models of thought that tacitly direct philosophical and scientific conceptualizations of, for instance, memory. Furthermore, Weinrich documents the dangers inherent in an unconscious use of metaphoric models for scientific understanding with a quote from Henri Bergson; Bergson criticizes the assumption that memory is indeed, and literally, a storehouse in the mind: "Therefore, there is not, there cannot be a region in the brain where memories are preserved and accumulated" (Bergson 1946).

Parallel to the image field memory as storehouse, Weinrich identifies memory as a wax tablet as the only other image field for memory that according to him has occurred in European literature since the classical period:

MEMORY AS A WAX TABLET

1. Sokrates says, "Please assume, then, for the sake of argument, that there is in our souls a block of wax, in one case larger, in another

smaller, in one case the wax is purer, in another more impure and
harder, in some cases softer, and in some of proper quality. . . . Let us,
then, say that this is the gift of Memory, the mother of the Muses"
(Weinrich 1976, 292; trans. Harold N. Fowler).

2. "Look at the soft substance of the brain as a mass of sensitive and
living wax, but capable of having all sorts of forms, not losing any of
those that it has received, and incessantly receiving new ones that it
preserves" (Diderot 1875, 368).

Weinrich draws several conclusions from these observations: first, he thinks
that it is impossible to conceive of an entity such as memory without using
metaphor; hence, he conceptualizes metaphor as a cognitive process, as a
form of thought. Yet this form of thought is rooted in language. The image
fields derive from the use of language mostly in literature, but they have the
status of mental models: "We cannot conceive of an entity such as memory
without metaphors. Metaphors, particularly when they occur in the stability
of image fields, have the value of (hypothetical) mental models. Used critically, they help us to raise questions" (Weinrich 1976, 294). These models
guide the ways in which the members of a particular language community
think, infer, and construct scientific models. Weinrich also finds that one
subject, such as memory, may be structured by more than one image field,
whereby each image field addresses a different aspect of the subject in question (the wax tablet model concerns the nature of mental representations;
the storehouse model informs about the ways in which representations are
assembled in memory).

Apart from these apparent parallels with Lakoff and Johnson's theory of
conceptual metaphors, there remains one fundamental difference: Weinrich
locates these groups of verbal expressions on the level of Saussure's *langue*;
they are an organizational structure of the lexicon of a given language, and as
such, they constitute the supraindividual, collective realm of a linguistically
transmitted world of images. This world of images is passed on via mother
tongues and literature and constitutes a linguistic-literary worldview.

Using the first method I mentioned, it cannot be observed that there is,
however, beyond the good or bad metaphors of an author or a man on
the street, yet another supra-individual world of images: the objective,
material store of metaphors belonging to a community. And nevertheless,
it is hardly likely that the extraordinary, extensive agreement regarding
metaphor usage among the members of a cultural group, and particularly
of an era, is based on chance. The individual is always placed within a

metaphoric tradition that is communicated to him, partly through his mother tongue, partly through literature, and which is present to him as a linguistic-literary worldview. (Weinrich 1976, 277–78)

It is interesting to see that Weinrich appears to struggle with a problem that is similar to the one confronting Lakoff and Johnson, namely, the fact that there is a form of lexical organization—groups of verbal expressions—that appears to transcend individual languages. Unfortunately, Weinrich does not systematically follow up these two threads of his argument. He simply states that, on the one hand, image fields are structures of *langue* (i.e., relate to one specific language), while at the same time he says that they may crosscut all European languages and are a part of European culture. The relation between the level of a *langue* and European culture does not receive further discussion.

Lakoff and Johnson, on the other hand, do not consider a level of purely linguistic organization at all. They progress directly from the linguistic system to general conceptual structures. All three authors hypothesize a general level of cognitive organization: be it in terms of conceptual metaphors or mental models. And all three derive it from instances of language use, yet none of them works out in detail the relation between the verbal and the general level of conceptualization. This is where the study presented in this book seeks to offer some insights.

To conclude, the role philosophy attributes to language in human understanding, reason, and imagination obviously informs the role attributed to metaphor in this process. And we shall bear in mind the philosophical issues involved in the study of metaphor, although they will not be a core feature of this book. The enterprise of this book is to firmly base the study of metaphor in linguistics proper and to relate a close analysis of verbal metaphors in use to what is known about metaphorical conceptualizations, be they conceptual metaphors or image fields. Although the fundamental claims of Lakoff and Johnson's conceptual metaphor theory now appear to be empirically validated, as I have mentioned before, there is a growing recognition of the need to root the theory more firmly in a close linguistic analysis of metaphors (cf. Cameron 2003; Cameron and Low 1999; Deignan 2005; Gibbs 1999a; Gibbs and Steen 1999; PragglejazGroup 2007; Steen 1999, 2002a, 2002b, 2007; Stefanowitsch and Gries 2006).[16] I am much in favor of this recent development in cognitive linguistic studies of metaphor, for if we take language to contain resources for reconstructing conceptualization, our reconstructions will only be as good as our linguistic analyses. Therefore, I see the cognitive linguistic analysis of metaphors (be they verbal, conceptual, or multimodal) as integral to the core of language and hence as a focal aspect of the field of linguistics.

A final remark: although the sketch of the epistemology of metaphor provided in this section is only meant to serve as a rather crude background for our further discussions, it should have at least made clear that any theory of metaphor implies a specific philosophy and that any philosophy has, of course, to be accounted for within its network of philosophical debates and controversies. Wallace Martin (1993), in his entry on metaphor in *The New Princeton Encyclopedia of Poetry and Poetics*, makes this very point, underlining it with a quote from Derrida: "As Derrida says (1972), 'each time that a rhetoric defines metaphor, not only is a philosophy implied, but also a conceptual network in which philosophy itself has been constituted.' Thus agreement about the status of metaphor will be deferred until all other philosophical disputes have been resolved" (Martin 1993). In other words, this means that for the present purposes I will accept the philosophically provisional status of the accounts of metaphor sketched above and go ahead with a linguistic and cognitive study of metaphor, which in turn may feed back into the philosophical discussion concerning metaphors and into their role in processes of thinking for speaking.

2.2 The Nature of Metaphor: Cognitive or Linguistic?

As we have seen above, some philosophers have placed metaphor outside of the sort of linguistics that aims to reveal true descriptions of the world; quite astonishingly, some linguists have placed metaphor outside of linguistics proper—and this is not just a consequence of situating the study of meaning outside of linguistics (cf. Arens 1967, 686–87). One such case is Jerrold M. Sadock, who deliberately and provocatively locates all figurative speech outside of linguistics; he adopts a structuralistic conception of linguistics with its characteristic approach to explaining language on the basis of its system-internal relations, not its system-external relations.

> I take synchronic linguistics to be the study of those aspects of human communication that are unique to natural language, no matter whether they are principled and inhere specifically in the nature of human language or are arbitrary features of particular languages. All nonliteral speech, then, including metaphor, falls outside the domain of synchronic linguistics, for nonliteral acts having nothing to do with natural language occur and parallel those that we perform by using language. (Sadock 1993, 42)

He further underlines this assessment by pointing out that the psychological basis of metaphor is analogical reasoning, which as a general cognitive principle is not part of what linguistics should be concerned with.

> I take it for granted that the underlying principles governing metaphor are of a general psychological sort and are thus not specifically linguistic. While the intellectual faculties that are involved might be *prerequisites* to speech, they are independent of it. The fact that a certain group of stars in the night sky reminded someone of a bull and the fact that a lion on a warrior's shield suggests that its bearer is brave are, I think, nonlinguistic instances of the same analogical urge that functions in the issuance and apprehension of metaphor. (Sadock 1993, 42; emphasis in the original)

Yet, in spite of locating the study of metaphor outside of linguistics, Sadock does work on metaphor, and he does so from a linguistic point of view. This reintegration of metaphor into linguistics is realized via a Gricean perspective, for example, by regarding language as communication governed by rules of social interaction (H. P. Grice's cooperative principle; cf. Grice 1975). The foundation of metaphor in general processes of analogical reasoning does not receive further attention; instead, Sadock conceptualizes metaphor as a form of nonliteral or figurative use of language, which he explains as a violation of one of Grice's maxims of conversation. Taken as a whole, Sadock's argument appears to follow a specific rhetorical aim, namely, to characterize the nature of metaphor as a nonliteral or figurative aspect of language that is not only different from literal language but that is only accountable via literal meaning. We will return to this concept of metaphor in chapter 4, in the context of John Searle's analysis of metaphor in terms of indirect speech acts. For the purposes of this section, the brief account of Sadock's argument should have sufficiently illustrated what are the two disparate poles governing the controversies about the nature of metaphor: metaphor as a specific form of language and metaphor as a general form of thought, or, in short, metaphor as a cognitive or/and linguistic phenomenon.

Traditionally (e.g., in rhetoric, stylistics, philology, literary criticism, semantics, and historical linguistics), metaphor has been primarily regarded as a matter of language that serves a multitude of functions, with the most pertinent ones operating in language change and in poetic language. Stephen Ullmann (1967), in his landmark treatment of linguistic semantics, conceives of metaphor as a multifunctional device of human speech that languages exploit in various different ways: "Metaphor is so closely intertwined with the very texture of human speech that we have already encountered it in various guises as a major factor in motivation, as an expressive device, as a source of synonymy and polysemy, as an outlet for intense emotions, as a means of filling gaps in vocabulary, and in several other roles" (Ullmann 1967, 212). It is noteworthy that another classical treatment of linguistic semantics, the one by John Lyons, also mentions metaphor as a phenomenon of polysemy and language change; but Lyons also points out that metaphor, because of its extension of lexical meaning, poses severe problems for any formalization of the semantic structure of language. Formal accounts of semantic structures should be able to predict all possible sentence meanings—and, apparently, metaphorical meaning is not predictable by formal rules (cf. Lyons 1977).

Further advocates of a primarily linguistic view on metaphor can be found in structural semantics (Cohen 1993), in formal semantics (Abraham 1998; Davidson 1978; van Dijk 1975), in pragmatics (Cohen 1975; Sadock 1993; Searle 1993; Sperber and Wilson 1986), in semiotics (Eco 1984; Köller 1975, 1986), and in stylistics and literary criticism (Friedrich 1968; Kayser 1976; Bertau 1996; Brooke-Rose 1958; Coenen 2002; Lausberg 1960; Kubczak 1978; Meier 1963; Mooij 1976). In the following discussion, I shall refer to these approaches to metaphor as linguistic metaphor theories (LMTs), whereas approaches that regard metaphor as a cognitive phenomenon will be called cognitive metaphor theories (CogMTs). Cognitive metaphor theories share the assumption that metaphor is a cognitive phenomenon, a specific structure or process of thought.

Since contemporary controversies in metaphor theory oscillate not only between the poles "linguistic" and "cognitive nature of metaphor" but also between the two subpoles "linguistic" and "general cognition," it is necessary to introduce a further distinction: the distinction between CogMTs with a bias toward the assumptions of LMT and CogMTs with a bias toward grounding metaphor in general cognition.[17]

LMTs	CogMTs
→ Metaphor as a specific form of language	→ Metaphor as a specific form of thought
→ Metaphor as a linguistic phenomenon only	→ Metaphor as a cognitive phenomenon

Cognitive metaphor theories with an inclination toward LMTs share the belief that metaphor is a linguistic phenomenon, and they demand its integration into theories and models of language production and comprehension.

Adherents of these theories are typically psycholinguists or cognitive scientists (cf. Glucksberg and Keysar 1990, 1993; Keysar and Bly 1995; McGlone 1996; Miller 1993; Murphy 1996, 1997; Ortony 1988; Paivio and Walsh 1993; Stock, Slack, and Ortony 1993; Winner and Gardener 1993). These scholars tend to found their theories on a set of basic assumptions regarding the nature of language and of metaphor whose correctness is often tacitly assumed:

- Language is primarily literal,
- Metaphor is a matter of poetic language (primarily),
- Literal language is the default case (ubiquitous and accessible to truth-conditional and pragmatic analysis),
- Figurative language is an aberration of the default (a violation of a proposition and/or of a pragmatic rule),
- Literal language reflects reality in an objective manner, and
- Figurative language distorts reality (because it violates truth conditions).

The cognitive processing of metaphor has received quite a lot of attention in psycholinguistics and cognitive science in the past two decades. Because of its assumed aberration of the default processes of language comprehension, it has been widely studied. For psycholinguists, metaphor constitutes a challenge to models of language production and comprehension because of the way it supposedly differs from or is indifferent to literal language processing. In short, even though this interest focuses on cognitive processing of metaphor, the nature of metaphor is conceived of as inherently linguistic.

Another type of CogMT showing a certain bias toward LMT can be found in philosophical, rhetorical, linguistic, and stylistic approaches to metaphor. Thus, Richards's *The Philosophy of Rhetoric* (1936), Black's *Models and Metaphors'* (1962), and Weinrich's *Sprache in Texten* (1976) conceive of metaphor as linguistic and hold the following assumptions:[18]

- Language is primarily literal,
- Metaphor is a matter of poetic language (primarily),
- Metaphor is an aberration of the default,
- Metaphor is a violation of a proposition and/or of a pragmatic rule,
- Metaphor is the result of a tension between focus and frame,
- Metaphor is a contradictory predication,
- Metaphor is an omnipresent principle of language,
- Metaphor is structured in terms of image fields (within the lexicon of a language), and
- Metaphors are mental models.

One interesting—and in the current debates insufficiently accounted for—
aspect of these older conceptions of metaphor is that they conceive of
metaphor as both a specific form of language, *and* a specific form of thought.
In this view, metaphoric language provides mental models that structure
processes of categorization and inferencing and that structure experience
to a very large extent. To my knowledge, Richards in his *Philosophy of
Rhetoric* gives the first explicit formulation of such a theory of metaphor
in the Anglo-Saxon world: "The traditional theory noticed only a few of the
modes of metaphor; and limited its application of the term *metaphor* to a
few of them only. And thereby it made metaphor seem to be a verbal matter,
a shifting and displacement of words, whereas fundamentally it is a borrowing between and intercourse of *thoughts*, a transaction between contexts.
Thought is metaphoric, and proceeds by comparison, and the metaphors of
language derive therefrom" (Richards 1936, 94; emphases in the original).
Before and in parallel with him, German psychologists and linguists such
as Wilhelm Wundt (1922), Friedrich Stählin (1914), and Karl Bühler (1936)
proposed similar views (cf. also Lieb 1964).

    And although scholars in this tradition do not explicitly claim that
metaphor is a form of general cognition, implicitly this idea is also present.
Hence, we find passages where they assume that

- Metaphor is having two thoughts of different things together (Richards
  1936);
- metaphors may reveal how things are; they are mental models (Black
  1962); and
- coupled image fields are mental models; they constitute a worldview,
  guide inferences, host and stimulate verbal metaphors (Weinrich 1976).

In the light of these historical precursors, the assumptions of Lakoff and
Johnson's conceptual metaphor theory (CMT) appear somewhat less radical,
and less novel. Therefore, it appears more appropriate to conceive of their
contribution as an important and significant step forward in the tradition of
philosophical, rhetorical, and psychological theories of metaphors.

    However, regarding its epistemological claims, conceptual metaphor
theory remains radical, for it conceives of the nature of metaphor not only as
primarily cognitive but also as a primarily nonlinguistic form of organizing
experience and thereby transforms metaphor theory into an experientially
grounded theory of human understanding. This generalization claim is in line
with a fairly broad range of research on metaphor in cognitive anthropology,

sociology, and linguistics. In this tradition, metaphors are regarded as conceptualizations of experiences that may have effects on learning, reasoning, and understanding. Metaphors as cultural models may shape collective views regarding various facets of everyday life:

- Reddy's conduit metaphor of communication (Reddy 1993);
- Schön's analysis of social policy (Schön 1993);
- Quinn's analysis of concepts of marriage (Quinn 1999a, 1999b); and
- Shore's analysis of baseball games (Shore 1996).

These approaches typically hold that ordinary language is often, if not pervasively, structured figuratively (with metaphor being the most pervasive among the tropes),[19] and that metaphor is a basic form of human creativity. Weinrich (1976), Oksaar (1988), and Störel (1997) regard metaphor as an important device for constructing scientific models of thought. Brünner (1987), Störel (1997), and Lakoff (2002) regard metaphors as an everyday and as a scientific means of conceptualizing abstract domains, such as communication, music, and morality. In the same vein, Schön (1993) takes metaphor to be a form of perspectivization of experience with consequences for social policy; Sternberg, Tourangeau, and Nigro (1993) view metaphors as cognitive constructions, and Gentner and Jeziorski (1993) as a form of analogical reasoning; in contrast, Reddy's (1993) notion of "conceptual frame" can be considered a precursor of Lakoff and Johnson's view of conceptual metaphor.

Lakoff and Johnson's CMT is certainly the most elaborate cognitive theory of metaphor currently under discussion. With its focus on metaphor as a general principle of human cognition, it has inspired a huge array of research, not only in cognitive linguistics and cognitive science, but also in anthropology and stylistics. Conceptual metaphor theory scholars tend to adhere to the following set of assumptions:

- Language is fundamentally figurative;
- metaphor is pervasive in ordinary language;
- the difference between literal and nonliteral meaning is a gradual, not a categorial one;
- metaphor is understanding one thing in terms of another;
- thought is fundamentally figurative;
- metaphor is a general principle of conceptual organization;
- metaphor is fundamental to human understanding; and
- metaphor is a general cognitive process.

It appears, therefore, that CMT has formulated the most far-reaching and, in this regard, radical and controversial position concerning the nature of figurative language; while being rooted in the history of a philosophy of rhetoric, it challenges widely held claims in linguistics, semantics, and cognitive science.

Proponents of CMT study metaphor from two points of view: what can language tell us about the nature of the human mind, and does the linguistic system use general cognitive mechanisms—or is it organized into modules that operate according to language-internal mechanisms? "Does language make use of general cognitive mechanisms? Or is it something separate and independent, using only mechanisms of its own? . . . The answer to this question will affect the study of cognition, since it will determine whether linguistic evidence is admissible in the study of the mind in general" (Lakoff 1987, 59).

Remember that Sadock used the argument that metaphor is based on the general cognitive principle of analogy as a reason to rule out its study within linguistics (by bringing it back in via the back door of a Gricean approach). I think Sadock's position is more than rhetoric—it reveals a fundamental rift in linguistics by raising questions concerning the nature of language: is language a self-sufficient system that has to be accounted for only in its own terms, that is, in terms of system-internal principles (as in structural linguistics or in Chomskyan linguistics), or is it to be explained in terms of system-external principles (as in cognitive linguistics)? Linguistic metaphor theories tend to be compatible with modularistic views of the mind, whereas CogMTs with a bias toward CMT tend to be compatible with network and constructivist models of the mind. For an overview of the fundamental assumptions of LMTs and CogMTs, see. Table 1.

2.3 Conclusion: Establishment and Creation of Metaphoricity Is a Cognitive Process with Multimodal Products

The stance advocated throughout this book is one that seeks to narrow down some of the divisions outlined above. Notably, I shall argue that metaphors are neither language nor thought; rather their establishment and their construction is a form of thought, a cognitive activity that makes use of different representational modalities—such as language, picture, and gesture—of which language is certainly the most elaborate one. In short, metaphors are thought and language (in conjunction with other modalities or even independent of language).

Table 1. Overview of linguistic and cognitive metaphor theories (LMTs and CogMTs)

Linguistic metaphor theories (LMTs)	Cognitive metaphor theories (CogMTs)	
→ Metaphor as a specific form of language → Metaphor as a linguistic phenomenon only	→ Metaphor as a specific form of thought → Metaphor as a cognitive phenomenon	
	Linguistic cognition	General cognition
• Language is primarily literal • Metaphor is a matter of poetic language (primarily) • Literal language is the default case (ubiquitous and accessible to truth-conditional and pragmatic analysis) • Figurative language is an aberration of the default (violation of a proposition and/or of a pragmatic rule) • Literal language reflects reality in an objective manner • Figurative language distorts reality (because it violates truth conditions)	• Language is primarily literal • Metaphor is a matter of poetic language (primarily) • Metaphor is an aberration from the default • Metaphor is a violation of a proposition and/or of a pragmatic rule • Metaphor is the result of a tension between focus and frame • Metaphor is a contradictory predication • Metaphor is an omnipresent principle of language • Metaphor is structured in terms of image fields with the lexicon (language) • Metaphors are mental models	• Language is fundamentally figurative • Metaphor is pervasive in ordinary language • The difference between literal and nonliteral meaning is a gradual one, not a categorical one • Metaphor is understanding and experiencing one thing in terms of another • Thought is fundamentally figurative • Metaphor is general principle of conceptual organization • Metaphor is fundamental for human understanding • Metaphor is a general cognitive process
Formal semantics (proposition analysis) Pragmatics	Psycholinguistics (language production, comprehension, development) Cognitive science (artificial intelligence)	Conceptual metaphor theory Cognitive anthropology Cognitive science
Examples		
Van Dijk: Determine the conditions under which metaphorical sentences may have a truth value Grice: Metaphorical utterances violate the cooperation principle when understood literally Searle: Metaphor is a form of indirect speech act	Glucksberg/Keysar: Metaphors are assertions of categorizations speakers mean what they say Winner/Gardener: In nonliteral discourse speakers do not mean what they say	Lakoff/Johnson: Conceptual metaphors are entrenched cognitive structures that inform thought, action, and language. Gibbs: Figurative language provide basic schemes that organize experiences and the external world
	Rhetoric and stylistics	Rhetoric and stylistics
	Weinrich: Metaphor is structured in terms of image fields within the lexicon Richards: Metaphor is an omnipresent principle of language Black: Metaphor is a tension between focus and frame	Richards: Metaphor is having two thoughts of different things together Black: Metaphor may reveal how things are; they are mental models Weinrich: Coupled image fields are mental models; they constitute a worldview, guide inferences, and host and stimulate verbal metaphors

As we proceed, a view of metaphors will be presented that seeks to honor the cognitive, procedural, and multimodal nature of metaphor. Hence, it is one goal of this book to propose further steps toward an overarching cognitive approach to metaphor by systematically incorporating its multimodal, procedural, and discursive nature. As such, it is a core element of the cognitive linguistic enterprise; more specifically it falls within the scope of its applied linguistics branch. The view advocated in this book focuses on a still nonmainstream aspect of the relation between language and cognition. Whereas cognitive linguists have so far accumulated considerable knowledge about the structures of understanding via the study of language (i.e., focused on the level of the system), the ways in which structures and processes of cognition interact and draw upon linguistic and conceptual structures have only been a topic of research that sets out to test the psychological validity of the various claims. The cognitive processes engaged during metaphor production in naturalistic situations of language use, as well as the characteristics of metaphors as language, have received only scant attention.

Psycholinguistic experiments aimed at testing the psychological reality of conceptual metaphors and so-called dead metaphors (cf. Gibbs 1994; Katz et al. 1998; Ortony 1993a) have not stimulated a theoretical reconceptualization of Lakoff and Johnson's CMT. Rather, they have served as evidence for the psychological plausibility of some of the fundamental assumptions of metaphor theories. Here are the three main questions under discussion:

- Is figurative language processed differently from literal language?
- Are dead metaphors vital, or are they processed as literal expressions?
- Are conceptual metaphors activated online during speaking?[20]

The point of departure taken in this book—the dynamic view—foregrounds the constraints that are imposed on linguistic and conceptual structures of metaphors by the conditions of processing metaphoricity online during discourse, or, put another way, how and to what degree are metaphors (conceptual and verbal) activated online during speaking and writing? This shift in perspective bears upon some fundamental theoretical issues: it demands a cognitively realistic conception of metaphoricity—in whatever medium metaphor may be instantiated—and a systematic integration of the conditions governing usage into a theory of metaphor. In doing this, it seeks to overcome the simple *langue-parole* or competence-performance projection that tacitly guides most of the theoretical work in cognitive linguistics. Instead of regarding language use as an epiphenomenon of static linguistic and conceptual structures, the dynamic view takes the facts that language needs to be processed internally and needs to be adapted to specific contexts of use to be primordial for a theory of metaphor. In taking this perspective, the book constructs a small bridge between more traditionally linguistic and more radically cognitive linguistic conceptualizations of metaphor; it does this by taking language seriously as a phenomenon of use that is tightly integrated into the intellectual architecture of human beings.

CHAPTER THREE

Realms of Metaphors: Activation in Language Use

What are the cognitive realms of metaphor in speaking and writing? Or, put another way, what exactly is activated when a metaphor is used and is active for a given speaker or writer? As we have seen in chapter 2, a critical and highly controversial issue in theories of metaphor is the question of the ontology of metaphor. Is it a uniquely verbal phenomenon or a primarily conceptual phenomenon? The discussions are, to a large degree, conducted on a purely theoretical level, mainly based on invented examples of sentences or on dictionaries of idiomatic expressions, with psycholinguistic research testing the theoretically generated hypotheses. The qualitative analyses of spontaneous language uses to be offered in this chapter will uncover new theoretically relevant facets of the realms of metaphor.

The conceptual, verbal, verbo-gestural, and verbo-pictorial realms of metaphors will be considered in this chapter. I shall address the following questions with respect to each of them:

1. Are they activated online during speaking?
   a. What are the empirical indications for this?
2. If yes, how are they activated?
   a. Always in the same manner
      i. Always as conceptual metaphors, which would be a logical consequence of the CMT assumption that lexical meaning equates with conceptual meaning.
      ii. Always as verbal metaphors, which would be a logical consequence of the LMT assumption that metaphors reside on a verbal level of cognitive organization.
   b. Selectively

i. If they are activated selectively, then this would mean that both assumptions are false, and that we must assume various levels of cognitive organization on which metaphors may rely.

These questions will be addressed by first reviewing the different theoretical conceptions of these realms and then by discussing each of them in the light of exemplary cases of metaphor use, such as spontaneous speech production, works of art, and newspaper photographs that incorporate metaphors in their headlines and/or their captions.

3.1 Conceptual Metaphors

Conceptual metaphor theory claims that conceptual metaphors are modality-independent cognitive structures that may be manifested in all kinds of forms: "It is also important to stress that not all conceptual metaphors are manifested in the words of a language. Some are manifested in grammar, others in gesture, art, or ritual. These nonlinguistic metaphors may, however, be secondarily expressed through language and other symbolic means" (Lakoff and Johnson 1999, 57). In other words, conceptual metaphors are not conceived of as simple projections of verbal metaphors, or systems of verbal metaphors, into the cognitive system. Rather, it is suggested that they are abstract structures of thought that function as a conceptual frame in terms of which single lexical items are produced and comprehended. This means that they are assumed to be cognitively real (which is a logical consequence of one of the two commitments of cognitive linguists).[1]

In the section 3.1.1, the concept of conceptual metaphors will be introduced based on a specific example: the conceptual system of anger inherent in American English as presented by Lakoff and Kövecses (1987). This will be related to the typical twofold argument of CMT: on the one hand, to conceive of conceptual metaphors as active cognitive realms of verbal metaphors in language use and on the other hand, to describe conceptual metaphors as the entrenched patterns of thought of a cultural community. Specific attention will be paid to the distinction between the individual level of use and the collective level of established usages, which I believe CMT tends not to account for systematically.[2] This distinction will be related to the claim of their psychological plausibility.

3.1.1 An Example: Lakoff and Kövecses's Conceptual System of Anger

Conceptual metaphors constitute larger systems of conceptual organization, of which the conceptual system of anger is an example. ANGER IS HEAT belongs to a complex conceptual system consisting of conceptual metaphors, conceptual metonymies, a cultural model of anger, and primary bodily experiences of the emotion of anger.

The conceptual metaphor ANGER IS HEAT is visible in verbal expressions, such as "you made my blood boil," "simmer down," and "let him stew." Note that the conceptual metaphor is not conceived of as an abstraction from these uses of language. Rather, it is claimed that the verbal expressions are derived from, are instantiations of, a conceptual metaphor, which in itself is grounded in the ways in which humans experience the emotion of anger and in a cultural model of the physiological effects of anger. The physiological effects of anger are filtered into a cultural model or a folk theory of anger. According to Lakoff and Kövecses' (1987) analysis, "The Cognitive Model of Anger Inherent in American English," the model contains the following physiological effects: body heat, internal pressure, agitation, and loss of accurate perception. And as anger increases, all the physiological effects also increase. The conceptual metaphor ANGER IS HEAT is based on this cultural model through the metonymic principle EFFECT FOR CAUSE or, as Lakoff and Kövecses put it, THE PHYSIOLOGICAL EFFECTS OF AN EMOTION STAND FOR THE EMOTION. This metonymic principle produces a system of metonymies for anger that operates on the physiological effects fixed in the folk model: BODY HEAT, INTERNAL PRESSURE, REDNESS IN THE NECK AREA, AGITATION, and LOSS OF ACCURATE PERCEPTION. These conceptual metonymies give rise to verbal expressions, such as "don't get *hot under your collar*," "Billy is a *hothead*" (ANGER IS INCREASED BODY HEAT), "she was *blind with rage*," and "I was so mad I *couldn't see straight*" (LOSS OF ACCURATE PERCEPTION). These metonymies, in turn, motivate the emergence of more general conceptual metaphors, such as ANGER IS HEAT. In this conceptual metaphor, anger is not necessarily body heat, but it can be attributed to different entities and to different aspects of a person (which is the point where metonymy turns into metaphor). Thus, arguments may be "heated," or people may "stew" like a piece of meat in a pot. Solid and fluid entities may become heated, and this is captured in the conceptual metaphors ANGER IS FIRE and ANGER IS THE HEAT OF A FLUID IN A CONTAINER. They, in turn, may motivate verbal expressions, such as "you make my *blood boil*," "*simmer* down," and "let him *stew*." Furthermore, the conceptual metaphor ANGER IS THE HEAT OF A FLUID IN A CONTAINER is motivated by another type of conceptual metaphor: the body is a container for the emotions, which shows up in verbal expressions, such as "he was *filled* with anger," "she couldn't *contain* her joy," and "she was *brimming* with rage."[3] The conceptual system rests upon two cognitive principles and is grounded in the physiological experience of anger:

Physiological experience:

anger produces body heat

Metonymic principle:	Metaphoric principle:
physiological effects for the emo-tion	one conceptual domain is understood in terms of another

The diagram (figure 11) below gives an overview of the complex set of conceptual metonymies and metaphors, which, according to Lakoff and Kövecses, structure the concept of ANGER in American English.

Lakoff and Kövecses' system assumes a network of interrelated concepts that are established via two ways: the cognitive principles of metonymic and metaphoric thinking on the one hand, and physiological and cultural experiences on the other hand. Metonymic and metaphoric principles operate upon experiences and create new concepts. The system of conceptual metaphors that results from such an analysis is clearly one that is collective and evolutionary by nature. Put another way, the cultural model of anger, as reconstructed by Lakoff and Kövecses through an analysis of verbal expressions, is a system that exists on the level of a language community; it is situated on the level of a linguistic system, or more specifically, on the lexicon of American English (at least this is what their investigation documents and what the title of their article claims). Moreover, what they document is the historical motivation of this system. How do expressions such as "he was filled with anger" evolve? Once again, their answer indicates a process operating on the collective level: by means of collectively shared ways of experiencing a certain emotion, which in our case is anger. However, when turning to the grounding of the cultural model of anger, the assumed process appears to become subjective and shifts to the individual level. Experiences of anger are manifold (and subjective) and are filtered into a collective cultural model of anger. Once they have been filtered to a cultural model, it is unclear whether they are still connected to individual experiences. In addition, the status of the cognitive principles involved is somewhat vague: although the formulation chosen points to a subjective level—the authors speak of "metaphoric and metonymic thinking" (Lakoff and Kövecses 1987)—in order to become collectively shared ways of conceptualization, these principles must function on a collective level too.

Unfortunately, Lakoff and Kövecses only scarcely discuss the relation between the collective and individual levels of cognitive organization. Consider the quotes taken from their concluding section of the article:

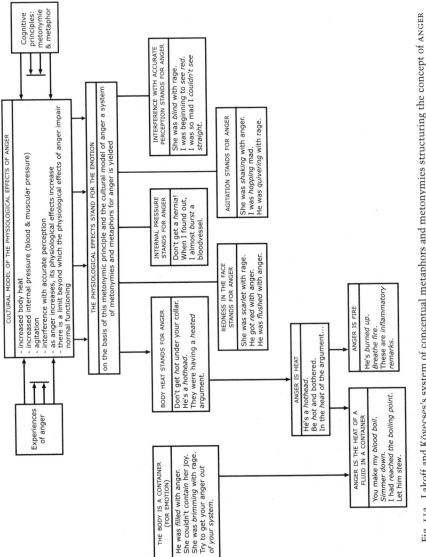

Fig. 11a. Lakoff and Kövecses's system of conceptual metaphors and metonymies structuring the concept of ANGER inherent in American English. Lakoff and Kövecses (1987).

[T]he study of the language as a whole gives us no guide to individual variation. We have no idea how close any individual comes to the model we
have uncovered, and we have no idea how people differ from one another. . . . our methodology does not enable us to say much about the exact
psychological status of the model we have uncovered. How much of it do
people really use in comprehending anger? Do people base their actions
on this model? Are people aware of the model? How much of it, if any,
do people consciously believe? And most intriguingly, does the model
have any effect on what people feel? (Lakoff and Kövecses 1987, 220–21)

It is based on the authors' "intuitive observations" that these collective
structures are psychologically real for every speaker of American English.
The authors add that this claim demands firm empirical testing before it
can be really established. Yet, implicitly, the assumption that conceptual
metaphors have a psychological reality has been a characteristic of CMT
right from the start. Even the book title Lakoff and Johnson chose for their
influential monograph, *Metaphors We Live By*, indicates that the collective
and the individual aspects of metaphors merge ("we" implies that all speakers of American English live by metaphors; Lakoff and Johnson 1980). In the
very first lines of this book, this argument is made quite explicitly:

> Metaphor is for most people a device of the poetic imagination and the
> ·rhetorical flourish—a matter of extraordinary rather than ordinary lan-
> guage. Moreover, metaphor is typically viewed as characteristic of lan-
> guage alone, a matter of words rather than of thought or action. . . . We
> have found, on the contrary, *that metaphor is pervasive in everyday life,*
> *not just in language but in thought and action.* Our ordinary concep-
> tual system, in terms of which we both think and act, is fundamentally
> metaphorical in nature. (Lakoff and Johnson 1980, 3; my emphasis)

The argumentative move of CMT is to project the linguistic system into
the individual minds of speakers. Every linguistic structure is assumed to
be cognitively real in that it guides the thought and action of individual
speakers. The use of the first person plural—"we" and the pronoun "our"—
indicates the shift from the collective to the individual level. Although
the plural form indicates that it is the same for each and every speaker of
English, it is clear that the assumed processes must be individual processes.
This reading of Lakoff and Johnson's argument is in harmony with one of the
above-mentioned commitments of cognitive linguistics that Lakoff himself
has formulated, namely, that the principles and structures that cognitive

linguists are interested in should be cognitively real, that is, in accordance with what is known about the mind and the brain. This means that they must also be functional in the online processes of language production.

Departing from this basic assumption, it appears that CMT tacitly assumes that conceptual systems like the ones for anger are collective in nature (in that they reside in the lexicon of American English) *and* (at least partially) psychologically realistic (in that they guide "our" thought and language, i.e., that of the speakers using this system). If this were true, then this conceptual system of anger should be available, if not active, every time a speaker uses one of the linguistic expressions that are derived from conceptual metaphors. Is this plausible?

I do not think so. At least the assumed relations between such systems and cognitive processes during speaking demand further specification. As it is, the conceptual system of anger is rather complex, and, simply for reasons of procedural economy, it seems hardly probable that it is accessed as a whole each and every time a linguistic metaphoric expression based on it is used. Moreover, given that the system only accounts for the semantics of one lexical item or idiom, nothing is said about how other metaphors in the same sentence, "literal" meanings or the "meanings or functions" of syntactic structures, relate to these processes.

It just seems highly implausible that, under normal conditions of language production, each and every time such a metaphor is used, activation would have to run through the entire system. Gibbs is aware of this problem and argues that "this does not mean . . . that these metaphorical schema are ordinarily accessed each and every time a metaphor is read and heard" (Gibbs 1998, 92). Take the conceptual metaphor ANGER IS THE HEAT OF A FLUID IN A CONTAINER as an example. If we were to assume that during cognitive processing the whole network is built up, the following experiences, cultural models of experiences, principles, and concepts would have to be active at the very moment of producing a sentence like "you make my *blood boil*":

Cultural model	CULTURAL MODEL OF ANGER
	The physiological experience "anger produces body heat" is part of the cultural model of anger
Conceptual metonymy	BODY HEAT STANDS FOR ANGER
Conceptual metaphor	ANGER IS HEAT
Conceptual metaphor	THE BODY IS A CONTAINER FOR EMOTION
Conceptual metaphor	ANGER IS A HEATED FLUID IN A CONTAINER

These are five aspects of the conceptual system of anger active to produce "boil" in "You make my blood *boil.*" It hardly seems plausible that all these concepts and conceptual operations need to be active to ensure metaphor production or comprehension. This becomes even more obvious when we consider this supposed procedure in the context of the entire system of anger as reconstructed by Lakoff and Kövecses (1987). A mere glance at the diagram of the above system reveals that, as a model of "concept" and/ or "language production," this does not appear to be straightforward enough. As mentioned above, Lakoff and Kövecses themselves and the psycholinguist Gibbs have argued along similar lines, pointing out that not all conceptual metaphors that underlie a specific verbal expression need to be active during speech production or comprehension or that the complexity of these systems of conceptual metaphors simply lacks the elegance required for a theory that claims to be both experientially grounded and cognitively realistic (cf. Grady, Taub, and Morgan 1996).

A close inspection leaves us with the impression that, despite their commitment to cognitive plausibility, Lakoff and Kövecses' perspective continues to be—albeit tacitly—grounded in a kind of Saussurean view of the linguistic system as a collective and static entity that only needs to be realized in language use. The motivation for the conceptual metaphor ANGER IS HEATED FLUID IN A CONTAINER sketched above reveals this quite clearly. This holds even though conceptual metaphors are assumed not to be linguistic in nature. Even if they are modality-independent conceptual structures on the level of general world knowledge, they remain collective. And as collective systems, they are projected into the minds of individual speakers whose thinking and acting are supposedly organized in their terms (even if they are only selectively represented and/or accessed).

Therefore, it seems crucial to devote more energy to clarifying the relation between the collective system and its individual availability and activation during the online processes of thinking, speaking, and acting. From a historical point of view, such motivations of word meanings appear plausible, and they are not—as I have documented in chapter 2—a new discovery. From the point of view of cognition in language use, their plausibility is not as obvious.

Therefore, in order to gain support for the claim that systems of conceptual metaphors are cognitively real and exist independently of language, empirical evidence of nonverbal instantiations of conceptual metaphors is needed. But before turning to the discussion of an example of a bodily realization of conceptual metaphor, it is necessary to introduce two fundamental forms of conceptual metaphors: primary and complex metaphors.

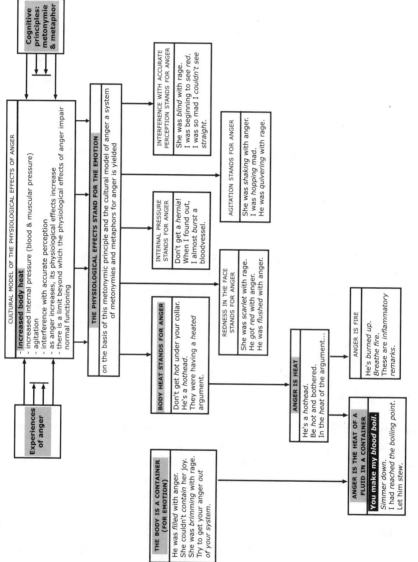

Fig. 11b. Conceptual system of anger with (supposedly) active building blocks when uttering the sentence "You make my blood boil."

Experiences of anger

Cognitive principles: metonymie & metaphor

CULTURAL MODEL OF THE PHYSIOLOGICAL EFFECTS OF ANGER
- **increased body heat**
- increased internal pressure (blood & muscular pressure)
- agitation
- interference with accurate perception
- as anger increases, its physiological effects increase
- there is a limit beyond which the physiological effects of anger impair normal functioning

THE PHYSIOLOGICAL EFFECTS STAND FOR THE EMOTION

on the basis of this metonymic principle and the cultural model of anger a system of metonymies and metaphors for anger is yielded

INTERFERENCE WITH ACCURATE PERCEPTION STANDS FOR ANGER

She was *blind* with rage.
I was beginning to *see red*.
I was so mad I *couldn't see straight*.

INTERNAL PRESSURE STANDS FOR ANGER

Don't get a *hernia*!
When I found out, I almost *burst a bloodvessel*.

AGITATION STANDS FOR ANGER

She was *shaking* with anger.
I was *hopping* mad.
He was *quivering* with rage.

BODY HEAT STANDS FOR ANGER

Don't get *hot* under your collar.
He's a *hothead*.
They were having a *heated* argument.

REDNESS IN THE FACE STANDS FOR ANGER

She was *scarlet* with rage.
He *got red* with anger.
He was *flushed* with anger.

ANGER IS HEAT

He's a *hothead*.
Be *hot* and bothered.
In the *heat* of the argument...

ANGER IS FIRE

He's *burned up*.
Breathe fire.
These are *inflammatory* remarks.

THE BODY IS A CONTAINER (FOR EMOTION)

He was *filled* with anger.
She couldn't *contain* her joy.
She was *brimming* with rage.
Try to get your anger *out of your system*.

ANGER IS THE HEAT OF A FLUID IN A CONTAINER

You make my blood boil.

Simmer down.
I had reached the *boiling point*.
Let him *stew*.

3.1.2 *Primary and Complex Conceptual Metaphors*

John Grady introduces the concept of primary and complex conceptual metaphors in order to cope with some of the apparent structural and evolutionary differences inherent in conceptual metaphors.[4] As we have seen
above, the conceptual system of anger not only contains metonymies as
well as metaphors but also metaphors of varying complexity. Hence, the
conceptual metaphor ANGER IS HEAT appears to be less complex, less internally structured, and therefore more general than ANGER IS A HEATED FLUID
IN A CONTAINER. In a joint article, Grady, Taub, and Morgan (1996) argue
that metaphors such as THEORIES ARE BUILDINGS or LOVE IS A JOURNEY are
complex in that they are composed of experientially based primary metaphors.[5]

Grady et al. present the conceptual metaphor LOVE IS A JOURNEY as a
subcase of the more general conceptual metaphor RELATIONSHIPS ARE VEHI-
CLES, and they argue that the latter consists of a set of primary metaphors
that combine on two levels. On the first level, the two primary metaphors,
ACTION IS MOTION and PURPOSES ARE DESTINATIONS, combine to LONG-TERM
PURPOSEFUL ACTIVITIES ARE JOURNEYS. On the second level, there are three
primary metaphors: ACTION IS MOTION, INTIMACY IS PROXIMITY, and CON-
STRAINTS ARE BOUNDARIES combine to form the conceptual metaphor RE-
LATIONSHIPS ARE CONTAINERS. Together, these combinations amount to the
complex metaphor RELATIONSHIPS ARE VEHICLES. See the graphic representation below provided by Grady and his coauthors.

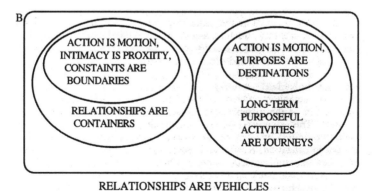

RELATIONSHIPS ARE VEHICLES

Fig. 12. Grady, Taub, and Morgan's decomposition of the conceptual metaphor
RELATIONSHIPS ARE VEHICLES into its primary metaphoric components.
Grady, Taub, and Morgan (1996, 185).

For three of the four primary metaphors involved, Lakoff and Johnson (1999, 51–53) report on Grady's (1997) analysis of their ontogenetic, experiential foundation:

INTIMACY IS CLOSENESS
Subjective judgment: Importance.
Sensorimotor experience: Being physically close.
Example: "We've been *close* for years, but we're beginning to *drift apart*."
Primary experience: Being physically close to people you are intimate with.

ACTIONS ARE SELF-PROPELLED MOTIONS
Subjective experience: Action.
Sensorimotor experience: Moving your body through space.
Example: "I'm *moving* right along on the project."
Primary experience: The common action of moving yourself through space, especially in the early years of life.

PURPOSES ARE DESTINATIONS
Subjective judgment: Achieving a purpose.
Sensorimotor experience: Reaching a destination.
Example: "He'll ultimately be successful, but he isn't *there* yet."
Primary experience: Reaching destinations throughout everyday life and thereby achieving purposes (e.g., if you want a drink, you have to go to the water cooler).

Apparently, Grady has reanalyzed the 1996 version of the conceptual metaphor RELATIONSHIPS ARE CONTAINERS documented above, conceiving of them as directly emerging from everyday experiences in ontogenesis. Lakoff and Johnson (1999, 53) list it as a primary conceptual metaphor which is now termed RELATIONSHIPS ARE ENCLOSURES.

RELATIONSHIPS ARE ENCLOSURES
Subjective experience: An interpersonal relationship.
Sensorimotor experience: Being in an enclosure.
Example: "We've been *in* a close relationship for years, but it's beginning to seem *confining*."
Primary experience: Living in the same enclosed physical space with the people you are most closely related to.

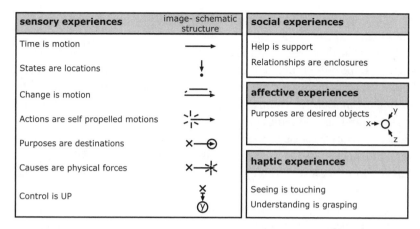

Fig. 13. Primary metaphors based on sensory, social, affective, and haptic experiences.

Grady's attempt to increase the parsimony, systematicity, and cognitive plausibility of the presumed systems of conceptual metaphors is doubtlessly an important step toward the ambitious goal of reconstructing the conceptual systems of individual and collective minds.

At the same time, Grady's analyses indicate how much work remains to be done before even a basic understanding of the "building blocks" or "atoms" of conceptual structure can be achieved. Although Lakoff and Johnson's (1999, 49–54) version of Grady's list of primary metaphors is assumed to give a representative overview of primary metaphors, it is obvious that this list provides (and can only provide) a glimpse at the actual foundational elements of conceptual structure. Unfortunately, it also lacks a connection to other forms of conceptual metaphors that have been proposed by both authors, such as orientational, ontological, image schematic, and structural metaphors. It appears, however, that the first three forms of metaphors listed are implicitly related to the category of primary metaphors because they appear to share an important structural feature, namely, an image-schematic structure. Primary metaphors, as well as orientational and ontological metaphors, tend to have an image-schematic structure. Let us first focus on the image-schematic structure of primary metaphors. This is an important trait, and a large number of the conceptual metaphors listed as primary metaphors also show an image-schematic structure.[6] The other primary metaphors mentioned by Lakoff and Johnson (1999) relate to other kinds of "primary experiences," such as social experiences (help is support, relationships are enclosures), affective experiences (purposes are desired objects), and modality-specific bodily experiences (seeing is touching, understanding is grasping).

Note that the skeletal and highly abstract structure of image-schemata appears to be quite functional in that it is applicable to a wide array of different target domains and allows for a layering of different functions.[7] For example, "motion" as an image-schema accounts for the concepts of TIME, CHANGE, and, as a specific form of motion, ACTIONS as self-propelled motions. Probably because of their relatively simple internal structure, these kinds of conceptual metaphors have also been termed "simple" metaphors; furthermore, because of their general applicability, they have been termed "generic-level" metaphors. As a whole, they have been contrasted with conceptual metaphors, which show a high degree of internal complexity and reflecting specific knowledge of a conceptual domain. Such conceptual metaphors have been termed "complex," "structural," and "specific-level" metaphors. They typically provide a rich image of a scene (ANGER IS A HOT FLUID IN A CONTAINER would be an example), and accordingly they apply to a relatively specific level of conceptual structure.

Apart from primary metaphors showing image-schematic structures, orientational as well as ontological metaphors are also supposed to be image-schematically structured, and, hence, they also presumably belong to the group of primary metaphors. Orientational metaphors use basic, spatial orientations, such as up-down (HAPPY IS UP, SAD IS DOWN)[8] or front-back (the past is behind, the future is in front); ontological metaphors substantiate nonphysical entities, that is, they transform nonphysical objects into objects (EVENTS ARE PHYSICAL OBJECTS, ACTIONS ARE PHYSICAL OBJECTS) or containers (UNDELINEATED OBJECTS ARE CONTAINERS, NONPHYSICAL OR ABSTRACT ENTITIES ARE CONTAINERS).

It is somewhat unfortunate that scholars in the field of CMT have not paid more attention to the ways in which these different forms of conceptual metaphors are interrelated. Until now, they have merely been presented as different kinds of metaphors resulting from different ways of categorizing conceptual metaphors (cf. Kövecses 2002, 29–41). It is not possible to go into the details of the different forms of conceptual metaphors here, but an overview of how they seem to be related is provided in figure 14 , which shows forms of conceptual metaphors and how they relate to each other.

Conceptual metaphors tend to differ fundamentally with regard to their structural complexity: image-schematic, generic level, primary, simple, ontological, and orientational metaphors are all structurally simple; specific-level, domain-specific, complex, and structural metaphors are structurally

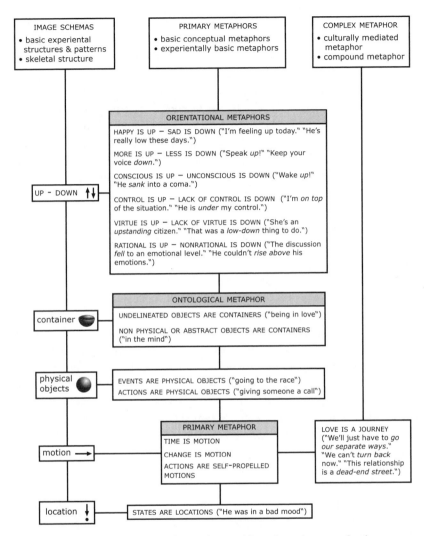

Fig. 14. Forms of conceptual metaphors and how they relate to each other.

complex.[9] This basic opposition between simple and complex structure is represented in the dichotomic order presented in figure 14 above.

Why is it necessary to go into these details of the different forms of conceptual metaphors? Because clarifying the relation between these forms would be a first step toward a systematic documentation of the "system of conceptual metaphors" as a fundamental structure of the collective and of the individual mind. I wish to emphasize that the perspective applied in such an enterprise is necessarily a collective one in the first place. The reconstruction of these conceptual metaphors is methodologically based: (primarily) either on the analysis of lexical entries in dictionaries (cf. Lakoff and Johnson 1999; Lakoff and Kövecses 1987; Kövecses 1986, 1988, 1990, 2002; Liebert 1992) or in analyses of larger corpora of written language (cf. Baldauf 1997; Störel 1997). In any case, it is a reconstruction of conceptual structure that is supraindividual and supralinguistic, that is, it is supposed to entail more than the linguistic system or the Saussurean socially established *langue*. The degree to which this conceptual system is indeed mirrored in the individual minds of speakers is then an empirical question, which will be addressed in the subsequent section.

3.1.3 How Are Conceptual Metaphor Systems Activated during Speaking?

In the analysis of metaphor in language use, one fundamental issue that inevitably comes into play is the multilayering of conceptual metaphors, both in a paradigmatic perspective and in a syntagmatic perspective. Paradigmatically, the verbal metaphor in the sentence "he is *steaming with anger*" is supposedly constructed out of a multilayered system of conceptual metaphors. From a syntagmatic viewpoint, it is not clear how the metaphorical meaning of one verbal metaphor (say of "steamed") relates to other elements of meaning within a given utterance: it is not clear how verbal metaphors relate to other lexical metaphors ("He steamed for hours before he exploded"), how they relate to grammaticalized metaphors (as in prepositions like "before"), or how they relate to the remaining literal parts of the utterance.

These kinds of questions immediately arise once the object of investigation shifts from the analysis of the linguistic system, which uses sentences in the traditional linguistic way as examples, to the analysis of actual language use. When analyzing language in use, the researcher is faced with a different kind of complexity. The ways in which sentences are treated in CMT do not seek to provide explanations of how the elements within a sentence build up a coherent meaning. So far, CMT has continued to take a basically lexical-semantic approach. Still, as we have seen above, the problem of this kind of paradigmatic multilayering of conceptual metaphor systems has escaped the attention of advocates of CMT. Indeed it hardly seems likely that all the building blocks of a conceptual system that are semantically connected with a given verbal metaphor need to be activated during language production. Furthermore, it appears at least not to be self-evident that uttering a verbal metaphor implies the activation of a conceptual one (or ones). Of course, this ultimately remains an empirical question that cannot be convincingly answered on the grounds of the analysis of verbal data only. Therefore, an example of a dead metaphor accompanied by a metaphoric gesture will be presented, which will shed some light on this complex issue.

Example 4 is interesting because it indicates that the source domain of a conceptual metaphor might be active while a highly conventionalized, supposedly dead verbal metaphor is being used in spontaneous speech. Note that this refers to a "truly" dead metaphor in the sense that it lost its transparency a long time ago—it is dead, because its historical source is even potentially unavailable to the average speaker of German. The metaphoric lexeme is "Depressivität" (depressiveness), that is, a borrowing from Latin via French (Latin: *deprimere, depressio:* "to press down"; French: *dépressif, dépressivité;* English: depressive, depressiveness).

Example 4 is taken from a narrative interview about the first love of a woman in her forties. She is describing the atmosphere of her first week of being in love for the first time in her life. This coincided with a one-week school excursion to a small island in the North Sea, and she fell in love with a boy in her class on her way to this island. In the short sequence below, she describes the atmospheric quality of their respective feelings during this stay. She says that she felt sad because he was depressive:

Example 4: "Dieses Depressive" (*this depressiveness*)

```
              point upwards                  Ring PA, fast forward movements
1   [also es war nICHt getrÜBt (.h) || ich denke das war
    getrübt
    well it was not gloomy                I think it was gloomy


              PDOH moves down              Ring PD, moves down repeatedly
2   eher || (.h) durch dieses (.h) || durch dieses
    depressIve/]
    more       because of this   because of this depressiveness


              Ring PD opens to PDOH        PDOH held
3   (.) [das hab ich damals schon gemerkt\ || auf dieser
    insel \
       this I already realized at the time         on that island
```

The important point she makes is that while she was in love and in high spirits, this week was overshadowed by the depressiveness of the young boy. The lexeme "dieses depressive" is the only verbal expression in this

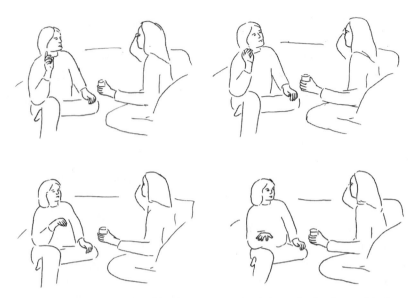

Fig. 15. "Dieses Depressive" (this depressiveness) and ring and palm down with slow downward motion in gesture. A conceptual metaphor activated visible in gesture only. Top left: point upwards; top right: ring, fast forward movements; bottom left: palm-down open hand, slow downward movements; bottom right: Palm-down open hand, moves down.

sequence in which her sadness is expressed as something that is "down." As mentioned above, the German lexeme "depressiv" is ultimately derived from the Latin word for "press down," but of course this downward dimension is not transparent for the average speaker anymore. Etymological reconstruction is needed to discern it. And as Alina, who is telling this story, is not familiar with its etymology, it does not appear likely that her use of the words "dieses depressive" (this depressiveness) is being actively sustained online by a conceptual metaphor SAD IS DOWN during speech production. Furthermore, in the remaining parts of her utterance, she uses different experiential source domains to describe the more negative facets of this week by employing verbal metaphors that draw upon sight and vision. She uses, for instance, the transparent verbal metaphor "getrübt" (gloomy) to characterize the atmosphere as a whole and only employs "depressiv" (depressiveness) to account for the mood of her boyfriend. In short, on the verbal level, there is no indication whatsoever of the active conceptual metaphor SAD IS DOWN. This changes when we consider the gestures that she makes as she speaks. Take a look at the pictures and the gestures:

Apart from the first two gestures, all her movements show a distinct, slow, downward pattern. The first two gestures accompany the production of a verbal metaphor that draws upon the domain of vision: an upward point and a ring gesture, which are performed along with a verbal metaphor "es war nicht getrübt, ich denke das war getrübt" [it was not gloomy, I think this was gloomy]. In both cases, the gesture does not bear upon the semantics of the verbal metaphor. The upward point functions as an indication marker in much the same way that the ring (also known as the precision grip) maybe used as an indication of the verbal elements in discursive focus (cf. Kendon 1995; Neumann 2004). The remaining gestures all have a downward movement. Moreover, they are performed not just with a downward motion but with a *slow* downward motion—as if something heavy were pulling her hands downward. Yet this slow, downward motion combines with different configurations: first, with a palm-down open hand; second, with a ring; and finally, the ring opens with a palm-down open hand. What does this mean?

Note that in her utterance no metaphor is produced simultaneously with these downward movements. On the contrary, when she makes the first downward movement (the one with the palm-down open hand), she does not even utter the noun that is indicated by the demonstrative pronoun "dieses" (this); instead, she accompanies the demonstrative with a palm-down open hand moving slowly downward. Taken together, this speech-gesture combination might be paraphrased as "this state of being down." Then she re-formulates. She repeats the demonstrative with the respective noun, "this depressiveness." It is likely that this was exactly the word she was looking for a moment before, as she was producing a downward gesture. At least the idea of being down was already there in the gesture. The striking fact is that, although there is no hint of an activation of the conceptual metaphor SAD IS DOWN in the verbal part of her utterance, the two gestures show a significant, downward-motion pattern, which indicates that the idea of conceptualizing depressiveness in terms of being down was active for the speaker at that very moment. Now, one could argue that this downward motion is neither significant nor systematically related to this idea. At least three arguments provide support in favor of regarding it as significant: First, there is a change in the direction of movement of the gestures performed during this stretch of talk (first the ring gesture is performed with forward movements, and only when she talks about depressiveness does the motion change direction downward). Second, the downward movement continues throughout the passage in which she formulates the point she is trying to make (the fact that she had already realized that he was depressive during this first week). Third, the downward-motion pattern remains constant in spite of the changing configurations of the hands.

Let us take a brief look at these changing configurations. Alina uses a ring and a palm-down open hand configuration with this downward motion. Combining a ring configuration with a downward movement represents the blending of a semantic and a pragmatic facet of this gesture: the slow downward motion indicates that something is located below or in a downward direction, while the ring configuration represents the exactness and precision of the discourse object that she is looking for. The combination of the palm-down open hand configuration and the downward movement represents the idea of something being below or of pushing something down. The pushing of objects downward is typically performed with the open palms oriented downward (depending ultimately, of course, on the shape of the object to be pushed down). Hence, in this gesture the configuration as well as the direction of movement represents something moving down or something being below.[10] Apparently, important additional semantic information is provided through the gestural medium of expression. The kind of information is interesting because it points to the activation of a conceptual mapping that connects sadness and depressiveness with a location at the lower end of a vertical scale. Put another way, the gestures are most likely based on an active conceptual metaphor along the lines of the conceptual metaphor SAD IS DOWN. This means that the gestures provide support for the assumption that conceptual metaphors constitute a potentially active realm that is available online during speaking and gesturing.

To be clear, this does not imply that conceptual domains with a label SAD IS DOWN do indeed exist; assuming this is clearly too simplistic, and nothing of the sort is claimed by CMT (Lakoff 1993).[11] Rather, what seems to be the case is that two mental domains are connected with each other and that this connection is active at the moment of producing these downward-motion gestures. Note that this provides support for one controversial claim put forward by Lakoff and Turner (1989), namely, that conceptual metaphors may be active although some of their lexical instantiations are no longer transparent metaphors.[12] In our case, the conceptual metaphor underlying the SAD IS DOWN mapping continues to be active for German speakers, even if they use a dead metaphor, that is, a conventionalized metaphor that has lost its transparency.

To conclude, this example of the spontaneous use of speech and gesture demonstrates three rather important points: First, it supports the assumption that conceptual metaphors constitute a specific realm of conceptual structure. Second, it indicates that conceptual metaphors may be activated during speaking independently of verbal metaphors. And third—as a consequence—it documents that conceptual metaphors are not reduced to triggering verbal metaphoric expressions.

3.2 Verbal Metaphors

Is there a cognitive realm of verbal metaphors that is different or separated from conceptual metaphors? How are verbal metaphors treated in CMT? And how does this relate to Weinrich's Bildfeldtheorie? The close analysis of verbal metaphors as such is not a topic that has received profound treatment in CMT. "Surface" differences between verbal metaphors are not considered as relevant for a cognitive theory of metaphors. Differences regarding formal structure (metaphoric expressions comprise single lexemes, compounds, idiomatic expressions, sentences, utterances, and textual metaphors) or regarding novelty or conventionalization are not considered as substantial dimensions of verbal metaphors; at least they do not appear to bear upon the central claim, namely, that the overwhelming majority of verbal metaphors are rooted in conceptual metaphors. As already mentioned, verbal metaphors attract the interest of CMT scholars only insofar as they are revelatory of conceptual metaphors. And—as we have seen above—they do this when they group into semantic clusters. Conceptual metaphors are identified via the collection of semantically related verbal expressions, but the verbal expressions as such are not the object of a separate analysis. Thus, as we have seen in chapter 2, conceptual metaphors, such as LOVE IS A JOURNEY, LOVE IS MADNESS, THEORIES ARE BUILDINGS, and ARGUMENT IS WAR, are identified through the collection of semantically related verbal expressions (this characteristic shift in argumentation has already been introduced in chapter 2). We have also seen that Weinrich developed a similar, although not identical, theory of metaphors in the 1960s and 1970s. We will now consider in more detail how Weinrich and Lakoff account for verbal metaphors. This comparison imports on the issue of realms of metaphors, insofar as Weinrich assumes a verbal level of metaphorical organization, that is, verbal domains of sense, whereas CMT does not. Conceptual metaphor theory assumes, in contrast, that lexical meaning is always conceptual meaning or, more specifically, conceptual meaning that is embedded in conceptual domains. No systematic difference is made between a lexical and a general conceptual level.

3.2.1 Weinrich's Image Fields (Bildfelder), and Lakoff and Johnson's Conceptual Metaphors

Weinrich observes the same phenomenon as Lakoff and Johnson did: conventionalized "dead" metaphors are not isolated occurrences in the lexicon of a language but group into semantic clusters. Yet for him, this is not an isolated observation but an observation that relates to a theory of the lexicon

proposed by Jost Trier in the first decades of the twentieth century. Trier's
Wortfeldtheorie (word-field theory) proposes that lexical fields are structured
around core terms (Trier 1931, 1934a, 1934b, 1968).[13] Weinrich explicitly relates his theory of metaphors to Trier's conception of word fields. He argues
that metaphors are not isolated and randomly distributed occurrences in the
lexicon of a language, but that they are clustered in fields. Therefore, he proposes that, in reality, the use of a verbal metaphor involves the coupling of
two verbal domains of sense ("sprachliche Sinnbezirke"): "In the case of the
actual and apparently punctual metaphor, what really happens is the coupling of two verbal domains of sense" (Weinrich 1976, 283). More specifically,
Weinrich assumes that the two verbal domains of sense are coupled by a verbal act and a mental process for establishing analogical relationships: "It is
only decisive that two verbal domains of sense are coupled and established as
analogies through a verbal act" (Weinrich 1976, 283). Two verbal domains of
sense coupled together constitute an image field (Bildfeld). As an illustration
of such an image field, Weinrich offers a collection of metaphoric expressions
that use the domain of money or, more generally, financial transactions, which
are taken from literary and philosophical writings (Weinrich 1976, 280):

> The image field "Wortmünze" (word-coin)
> ein Wort wird geprägt
> Lehnwörter (ausleihen)
> Schlagwörter/Prägewörter
> Wortschatz/Thesaurus
> Reichtum der Sprache (Leibniz)
> Sprache hat baren Vorrat, der im Umlauf ist, Sparpfennige und seltene
>   Münzen (J. Grimm)
> Les traductions sont comme ces monnaies de cuivre qui ont bien la
>   même valeur qu'une pièce d'or . . . . (Montesquieu, Lettres persanes)
> vermeintliches Gold wird durch schmutzige Papierscheine ersetzt (Valéry)
> alte Goldgruben öffnen (Jean Paul)
> Goldene Worte
> A word is coined
> Loan words (to lend/borrow)
> Key words ("punch-words" lit.; Prägewörter = "coin-words" lit.)
> Vocabulary ("word-treasure" lit.; thesaurus)
> Language wealth
> Language has a cash supply in circulation, little nest eggs and rare coins
> Very old coins keep their collector's value that have the same value as a
>   piece of gold

Translations are only coppers
To open up old gold mines
Golden words

Weinrich gives these examples to show that verbal metaphors using the
domain of money or financial transactions appear in groups, that they are
interrelated and, hence, constitute an image field. This field is named after
its central metaphor, "word coin" (Wortmünze). Consider the diagram (figure 16) for a first glimpse at Weinrich's conception of the image field word-
coin."

The image field "Wortmünze" consists of an image-offering and an image-
receiving field. The domain of financial transactions acts as the image-
offering field, and the domain of words or language is the image-receiving
field. The two fields are conventionally coupled via analogy and merge into
one consistent field. According to Weinrich, the local meaning of a verbal metaphor is established through the activation of this coupled image

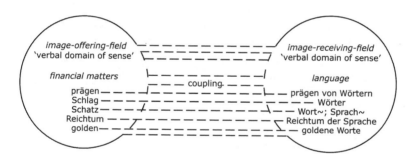

conceptual metaphor

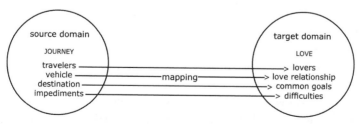

Fig. 16. Weinrich's image field "Wortmünze" (word-coin).

field. The lexical meaning of a verbal metaphor resides in an entrenched image field.

Note that this explication of metaphoric meaning is very similar to the one proposed in CMT, but it is not identical. Conceptual metaphor theory also holds that single verbal metaphors are meaningful because they reside in conceptual domains, which are connected via entrenched mappings. In fact, the very notion of metaphor in CMT is defined as a "cross-domain mapping in the conceptual system" (Lakoff 1993, 203) in which mappings establish ontological correspondences between conceptual domains. Thus, in the LOVE AS A JOURNEY mapping, the love relationship corresponds to a vehicle, the travelers in the vehicle are the lovers, the movement of the vehicle is the movement of the lovers through time, and the goals of the lovers are the destinations in a journey. These mappings are projections of knowledge structures that allow for a creative exploitation by providing the possibility and the frame for reasoning about love relationships in terms of vehicles moving through space and time (Lakoff 1993, 207). Lakoff, furthermore, underlines that an important characteristic of these mappings is that they are supposed to reside at a superordinate level of conceptual categorization and not at the level of basic categories. Therefore, because we find a range of basic level lexemes that all fall into the higher level category of vehicle, it is assumed that the higher level category is the place where the mapping is established. Lakoff (1993, 203) gives the following examples of vehicles that are used to conceptualize a love relationship:

Car	→	long bumpy road, spinning our wheels
Train	→	off the track
Boat	→	on the rocks, foundering
Plane	→	just taking off, bailing out

Lakoff infers from this kind of variation of verbal metaphoric expressions that the actual mapping takes place on a superordinate, more general level of categorization, with verbal metaphors being merely instantiations of this more general level.

Thus, a prediction is made about conventional mappings: the categories mapped will tend to be at the superordinate rather than the basic level. One tends not to find mappings like A LOVE RELATIONSHIP IS A CAR or A LOVE RELATIONSHIP IS A BOAT. Instead one tends to find both basic level cases (e.g. both cars and boats), which indicates that the generalization is one level higher, at the superordinate level of the vehicle. In the hundreds of cases

of conventional mappings studied so far, this prediction has been borne out:
it is superordinate categories that are used in mappings. (Lakoff 1993, 212)

Yet, what exactly does this mean: "it is the superordinate categories that are
used in mappings"? Does this mean that there is no mapping on the basic
level? And what exactly is a mapping? What is its ontological status? Is it
a conceptual structure of a collective mind that enters the individual mind?
If so, then how? If it is experientially based, then the individual experiences
need to be matched with the collective ones that are encoded in the linguistic system of a language. And what about the psychological reality of these
mappings? Are they supposed to be active online during language production? And what would this imply for the cognitive construction of lexical
meaning? If, as Lakoff says, mappings are at the superordinate level, does
this mean that there is no mapping between basic level categories? A lot of
open questions emerge once we seek to relate the collective and the individual facets of conceptual metaphors. Weinrich does not address this issue
either, at least not systematically.

   We shall return to the problem of the localization and activation of
mappings and of image fields online during speaking. For now, we shall bear
in mind that CMT assumes that metaphoric expressions are based on cross-
domain mappings at the level of general conceptual organization. The diagram below shows this general level of mapping between the source domain
of journeys and the target domain of love. The mappings indicate that ontological correspondences have been established that speakers are assumed
to use as a source of knowledge to reason about love relationships.

   Thus, the metaphorical expression "we're *stuck*" is not meaningful because of a mapping that takes place on the lexical level, say, between being
physically stuck and being nonphysically stuck but because of the activation of a metaphorical scenario based on the knowledge structures that are
projected from the source domain of journeys to the target domain of love
relationships.

   To conclude, it appears that Weinrich's account of verbal metaphors has
much in common with Lakoff's proposal but also differs crucially. In both
cases, word meaning is equated with the activation of a field or domain and is
not a matter of single isolated lexemes; but for Weinrich, the activated field is
a verbal field, while for Lakoff, it is a domain of general conceptual organization.
Conceptual metaphors are supposed to be general cognitive structures, whereas
image fields are verbal structures with cognitive implications. Recall that
Weinrich situates image domains on the level of *langue*, that is, on the level
of the linguistic system, not on the level of a general conceptual organization,

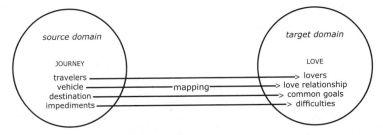

Fig. 17. Lakoff and Johnson's conceptual metaphor LOVE IS A JOURNEY (or the LOVE AS
JOURNEY MAPPING). Cf. Lakoff and Johnson (1980).

as Lakoff and Johnson suggest: "They [the image fields] are unmistakable,
mental and material images of language (*langue*)" (Weinrich 1976, 285). A
basic difference between the two approaches is the motivation of these higher
order structures. Whereas CMT grounds them in various kinds of experiences (as we have seen above), that is, they are nonverbal, in Weinrich's theory
of image fields they are rooted in the use of language. Image fields develop
as a form of verbal structure: they evolve with language and change through
language contact, through conditions of use and literary tradition.

3.2.2 Activation of Verbal Metaphors

Let us devote some more attention to how these approaches characterize
the vitality of verbal metaphors. As we have seen above, they fundamentally
agree, in that the vitality of a verbal metaphor involves the activation of
higher level structures, be they image fields or conceptual metaphors. Weinrich argues that "[a]s long as one does not simultaneously have one's eye
on the image-offering and the image-receiving field, metaphoricity is abso-
lutely out of the question" (Weinrich 1976, 284). According to Lakoff, "What
constitutes the LOVE IS A JOURNEY metaphor is not any particular word or expression. It is the ontological mapping across conceptual domains, from the
source domain of journeys to the target domain of love" (Lakoff 1993, 209).
For Lakoff, these domains are general cognitive ones, whereas for Weinrich,
they are primarily verbal. Both these accounts of vitality stand in opposition
to the mainstream in LMTs, which locates the vitality of a verbal metaphor
on the level of lexical meaning. Remember the quote in the introduction
from Max Black, who binds the vitality of metaphors to a "pregnant metaphorical use." Black's concept of use, implying the loss of transparency and
consciousness in verbal metaphors, does not envision any kind of higher
level organization of metaphors. It analyzes metaphors as single and unique

instances of language use, and vitality is a matter of conscious usage rather than of semantic structure. Weinrich and Lakoff stand in sharp contrast to such a view with regard to another assumption: not only do they propose a higher level order of metaphorical structure on the collective level of a language community, they also propose a metalinguistic and metahistorical level of metaphoric organization, a collective level of metaphorical structure that crosscuts linguistic and historic boundaries.

Thus, Weinrich suggests that the Occident is a "Bildfeldgemeinschaft" ("a community of image fields") because it disposes of a shared set of image fields that survive despite language change and despite single metaphoric expressions that lose their imagistic quality over time and turn opaque. Weinrich sees here what he terms a "harmony of image fields between the individual European languages." Consider the following quote: "There is a harmony of image fields between the individual European languages. The Occident is a community of image fields" (Weinrich 1976, 287). He even suggests that the translation of metaphoric expressions between the European languages is easier than the translation of "literal" language because the evoked image fields are the same (Weinrich 1976, 286). Hence, Weinrich clearly assumes a level of supranational metaphorical structure. It is not clear how this is to be related to his concept of image fields on the level of *langue*, which necessarily relates to one specific language, and he does not devote further attention to this issue. It appears important, however, to bear in mind that this is an issue for which metaphor theories need to account—if it is true. Furthermore, he does not suggest how these supranational structures of image fields relate to national structures and to verbal metaphors, let alone how all this might be activated in language use. Again, the problem is twofold: how are the assumed realms of metaphorical structures organized on a collective level, and how are the collective structures available on the individual level.

Consider a related line of argument (with similar open questions) in Lakoff and Turner's collaborative work on poetic metaphor, where they put forward the assumption that conceptual metaphors may be vital, while single lexical metaphors, which are historically derived from it, are dead:

> Compare, for example, the words "comprehend" and "grasp". Today, there is a live conceptual metaphor in which understanding is grasping, and we use the word "grasp" to mean understand. The same conceptual metaphor existed in Latin, where the word "comprehendere" meant basically to grasp, and, by metaphoric extension, to understand. Now we use it only in its metaphoric sense; its former central sense is dead for us. But

the old conceptual metaphor is still alive, though it is not used in this word. (Lakoff and Turner 1989, 129).

Hence, Lakoff and Turner's analysis also presupposes a supranational level of metaphoric organization—a level of cultural metaphoricity that may survive despite the loss of metaphoricity of single lexical instantiations.[14]

Lakoff and Turner also suggest the possibility that a conceptual metaphor may cease to be vital. Unfortunately, the example they give is not altogether clear. They say that "pedigree" is derived historically from Old French "pied de grue" (foot of a crane) and that this was an instantiation of the image metaphor in which the shape of a crane's foot was mapped onto a family tree diagram. The image metaphor is supposed to be dead by now: "That image-metaphor no longer exists at the conceptual level, and at the linguistic level we do not use 'pedigree' to mean 'crane's foot'. This is a truly dead metaphor—at both levels" (Lakoff and Turner 1989, 129). Somewhat unfortunately, there are no further instances of this image metaphor provided, which would be necessary to make the point that here we are looking at a higher level conceptual metaphor that has generated a wide range of lexical metaphors. As it stands, it is not clear whether or not it is a one-shot metaphor, that is, a metaphor that uniquely maps one concept onto another one and is not derived from a more general level of conceptual organization.

Let us sum up. Both approaches—Weinrich's and Lakoff's—hold that verbal metaphors are organized in larger scale structures, that is, structures above the level of individual verbal metaphors, and both suggest that these levels ensure the vitality of verbal metaphors. In short, both assume a level of supranational conceptual organization, but neither reflect upon the nature of the relation between the collective system and its individual realizations. Yet they do mention the need to account for an individual level of conceptual organization.

Weinrich points out that this activation of two fields is not just a matter of the collective mind of a linguistic or cultural community, but that they need to be activated each and every time a single individual realizes, produces, or comprehends a metaphor: "This [awareness of spheres—CM] is never lacking in a living metaphor. We can therefore say that the image field is not only available in the entire language system [*langue*—CM] as an objective social structure, but that it is also recalled subjectively in individual metaphorical speech acts, in that it is co-thought by the speaker, and counderstood by the listener" (Weinrich 1976, 288). Weinrich himself points out that the vitality of a metaphor is a psychological question and that the forms of activation are selective and maybe "spheric," a characterization inspired by Stählin's

(1914) impressive work on metaphor comprehension. Verbal metaphors are supposed to be vital in that they activate the image fields to which they belong, and as such they are actually seen to be activating mental models that are inherent in the respective image fields. As we have seen, Lakoff also holds that the metaphoricity of a verbal metaphor depends on the activation of a conceptual metaphor. But he also mentions that conceptual metaphor systems need not be activated completely each and every time a verbal metaphor is produced. Both approaches differ with regard to the ontology of the postulated realm that inhabits these larger scale structures. While Lakoff assumes that conceptual metaphors are a part of general cognition, Weinrich holds that image fields are a form of verbal structure with cognitive implications.

In section 3.2.3, we will investigate a spontaneously produced verbal metaphor and see what the verbal and bodily elaboration of it reveals with respect to potentially activated cognitive realms of verbal metaphors.

3.2.3 How Are Verbal Metaphors Activated during Speaking?

The example presented in this section brings us back to the general questions guiding the discussion in this chapter: what are the theoretically assumed realms of metaphor, and how are they activated online during speaking? Or, in other words, are there indications emanating from spontaneous speech production that provide support for active realms of conceptual metaphors, of image fields, or of individual verbal metaphors? If yes, does this hold for dead metaphors, that is, for conventionalized and transparent metaphors, or for novel, vital ones, or for both?

A particularly insightful case with regard to these issues is a spontaneous elaboration of a presumably dead verbal metaphor that results in a textual metaphor or an allegory. This spontaneous allegory is part of an account of the atmospheric change in a love relationship. Alina describes how, after returning from a week on holiday, her first love relationship changed profoundly in character. She makes a big effort to describe exactly how it felt when the young couple returned home after this first extraordinary week of being in love with each other. Something had changed. She still liked him, but being in love seemed to have attained a different quality. It had been stripped of its romantic aura and "exposed" (entblößt). She continues with an explication of this verbal metaphor, which consists of an elaborated textual metaphor. In order to explicate this feeling she invents a metaphorical scenario, a textual metaphor or an allegory. In this scenario, the first week of love in her life is a splendid ball—and returning home it is stripped of the magic of love. Here is a summary of her description:

When we returned home I still liked him, but the feeling of being in love was laid bare.

Falling in love is like embellishing yourself, preparing yourself to go out: you dress yourself up and put on a ball dress; and then, you somehow return home at night and begin to take off your makeup in front of the mirror, and all of a sudden you yourself reappear. It was as if this exposed or extraordinary situation (of being together on an island for one week) had provided the frame for and the possibility of being in love. After that, the tension was gone, it was dispelled, maybe it was like—yes, that's it—it had lost its magic. Yes, it's like going to a ball, and then you yourself take off the magic, and you face yourself in your nightdress in front of the mirror.

The listener sums up Alina's scenario and says that the situation of being in love had been deprived of its magic.

Alina confirms the conclusion: yes, it was deprived of its magic; it's like you go to a ball, then you return and face yourself wearing your nightdress in the mirror.

To begin with, laying bare, exposing (entblößt) is a typical case of what in German would typically be considered a dead metaphor. The expression is a conventionalized and an established part of the German lexicon. Yet it is transparent, and, parallel to its metaphoric usage, it is used in a literal sense, as a refined expression for "being naked" (or being in one's bare skin). It would be a perfect example of those metaphors that Black characterized as not having a "pregnant metaphorical use." As the example clearly shows, this is mistaken. The seemingly dead verbal metaphor inspires the spontaneous invention of an allegoric text, of a textual metaphor. Moreover, the idea of a love that is laid bare (exposed) triggers a scenario in which the laying bare (exposure) of love is allegorically transformed into a woman who embellishes herself for a beautiful ball. She enjoys the ball, and upon her return, she faces herself bare, without makeup, and without her ball dress, in her nightdress. Without the embellishment, the magic has gone. This embellishment metaphorically represents the one radiating week of their love, which they spent in such a special environment. The returning home from the ball, the taking off of makeup and nice clothes, represent the loss of magic on their return home after the extraordinary week.

Thus, "entblößt" is a conventional verbal metaphor that is active as a metaphor for the speaker in this context because it functions as the basis for the metaphoric elaboration, the allegoric story the speaker is telling. Hence, it appears more appropriate to regard this as a sleeping rather than as a dead metaphor.

Now, what else can we learn from this piece of metaphorical elaboration? I think it indicates that the lexical meaning of "entblößt" (exposed), of this sleeping metaphor, did not really trigger a lexical field of related expressions; rather, what appears to be activated is a scenario that is related to the verbal metaphor "entblößt." The scenario evoked is a conventionalized one: the ball as an extraordinary and exceptional situation and the evening after as disillusion and a return to gray normality. One could argue that this conventional scenario is not really active either. It could just provide an established conceptual schema or model for such a situation. Again, this is not how the speaker appears to experience it. This becomes apparent when, in addition to the verbal elaboration of the metaphor, we consider the bodily movements that accompany her speech. When we do this, there is no doubt that she does not simply elaborate the image domain on an abstract verbal level; rather, the opposite is the case. She actually enacts the scenario, she even embodies and inhabits it, by turning into a woman who looks into the mirror and takes off her makeup while she is wearing her nightdress. Hence, she does not just talk about taking off a ball dress and makeup; she enacts it: she posits herself in front of an imagined mirror, moves her hands as if they were taking off the makeup from her eyes, and only returns to looking at her conversational partner when she has finished. Consider the transcript with the bodily enactments and the sketches:

Example 5: "Das Verliebtsein war entblößt" (*falling in love was laid bare*)

```
1   und ich mOCHte den Imer nouch aber [dieses= dieses
    and I still liked him but        this= this

                           bh PUOH        auseinander
2   verLIEBtsein (-) wa:r (--) ehm (.) war irgendwie |
    entblÖSSt\
    being in love      was      er      was somehow exposed
3   (--) das war eh= (.) ja das ist so als wenn du dich
       that was er= it's like when you (make) yourself

                           bh OH model large object
4   (.) hÜBsch (.) machst und gehst irgendwie= gehst abend
    aus
       pretty (-)      and go somehow=      go out in the evening

                  bh OH expand large object
```

5 **und staffierst dich aus und | | hast ein bALLkleid an**
   und
   and dress yourself up and wear a   ball dress and

6 dann [gehst du (h) irgenwide (.) halt (-) dann nachts
   nach
   then   you go home   somehow   then at night

   enacting the taking off of eye make-up

7 hAUse und fängst an **dich vorm spiegel abzuschminken**
   und
   and begin in front of the mirror to take off your make-up and

8 **auf einmal kommst du selber da irgenwie** (.) zur ge=]
   suddenly (-) you yourself somehow (come)   to=

9 so wieder raus\ ja/ (laughter) das war auch als ob diese
   so out again\   yes/ (laughter) that was also as if this

10 situation\ diese exponierte situation/ EINfach diesen
   situation\ this exposed situation/ simply (had given this

11 rahmen und die möglichkeit gegeben hat und danach (-)
   frame and the possibility   and afterwards (-)

12 war die spannung raus/ (...) die spannung war weg\
   the tension was out   (...) the tension was gone\

13 das war ABgearbeitet vielleicht auch so was\
   that was worked off\ perhaps also something like that

14 C:und die= die veränderte situation/ des ist so als wär das
   and the= the changed situation/   it's like as if it

15   so entZAUbert
   somehow had lost its magic

16 A:ja genau\ (.) entzaubert\ (? 4 sec ?)
   yes exactly\   lost its magic\
   bh OH repeat modelling   repeat expanding large
   of object (cf. line 4)   object (cf. line 5)

17 **nach dem großen bALL** (.) || du **entzauberst** dich\ ja/ (.)
    after the great ball   you take off the magic\ yes/

18 und stehst dir dann gegenüber im=m nACHthemd
    and face yourself then   in your nightdress

19 vor dem spiegel\   ((laughter))
    in front of the mirror\ ((laughter))

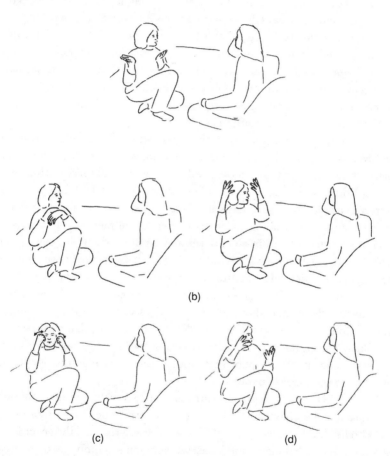

Fig. 18. (A): "Entblößt" (exposed); (B): "ausstaffiert" (dressed up); (C) "abschminken" (to take off make-up); (D) "du selber" (you yourself).

This way of enacting a prototypical scene of female habits shows that the verbally expressed metaphors are "inhabited" bodily; they are not just disembodied, abstract linguistic representations of source domains or of abstract lexical fields. Rather, they function as a "door opening," an invitation for the speaker to move into an imaginary world in which the disillusionment of the high feelings, the extraordinariness of being in love, becomes the disillusionment after a magnificent, beautiful ball. Weinrich says that the image field incarnates itself fully as a textual metaphor, as an allegory: "Only in the allegory do we find an image field 'completely' incarnated in the text" (Weinrich 1976, 288). Is the spontaneous allegory above an example of such an incarnation of a lexical field? I do not think so. But I do believe that it is an incarnation of a mental model or of a conceptual metaphor, to use Weinrich and Lakoff's terms, because here, it is clear that an entire scenario is being evoked, a scenario that transcends language, involves gestures, bodily movements, and routine motor programs that are habitually associated with a certain everyday pattern of action.

One could continue and argue that this is a clear example in favor of the CMT assumption that lexical meaning is located on the level of general cognitive concepts and not on the level of purely lexical organization. And indeed, I do wish to suggest that this kind of verbal elaboration points to a direct evocation of supralinguistic conceptual structures, such as mental models, cognitive scenarios, or probably conceptual metaphors. In this respect, it provides support in favor of the assumptions of Lakoff's conceptual metaphor and of Weinrich's mental model. It does not provide support for the idea of a lexical field as an internal structure of a language system. Yet it does indicate that the level of lexical meaning, viewed as a rich-image meaning, plays a role in metaphor production, because it is via this rich image inherent in the verbal metaphor, "entblößen" (to expose), that this scenario is evoked. The entrance to the scenario is the lexical level, not the level of a general conceptual metaphor that would supposedly map the domain of love onto exceptional situations.

Thus, what this example indicates is that two realms of metaphorical structure may be active at the same time: a verbal one with a rich image and a higher level one (conceptual) that is accessed through the specific semantics of the verbal metaphor. Thus, we cannot just simply say that verbal metaphors are instantiations of conceptual metaphors, but we must assume that verbal metaphors are active as verbal metaphors and provide access to different realms of conceptual organization. Here the verbal metaphor functioned as a kind of door opener to general cognitive structures. Thus, because the verbal metaphor was active at the moment of speaking, access to a metaphorical scenario was freed and liberated. Hence, it appears that verbal metaphors are vital on the lexical level and that they provide access to general realms of metaphorical and nonmetaphorical structures.

To conclude, the example "being in love was exposed" provides evidence of the activation of a level of general cognition that was accessed via a rich-image verbal metaphor. Hence, it appears that the so-called dead metaphor was actively processed by the speaker and triggered verbal and bodily elaboration. This observation supports, on the one hand, the assumption of a higher level metaphorical structure (be it in terms of conceptual metaphor or in terms of mental models), while suggesting, on the other hand, a highly active level of lexical structure.

Put another way, the above example supports both Lakoff's and Weinrich's assumption that verbal metaphors are embedded in larger scale structures: fields, domains, and mental models. It does not support Weinrich's assumption that allegory is the instantiation of an image field, at least not in this case of spontaneous language use.

This brings us back to our overarching questions in this chapter, namely, what are the theoretically assumed realms of metaphor, and how are they activated online during speaking? Apparently, we must assume that there is a level of highly active lexical structures that may provide access to higher level conceptual structures. It does not appear sufficient to simply characterize verbal metaphor in terms of conceptual metaphor. This misses the level and the potential role of lexical structure in cognitive processes during metaphor processing. Yet Weinrich's assumption that image fields are purely lexical structures also appears to be somewhat misleading, because it misses the fact that these lexical items may provide access to a nonverbal level of conceptual organization.

3.3 Verbo-gestural Metaphors

In this section, particular attention will be devoted to the ways in which gestures relate to verbal metaphors. This is important because it does not seem appropriate to reduce the role of gesture analysis to a mere "window" onto thought processes that are active during speaking—which is basically what I have done so far by using coverbal gestures and bodily enactments to argue for the activation of cognitive realms of metaphor.

The examples discussed so far merely document that bodily movements, and especially gestures, may relate in one way or another to supposedly dead verbal metaphors or even directly to conceptual metaphors. The kinds of relationships between verbal and gestural metaphors, with a clear focus on verbal metaphors accompanied by metaphoric gestures, will be investigated more systematically. Before turning to the analysis of an example that will document that metaphors may be multimodal, the following brief introductory overview documents what is currently known about metaphors in gesture and speech.

3.3.1 Gestural Metaphors and How They May Relate to Language

Research on gesture and speech has devoted surprisingly little attention to the issue of metaphor; for different reasons, the same holds for metaphor research. For both fields, it seems that this topic is a promising issue awaiting further in-depth investigation (Cienki & Müller forthcoming a, b).

Alan Cienki has conducted pioneering studies with regard to this issue. To my knowledge, he was the first person to systematically approach the issue of metaphor and gesture in the light of current and contemporary theories of metaphor (cf. Cienki 1997, 1998, 2003). Building on the work of Geneviève Calbris (1990) and David McNeill (1992), who paved the way by identifying the phenomenon of metaphoric gestures co-occurring with speech, Cienki began to study the ways in which metaphoric gestures may relate to speech. Cienki (1998, 2003) distinguishes five forms of gesture-speech relationships in the expression of metaphors:[15]

- Metaphoric speech with metaphoric gesture (shared source and target),
- Metaphoric speech with metaphoric gesture (different source, shared target),
- Metaphoric speech with nonmetaphoric or low metaphoric gesture,
- Metaphoric speech without gesture, and
- Nonmetaphoric speech with metaphoric gesture.

METAPHORIC SPEECH WITH METAPHORIC GESTURE (SHARED SOURCE AND TARGET)   Cienki (1998, 193) gives the example of somebody saying "it's like balancing all these things" and referring to the multitude of factors demanding consideration and integration in order to achieve a well-grounded point of view. While saying this, the speaker moves two cupped hands up and down and with the palms oriented upward (cf. Cienki 1998, 2003).

Cienki suggests that both gesture and speech express the conceptual metaphors FACTORS ARE OBJECTS and IMPORTANCE IS WEIGHT. This would mean that the abstract factors that need to be considered in working out a specific point of view are verbally and gesturally treated as concrete physical objects that are contained in the weighing dishes of a scale. The cupped hands represent the dishes of the scale, their position in space represents the position of dishes hanging down from the scale, and their movement up and down represents the movement of the dishes while balancing objects.

Cienki's point of view mirrors a characteristic analytic approach of CMT. It does so by merging the levels of lexical and conceptual meaning and by not envisioning the possibility of a separate lexical level of semantic structure. Rather, lexical meaning is embedded in conceptual domains, which are forms of general cognition. A level of lexical or linguistic semantic structure is not assumed. In suggesting a single level of meaning structure, which is conceptual, it is not surprising that Cienki does not discuss the possibility that coverbal gestures may relate to the lexical level of meaning structure directly, rather than to an abstract level of conceptual metaphors. Yet this is exactly what I would like to suggest, at least as a further possible interpretation of the semantic relation between gesture and speech that is apparent in the above example.

The gesture appears to embody exactly the same concrete, experiential source of the verbal metaphor so clearly, namely, a concrete balance, that grounding it in more general conceptual metaphors of FACTORS ARE OBJECTS and IMPORTANCE IS WEIGHT is not really convincing. Hence, I would propose characterizing it as a verbal and gestural expression of a shared source and target domain or of a more specific metaphoric mapping that could be paraphrased as BALANCING OBJECTS IS BALANCING ARGUMENTS/FACTORS, which seems closer to the image evoked on the verbal and on the gestural level. However, given the cultural and, more specifically, iconographic background of scales as a symbol of justice, that is, the "scales of justice," it appears probable that this metaphor exists on the level of nonverbal cognition.

METAPHORIC SPEECH WITH METAPHORIC GESTURE (DIFFERENT SOURCE, SHARED TARGET) It is not self-evident that each and every time a verbal metaphor is produced it is accompanied by a metaphorical gesture operating on the same source domain. This would be the case if a coverbal gesture were cognitively based and completely isolated in the lexical meaning of its lexical affiliate. Cienki (1998) provides us with interesting counterexamples of such a simplistic (albeit somewhat popular) view.

For instance, he describes a sequence in which two students discuss what they consider to be two typical forms of American morality (cf. Lakoff 1996, 2002). While characterizing it verbally in terms of colors (black and white versus "gray), it is depicted in gestures as two clear-cut moral spaces, as opposed to one curved, open space without boundaries.

Cienki concludes that "metaphors in speech and gesture draw on different source domains (those of color and spatial form), but in a coherent way" (Cienki

1998, 196). In other words, verbal and gestural metaphors draw on different source domains (color versus space) to characterize one target domain (morality).

METAPHORIC SPEECH WITH NONMETAPHORIC OR LOW METAPHORIC GESTURE   Here Cienki's distinction presupposes a specific understanding of what a metaphoric gesture is, namely, one that disregards the functional aspect of a gesture, while focusing on the cognitive procedure of activating two conceptual domains at once. Consider his characterization of metaphoric gesture: "Note that for the purposes of the present study, the criterion for establishing a gesture as (at least partially) metaphoric is that the gesture characterizes an abstract domain (here we will discuss mostly the domains of morality and time) in terms of the concrete (spatial form, location, and movement of the hands and forearms)" (Cienki 1998, 190). So far, we have only discussed examples in which metaphoric gestures have been characterized along the traditional lines of lexical semantics. Now, Cienki (2003, 5) also introduces beats (rhythmical movements beating out the rhythm of speech, thereby adding visual structure to the discourse) as metaphoric gestures. Even though one could argue that beating out a rhythm is creating discourse structure, in that it is a way of seeing-in -terms-of, it is nevertheless a fundamentally different way of seeing-in-terms-of because it does not have a referential function, that is, the speaker is not depicting a discourse structure as discourse structure, but he or she is creating it. A teacher of conversation analysis could depict discourse structure in a referential sense, that is, as a kind of spatial diagram (and this is indeed what we see in the gestures of linguists when they talk about grammar; cf. Mittelberg 2003, 2006, forthcoming; Mittelberg and Waugh forthcoming). Then the discourse structure would be the speaker's referential focus, his or her topic of speech. Considering discursive gestures only as metaphorical eliminates the difference between talking about discourse and structuring discourse or between the semantic and pragmatic functions of speech and gesture. Therefore, for the time being, it will be suggested that metaphoric speech may occur with different kinds of nonmetaphoric gestures, be they discursive or performative ones.[16]

METAPHORIC SPEECH WITHOUT GESTURE   It is noteworthy, and Cienki (1998, 2003) points this out, that metaphoric speech may occur, and indeed often does, without any gestural accompaniment whatsoever. We will return to the implications of this later in chapter 6 in the context of the proposal that metaphoricity is gradable. For now, it should suffice to mention that metaphorical gesture is not an automatic and random by-product of speech.

NONMETAPHORIC SPEECH WITH METAPHORIC GESTURE   Cienki (1998, 196–200) distinguishes two cases of nonmetaphoric speech accompanied by metaphoric gestures: in one case, the gesture embodies a metaphor that is also present in language; in the other case, the gesture rests on a gesture-specific conceptualization, that is, a metaphor that is not present in language. Thus, in the first case, there is only a lack of temporal synchronicity between the gesture and speech, but in the second, there is no parallel metaphor in the gesture and speech.

An example of the first case is the use of a straight gesture (the one we encountered in Cienki's example above), but now it is used without evoking a similar image verbally. While talking about dishonesty and truth, the speaker uses the straight gesture. This is example is somewhat similar to the "depressive" example 4 in that here nonmetaphoric speech combines with a metaphoric gesture. For an illustration of the second case, Cienki offers examples of gesture-specific conceptualizations of time. In the English language (and in Indo-European languages in general), time is conceptualized along a front-back axis in space, along which the past is behind the speaker, the present is the location of the speaker, and the future is the space in front of the speaker. In gestures, time may also be organized along a left-right axis, where the past is located on the left-hand side and the future on the right-hand side (cf. Borgschulte 2007). Both Calbris (1985, 1990) and Cienki (1998) observe this and suggest that this is a form of conceptualization that is derived from the conventional direction of writing in Western cultures.

For the present purpose, I shall focus on the first kind of relation between metaphor, gesture, and speech that Cienki distinguishes: metaphoric speech with metaphoric gesture, that is, instances in which gesture and speech share a metaphorical source and target. This focus promises further insights into the cognitive activation of so-called dead metaphors and potentially activated cognitive realms. More specifically, I shall devote attention to a possible level of lexical structure, rather than progressing directly to the level of conceptual metaphors, as Cienki does.

3.3.2 *How Are Verbo-gestural Metaphors Activated during Speaking?*

Let me briefly recall the specific concept of verbo-gestural metaphors that was introduced in chapter 1. The term "verbo-gestural metaphors" was used to characterize gesture-speech ensembles in which gesture and speech draw upon the same source domain. In example 3 in chapter 1, this kind of semantic relation was illustrated with the verbal metaphor it sparked ("es hat gefunkt"). Recall that this is an instance of a so-called dead metaphor. But because it is transparent, has a parallel "literal" use, and is used as the basis for a gestural enactment, it was conceived of as a waking metaphor in this very context of use (we will return to the distinction of waking and sleeping versus dead metaphors in detail in chapter 6). The gesture depicts the movement dynamics and the size of the "electric spark" that is encoded in the verbal metaphor and, hence, documents that the lexical meaning of the dead metaphor was available to gesture production and thus must have been cognitively active.

We will now readdress this issue based on a sequence in which the speaker uses a series of verbo-gestural metaphors.

The speaker characterizes the relationship between her first boyfriend and herself as somehow clingy ("klebrig"). She describes him as being too dependent, which felt as if he had "pulled and sucked" ("gezogen und gesaugt") on her.

Example 6: "klebrig" (sticky)

                    open palms touching each other repeatedly
1 [also da **hab ich schon gemerkt naja\ des is: ganz**

    well there I did already realize well\   this is really

            hands clap repeatedly
2 **schö:n** (-)   (mh)   (-)   **klebrig\ oder heftig**]

    pretty   (-)   (mh)   (-)   clingy or heavy

                    PUOH   point upwards
3 un[dadurch dass er so **depressiv** war] denke [ich

    letztendlich /]

    an because he was so depressive   I think finally

            grasping hds to body   squeezing vertically
4 [(.h) hat **er auch ganz schön gezogen**||**und ge** saugt\]]

    he also pretty much   pulled and sucked

Fig. 19. "Clingy" (klebrig) and open palms repeatedly touching each other. An activated verbal metaphor visible in gesture.

At a first glance, this extract appears relatively clear and simple, yet on closer consideration one sees that it does in fact document a rather manifold picture of how gestures may relate to verbal metaphor. First of all, the speaker performs a gesture that enacts the movement properties of clingy hands by two open palms repeatedly touching each other. The movement is slow; this is important because the slowness of the detachment expresses the difficulty of separating two surfaces that are stuck together. Note that in the first place this gesture is realized without a verbal metaphor. The speaker says, "well there I did already realize well\ this is really pretty" [also da hab ich schon gemerkt naja\ des is: ganz schön]—then she makes a speech pause—and then she utters the verbal metaphor "klebrig" (clingy). In other words, it is only at the very end of the utterance that she produces the verbal metaphor "clingy," while throughout this utterance she performs the "clingy gesture" with the open palms repeatedly touching each other. Thus, the metaphor was present in gesture before it was verbalized. Together, the gesture and the word constitute an extended verbo-gestural metaphor that shares the source and the target domain of the verbal metaphor.

When she continues, she describes her boyfriend as somehow depressive and reminisces that this might have been the reason why when she was with him she felt that he was somehow "clingy" (klebrig) and why it felt as if "he pretty much pulled and sucked on [her]" [hat er auch ganz schön gezogen und gesaugt]. This small sequence has four subsequent gestures: first, a two-handed palm-up open hand that coincides with "and because he was so depressive" [dadurch dass er so depressiv war]; second, an upward point with "I think finally" [denke ich letztendlich]; and third and fourth, respectively, grasping and seizing movements of the two hands that parallel "he pretty much pulled and sucked" [hat er auch ganz schön gezogen und gesaugt].

Again, the last two gestures clearly relate to the semantics of the verbal metaphor—or, put another way—the verbal metaphor and the gesture use the same source domain. The first two gestures are performative gestures, that is, gestures that perform a communicative activity (Müller 1998a, 2004; Müller and Haferland 1997). They do not depict a referent or enact aspects of a referent; rather they enact what they perform. In this case, this is presenting a discursive object on the open hand and focusing attention by pointing. The enactment of presenting does not serve to refer to presenting an object—rather it is used to do this—to present a virtual object on the open hand (cf. Kendon 2004; Müller 2004; Müller & Cienki forthcoming).

What we find in this little sequence are three verbo-gestural metaphors. In two of them, the verbal and the gestural part of the metaphor coincide in time, and in the third one, the gesture precedes the verbal metaphor. In other words, gestures and speech are semantically coexpressive in that they share their source and target domains. This shows that the metaphoricity of those conventionalized dead metaphors was highly active at the moment of speaking. This is why I consider them to be waking rather than sleeping or even dead metaphors. Moreover, this suggests that they reside in a cognitive realm of rich-image information, which triggers gestures before it triggers the verbal metaphor. This would, in fact, point to a kind of mental structure that has been proposed by Susan D. Duncan and David McNeill and that is termed the "growth point." This is the core of an "idea unit," whose characteristics encompass propositional as well as imagistic content. This concept would explain perfectly well why a gesture expresses the image of verbal content (which is propositionally structured) before it is even uttered.

Before concluding this section, a brief aside will be devoted to the grounds on which my conception of verbo-gestural metaphors rest. Why should we talk about verbo-gestural metaphors and not about verbal metaphors that are activated? Because considering coverbal gestures solely as a window onto thought processes would devalue the role of gesture. The fact that metaphoric gestures may relate in a systematic fashion to verbal language calls for a theoretical consideration of gesture. Hence, it seems to me that in cases like the one above, we do not face a verbal metaphor here and a gestural metaphor there, but, in fact, a multimodal metaphor—a metaphor that uses two expressive modes conjointly (Müller and Cienki forthcoming). Adam Kendon (2004) speaks of gesture-speech ensembles to account for the tight interplay between gesture and speech in general. Yet, as we have seen even in the rough sketches provided in this chapter, the relations among gesture, speech, and metaphor are manifold, and they are functional. Thus, in Kendon's terms, we would need to be prepared to find not just one form of the gesture-speech ensemble, but systematic and functionally significant variation in the possible relations between speech and co-occurring gesture. We have seen above that Cienki has pointed this out for the relationship between metaphoric and nonmetaphoric speech and its relation to metaphoric and nonmetaphoric gesture.[17]

To conclude, in this section we have focused on metaphoric speech that is accompanied by metaphoric gesture. The point I wish to make is that not only is coverbal metaphoric gesturing revelatory regarding the activation of a so-called dead verbal metaphor, but it may also become a very part of that metaphor. What does this add to our reflections regarding the vitality of dead metaphors and about the realms of metaphor that are activated online during speaking? I believe that what this shows is, first of all, that metaphoricity is not restricted to the medium of verbal language; second, that it adds a further piece to the puzzle of our preceding observations regarding realms of metaphor that might be active online during speech production, namely, the possible activation of a conceptual, a verbal, and a verbo-gestural cognitive realm of metaphor.

3.4 Verbo-pictorial Metaphors

The last realm of metaphorical structure to be considered here is the one that underlies the use of verbo-pictorial metaphors. This offers a further interesting perspective because pictorial as well as verbo-pictorial metaphors provide us with further insights into the forms of metaphorical structure that are different from and independent of verbal language. Therefore, they may help to shed more light on the questions addressed in this chapter, namely, what kinds of cognitive realms are activated when presumably dead verbal metaphors are used in spoken or written language, and do they point directly to a level of conceptual structure or to a level of verbal structure? I am interested in pictorial and verbo-pictorial metaphors for additional reasons: they may accompany written language and in this way add a further perspective on the analyses of spoken language provided in this chapter so far. Moreover, they provide us with further evidence for the assumption that metaphors are the products of a modality-independent cognitive process.

Because of this book's primary focus on metaphor in language use, I shall devote relatively little attention to pictorial metaphors in isolation. It is clear that the issue of pictorial metaphor deserves much more detailed treatment than can be provided in this chapter, and I would like to draw your attention to Charles Forceville's (1996) monograph, *Pictorial Metaphor in Advertising*, which fills this gap in a very careful and competent manner and which has been a major source of inspiration for the subsequent section (cf. also Forceville 2000, 2002).

3.4.1 Pictorial Metaphors and How They May Relate to Language

Forceville's (1996) book on pictorial metaphor (in advertising) provides a differentiated survey of more recent theories of pictorial metaphor, and it develops what could be characterized as the foundations of a theory of pictorial metaphor. Based upon an in-depth examination and critique of the accounts of Richard Wollheim (1987), Carl Hausmann (1989), John Kennedy (1982), Bethany Johns (1984), Jacques Durand (1987), and Trevor Whittock (1990) of Black's interaction theory and of Sperber and Wilson's relevance theory, Forceville puts forward four criteria that a theory of pictorial metaphor should meet. Consider the overview below:

1. Literal reading as violation: "For a pictorial representation to be called metaphorical, it is necessary that a 'literal,' or conventional reading of the pictorial representation is felt either not to exhaust its meaning potential, or to yield an anomaly which is understood as an intentional violation of the norm rather as an error . . . " (Forceville 1996, 64).

2. Clarification of terminology: metaphor in a wide or in a narrow sense: "Considerable confusion has arisen from the fact that the word "metaphor" has both been used in the broad sense in which it is more or less equivalent with "trope," and in a much more narrow sense in which it is used as one trope among others . . . " (Forceville 1996, 64–5).

3. Semantic structure, feature transfer, identification mechanism: "An account of pictorial metaphor should show an awareness that a metaphor has two distinctive terms, one the primary subject or tenor, the other the secondary subject or vehicle, which are usually non-reversible. This entails that the transfer or mapping of features is from secondary subject (on)to primary subject, and not vice versa. The account must furthermore indicate by what mechanisms the identities of primary subject and secondary subject are established" (Forceville 1996, 65).

4. Various contextual levels: "For the identification of the two terms of the metaphor, their labeling as primary subject and secondary subject, as well as for the interpretation of the metaphor, it is necessary to take various contextual levels into consideration. These contextual levels are partly text-internal, partly text-external" (Forceville 1996, 65).

Forceville argues that at least two of the above criteria are met by Black's interaction theory of metaphor (criteria 2 and 3); and it is from Black's account that Forceville derives the questions guiding his investigations into pictorial metaphors in advertising: "What are the two terms of the metaphor and how do we know? Which is the metaphor's primary and what is its secondary subject and how do we know? What can be said about the feature(s) mapped from the secondary subject on to the primary subject?" (Forceville 1996, 65–6). We will return to Black's interaction theory and examine it more closely in chapter 4. For now, the quotes above may suffice as the background for a sketch of Forceville's approach to pictorial metaphors. For the present purposes, the most important distinction that Forceville introduces is the dis-

Fig. 20. "Shoe is tie." A pictorial metaphor with one pictorially present term (MP1).
Forceville (1996, 110).

tinction between pictorial metaphors with one and those with two pictorially present terms (MP1 and MP2). Consider the photograph in figure 20.

The striking violation of the normal appearance of the upper body of a
male businessman is a shoe that is placed where a tie would be located under
normal circumstances. Presupposing, in relevance theory terms, that the
communicator intends to be maximally relevant, Forceville argues that the
observers are led to infer that the depicted shoe suggests the concept TIE. Put
another way, the addressees are invited to conceive of the shoe in terms of
a tie, and this construction is clearly a seeing–in-terms-of process whereby
one thing is identified with something else. In this way, a metaphor with
the structure SHOE IS TIE is evoked in purely pictorial terms. Forceville
then goes on to argue that this is a metaphor with one pictorially present
term, in which the foregrounded object "shoe" is the primary subject, or
in Lakoff's and in Weinrich's terms, the source domain or image-offering
field, respectively. The distribution of primary and secondary subjects, or of
source and target, of image offerer and image receiver, is supported by a larger
pictorial and verbal context. This makes it clear that the advertisement is
about shoes and about taking them to be among the outstanding features
of a businessman's appearance, like a tie: "Hence it is the combination

Fig. 21. "Earth is candle." A pictorial metaphor with two pictorially present terms (MP2). Forceville (1996, 128).

of the understanding of the wider advertisement that is responsible for the distribution of primary subject and secondary subject" (Forceville 1996, 111). For an illustration of Forceville's conception of pictorial metaphor with two pictorially present terms, let us now turn to a second example.

What we see here is a photograph of a burning candle looking like a globe. A verbal paraphrase of the pictorial metaphor could be "earth is candle" or "candle is earth." Both terms of the metaphor "earth" and "candle" are represented pictorially. But the pictorial context does not provide sufficient evidence to clarify which is the primary and which is the secondary subject. Here the verbal context comes into play. It is the heading of the advertisement that offers the disambiguating information: "We extract energy from the earth as if it were inexhaustible" (Forceville 1996, 126). Both terms (primary and secondary, source and target, image offerer and image receiver) are visualized. "Earth" is to be taken as the primary term, and "the candle" is to be taken as the secondary term. The earth is to be regarded in terms of a candle that only provides a limited amount of energy. Hence, even though the metaphor is based upon two pictorially present terms, the verbal context is needed to disambiguate the distribution of the primary and secondary terms.

Note that the examples we have considered so far are all cases of novel creative metaphors in which the verbal context plays a relatively marginal role for their constitution as metaphors. Language was necessary, in that it created the disambiguating context, but it did not enter the multimodal metaphor as metaphor, which is the case of the pictorial metaphor that I will turn to now. Here Forceville introduces a third form of pictorial metaphor in which language does play a constitutive role; the example he gives for this type of metaphor is an advertisement for licorice. The picture is full of pieces of licorice candies, and in the middle of it, the words "Het zwarte goud" (the black gold) are written.

The verbal metaphor represents the secondary term, whereas the picture symbolizes the primary term of this metaphor. Hence, the verbo-pictorial metaphor could be paraphrased as "licorice is black gold." Thus, here we have again a truly multimodal metaphor with the metaphorical terms distributed across two modalities.

The philosopher of art Virgil C. Aldrich (1996) discusses some further interesting cases of pictorial metaphors that make use of language in a specific way. As we have already introduced Aldrich's conception of pictorial metaphor in chapter 1, there is no need to repeat his basic assumptions.[18] Let me just briefly recall that he conceives of the pictorial metaphor as dependent upon a process of seeing-in–terms-of: the process of the visual construction of a meaningful object. This is why he uses the term "visual metaphor" instead of

Fig. 22. (Het zwarte goud) "the black gold". A case of a verbo-pictorial metaphor in
Forceville's terms. Forceville (1996, 150).

"pictorial" or "sculptural metaphor." Aldrich grounds his explanation of visual metaphor in the philosophy of language, rhetoric, and the arts. As I have mentioned above, he uses Wittgenstein's notion of seeing-as and Owen Barfield's (1962) analyses of the semantic structure of simile, metaphor, and symbol. Additionally, his argument is influenced by Pablo Picasso's reflections upon sculpture, painting, and metaphor. Note that Picasso himself conceived of his sculptures as metaphors: "My sculptures are plastic metaphors. It is the same principle as in painting" (Gilot and Lake 1964, 296–97). Picasso uses *objets trouvés* to uncover the metaphoric structure inherent in sculpture. In addition, there is a very interesting case to which I would now like to briefly turn because it documents a specific kind of role that language may play in the construction of such a metaphoric sculpture. In his discussion of Picasso's *Vénus de gaz*, Aldrich writes that the perception of this sculpture as a sculpture depends upon its name. The sculpture is only perceivable as sculpture by taking into consideration the title Picasso gave it. The sculpture as such, for example, a gas burner on a pedestal, does not trigger a clear kind of reference to a female body or a Venus. This metaphoric view, this seeing-in-terms-of, is entirely motivated through its verbal title: *Vénus de gaz*. Thus, I would like to suggest that we may characterize this sculpture as a verbo-pictorial metaphor. The metaphorical target is only expressed verbally, while the source of the metaphor is represented both verbally and in sculpture. Only when we view both modalities together as a joint metaphor can we perceive the Venus in the form of the gas burner. Therefore, the sculpture critically rests upon the cognitive process of seeing-in-terms-of.

Let me conclude this chapter with an analysis of yet another different kind of verbo-pictorial metaphor that is nevertheless based on a seemingly dead metaphor. Let us see what this may import on our overarching question in this chapter regarding the cognitively active realms of metaphor and, more specifically, what answers it provides to the leading question in this book: are dead metaphors alive when they are used in writing or speaking?

3.4.2 How Are Verbo-pictorial Metaphors Activated during Writing?

The next example to be discussed is taken from a local Berlin newspaper. It shows a photograph of the distribution of trophies after a Formula 1 race. Michael Schumacher is pouring champagne into the mouth of Mika Häkkinen. The headline says: "Ein Gewinner. Zwei Sieger" (One winner. Two victors). The caption begins with the sentence "Siegestrunken in Silverstone" (drunk with victory in Silverstone). Consider the photograph below:

Ein Sieger, zwei Gewinner

SIEGESTRUNKEN IN SILVERSTONE. Mika Häkkinen feierte am Sonntag seinen ersten Saisonerfolg. Der Finne gewann im McLaren-Mercedes den britischen Grand Prix vor Michael Schumacher und Rubens Barrichello (verdeckt). Schumacher konnte seinen Vorsprung in der Fahrerwertung gegenüber David Coulthard ausbauen. Der Schotte schied früh aus. Foto: dpa

Fig. 23. "Drunk with victory" (Siegestrunken). A verbo-pictorial metaphor based on a dead metaphor. *Der Tagesspiegel*, July 16, 2001.

The German expression "siegestrunken" is a typical instance of a seemingly dead metaphor: it is conventionalized but transparent. Ordinary language is, indeed, full of this kind of dead metaphor. The metaphoric compound could be paraphrased "being a winner is being drunk." The picture instantiates both the source and the target, the secondary and primary terms, and the image offerer and image receiver of this conventionalized metaphor.

This example differs from the ones discussed above in that it really rests entirely upon a dead metaphor of ordinary language. It is not the novel creation of a metaphor, as in Forceville's pictorial and verbo-pictorial metaphors in advertisements and other visual media (1998, 2000, 2002, 2005) or in Picasso's *Vénus de gaz*. Therefore, it is particularly pertinent to our question regarding the cognitive realms of metaphor that are active during writing and speaking. Here we have a case in which a newspaper journalist was clearly playing with language and the available photos to generate a nice verbo-pictorial metaphor. And again, I would like to suggest that what is cognitively active is a level of rich-image verbal metaphoricity. Being drunk with victory is depicted as being drunk because the winner is drinking alcohol. Yet again, as in the ball in example 5 above, the rich image of the verbal metaphor appears to provide access to a domain of general cognition, a level of mental models that triggers a prototypical scenario: in this case, the means of getting drunk. Or it could have been the other way around, namely, that the photograph of this event—Schumacher pouring champagne into Häkkinen's mouth—could have inspired the choice of the verbal metaphor "drunk with victory" (siegestrunken). In both cases, this points to two things: the cognitively active level of metaphoricity of a seemingly dead metaphor and a tight connection to prototypical scenarios in terms of mental models.

Let me conclude this section with a fascinating instance of a verbo-pictorial metaphor that follows exactly the same principle as the one taken from the newspaper. Apparently, Picasso was highly sensitive to this kind of imagery in verbal language, and it appears as if one source of inspiration of his *objets trouvés* sculptures were the dead metaphors of ordinary language. Thus, Aldrich reports on an example where Picasso uses a wicker basket to represent the rib cage of a goat. In French and in Spanish (the two languages Picasso presumably used), the expressions "cage thoracique" and "caja torácica" contain the verbal image of a cage. In this case, the structure and form of a wicker basket clearly resembles the structure of a cage, and hence it is likely that Picasso's sculpture was, indeed, inspired by the image inherent in the supposedly dead metaphor. And this is precisely how Picasso appears to have conceived of it. Consider the quote from Francoise Gilot's biography of Picasso: "I follow the way back from the basket to the rib cage: from the metaphor to reality. I make reality visible, because I use the metaphor" (Gilot and Lake 1964, 176–77). Thus, the sculpture is seeing one thing (a basket) in terms of another (a rib cage), and Picasso reinforces this aspect of sculpting by using *objets trouvés*. Because *objets trouvés* have their own history and identity, this process of seeing one object in terms of another is especially clear, but the principle is the same regardless of whether marble or plaster is used. This is both Picasso's and Aldrich's idea. Hence, Picasso's goat sculpture is nourished by the active metaphoricity of verbal language.

3.5 Conclusion: Dead Metaphors Are Alive during Speaking and Writing

We have seen that, according to traditional accounts of metaphor, what should not have been accessible to the attention of a speaker or writer—the metaphoricity of dead metaphors—was in fact available to online cognitive processing. In other words, conventionalized, transparent, verbal metaphors of ordinary language were active in that their source domains engendered multimodal metaphors that combined gestures, pictures, sculptures, and language. As the example of "depressive" accompanied by a significant, downward-moving gesture indicates, even the source domain of a dead and opaque metaphor may be cognitively active online during speaking or writing. Taking nonverbal modalities into consideration breaks the vicious circle of cognitive linguistic claims based exclusively on the analysis of verbal language. Yet there is more to it than this. The theoretical and empirical studies presented in this chapter have offered insights into the specific forms of their "aliveness" or, put another way, into their cognitive realms.

Let us reconsider the leading questions in this chapter. We have seen that all theoretically assumed realms of metaphor—conceptual, verbal, verbo-gestural, and verbo-pictorial—are active online during metaphor production. They are active because they crosscut modalities and generate novel metaphors in modalities other than verbal language, such as gesture, picture, and sculpture. This does not imply, however, that they are all activated in the same manner. Thus, the claim that they would all reside in a general, cognitive structure, such as a conceptual metaphor, must at least be reformulated in a more specific and much more concrete manner than is common in CMT. Assumptions, such as lexical meaning equates with conceptual meaning, need to be specified in order to account for the apparent selectivity of activation that we have encountered in the examples discussed above. Thus, in one case, a conceptual metaphor on the level of a primary and image-schematic metaphor gave rise to a metaphoric gesture (SAD IS DOWN and significant downward motion), while in most of the other cases the rich-image level of the verbal metaphor informed the metaphor expressed in a gesture, picture, or sculpture. This in turn makes it necessary to postulate at least one more level of metaphoric conceptual structure: a level of active rich-image lexical structure that is tightly connected with other representational modalities, such as gesture, picture, and sculpture, and with general cognitive structures, such as cognitive scenarios, and mental models. This could presumably be modeled theoretically through an integrated account of the different forms of conceptual metaphors. Hence, instead of proposing primary metaphors here and complex metaphors there, it would be necessary to systematically reconstruct the integrated systems of conceptual metaphors with an additional level of rich-image verbal metaphor. Taken together, theoretical as well as empirical studies into the different possible realms of metaphor point to more than one single level of cognitive structure underlying the use of metaphoric language. This means that LMT assumptions concerning metaphor are contradictory, both with regard to the dichotomic assumption that verbal metaphors are either alive or dead and with regard to the claim that metaphor is primarily, if not only, a phenomenon of verbal language.

Both theoretical approaches lack a systematic theoretical reflection upon the relationship between the collective level of a conceptual system and the verbal metaphors within the collective system of verbal language. As the investigations in this chapter have shown, a cognitively realistic theory of metaphor needs to be well grounded in the online processes of metaphor use. The forms of language use we have studied here in the context of different realms of metaphors clearly document the theoretical relevance of an inductive perspective.

Having shown that conceptual and verbal metaphors may be cognitively active online during speaking and writing, we will now examine more closely what is meant by "activating a metaphor." This leads us to inquire into the nature of metaphoricity and what is at its core.

CHAPTER FOUR

The Core of Metaphors: The Establishment of a Triadic Structure

In chapter 3, we saw that dead metaphors may be alive during speaking and writing. We saw that what ought not to be accessible, according to linguistic accounts of metaphor, namely, the source domain or the literal meaning of a dead metaphor (including the activation of a conceptual metaphor in gesture only, that is, without a transparent verbal metaphor), was cognitively active online during speaking and writing.

In this chapter, attention will be paid to a more systematic exploration of what has been conceived of as the structure of metaphor. The first chapter briefly introduced the triadic structure, which I regard as the core of metaphors or as the inherent structure of metaphoricity. Now we will investigate historical and contemporary concepts of metaphor more closely and put forward the argument that explicitly or implicitly they all assume some kind of triadic structure. But, obviously, this does not mean that they are all similar.

Remember that we have distinguished a level of use on which the process of "seeing C in terms of B" (LOVE IN TERMS OF A JOURNEY, LOVE IN TERMS OF SUNSHINE, HERO IN TERMS OF LION) occurs and a level of the system on which the individual and singular process of seeing-in-terms-of is replaced with a conventionalized, collective sign (a lexeme, an idiom, a picture, a gesture, a conceptual metaphor, a primary experience). Hence a conventionalized, metaphoric structure (i.e., a sedimented product of collective processes of seeing B in terms of C) is constituted, and when it is used, it guides the individual process of seeing-in-terms-of along collectively paved paths. Moreover, I have also suggested that this triadic structure is highly abstract and ontologically neutral, that is, the relata may vary. This is important because it is the assumed nature of the relata that figures as a critical factor in metaphor theories. The assumption of such a triadic structure at the core of metaphors obviously relates directly to the central topic in theories of metaphor, namely, what exactly metaphor is. What are the specific properties that turn an entity, be it linguistic, pictorial, gestural, or conceptual, into a metaphorical one? Clearly, an in-depth treatment of this issue would easily fill a book on its own, which it would certainly merit. However, for the present purposes, we shall focus on two aspects of historical and contemporary concepts of metaphor: the constants and the variables in their assumed structure.

4.1 Duality of Meaning

A still very common way of characterizing the structure of metaphor is to assume a duality of meaning. Surprisingly, the structural properties of metaphors have received relatively little systematic attention, and eminent semanticists, such as Stephen Ullmann, have regarded duality of meaning as an unquestionable and almost trivial issue: "The basic structure of metaphor is very simple. There are always two terms present: the thing we are talking about and that to which we are comparing it" (Ullmann 1967, 213). An early psychological account of metaphor as a "double unit" is offered by Wilhelm Stählin (1914). His interest in describing the specific psychological processes of metaphor comprehension leads him to assume what he considers to be a specific form of awareness, "the state of awareness of a double meaning": "It is a characteristic state of awareness that is thus created, and I believe that I can appropriately call it the 'state of awareness of double meaning'" (Stählin 1914, 322). This unique state of awareness of double meaning (Bewußtseinslage der doppelten Bedeutung) is a merging or blending of two meaning spheres that are both active. The term "double meaning" refers to the parallel awareness of two spheres that inform each other reciprocally (Stählin 1914, 321–23).[1]

Stählin's analysis constitutes a highly important point of departure for subsequent treatments of metaphors, notably, not only psychological ones, such as the one outlined by Bühler (1982, first published 1936) in his "Sprachtheorie" (theory of language), but also, as we have seen above, linguistic and stylistic ones, such as the one offered by Weinrich (1976).

Stählin's linguistic and psychological characterization of metaphor is of central importance to the account of metaphor advocated in this book; it adds to the core of Western concepts of metaphor—"metaphor as a double unit"—the dimension of the active, cognitive establishment of metaphoricity. In his *Philosophy of Rhetoric*, Ivor A. Richards (1936) advocates a similar idea by characterizing metaphor as two thoughts that are active together.

And, as far as I know, Richards coined the expression "double unit" (Richards 1936, 94). The idea of conceptualizing metaphor in dualistic terms has become a standard way of characterizing the meaning structure of metaphor, and it is one that is present, for instance, in Black's concept of "duality of reference" (Black 1993, 27): "A metaphorical statement has two distinct subjects, to be identified as the 'primary' subject and the 'secondary' one.... The duality of reference is marked by the contrast between the metaphorical statement's *focus* (the word or words used non-literally) and the surrounding literal *frame*" (Black 1993, 27; emphases in the original). Duality of reference also continues to be taken for granted in more recent investigations into the parameters of language change. Elisabeth Closs-Traugott, in an article entitled "'Conventional' and 'Dead' Metaphors Revisited," distinguishes three crucial parameters in the historical changes of conventional metaphors: reference, conceptualization, and distance (Closs-Traugott 1985, 22–25). The reference parameter (a) concerns the duality of reference, the conceptualization parameter (b) concerns the reorganization of the belief system, and the distance parameter (c) concerns the position occupied within (b). We will return to Closs-Traugott's distinction in more detail in chapter 6. What is important for our present purposes is the mere observation that duality of meaning appears to be taken as an unquestioned trait of metaphoric structure.[2]

But, as I shall suggest in the subsequent section, the core structure of metaphors is not convincingly captured in a dualistic conception.

4.2 Triadic Structures in Historical Accounts: Constants and Variants

Historical concepts of metaphor that have evolved in the Western history of ideas from Aristotle to the first half of the twentieth century have been meticulously reconstructed by Hans Heinrich Lieb (1964, 1983). This is how he formulates his goal: "What do the terms denote (the individual expressions) that are contained in the historical concept metaphor, in particular, the terms currently used in the study of literature such as Metapher, métaphore etc.?" (1996, 342) Lieb's formal analysis of the varying concepts of metaphor provides us with a most valuable taxonomy of the kinds of structures that have historically been attributed to verbal metaphors. He considered 125 definitions of metaphor from eighty-five Western European scholars and a wide range of disciplines. He included definitions from philosophy, psychology, linguistics, and literary criticism with the following temporal distribution: (1) beginning with Aristotle and covering the period up to 1799, he considered twenty-five definitions and twelve authors; (2) for the period 1800–99, he considered twenty-one definitions and fifteen authors; (3) for the period 1900–63, he considered seventy-nine definitions and fifty-eight authors (cf. Lieb 1996, 343).

Lieb's procedure involved two methodological strategies: to collect and analyze definitions of metaphors from a wide range of disciplines, such as philosophy, psychology, linguistics, literary criticism, and ethnology; and to identify metaphors in literary texts. We will focus on the former aspect of his work. Lieb's analysis of this collection of Western definitions of metaphor revealed four basic concepts: metaphor in a wider and a narrower sense that is used either as a relational or as an attributive term.[3] We will begin with the distinction between the wider and the narrower concept of metaphor. Since Aristotelian times, metaphor (*metaphorá, trópos, metaphorá, translatio*) has been used in a wider sense referring to all figures of speech, including metaphor in a narrower sense, metonymy, and synecdoche.[4]

For the most part, metaphor was used as a relational term (metaphor is xyz), whereby a metaphor refers to a set of ordered entities with a specific structure. Fewer definitions apply an attributive concept of metaphor (xyz is a metaphor), whereby a metaphor refers to a set of single entities. Lieb illustrates these two versions of metaphor with two classical quotes from Aristotle's *Poetics*.

Relational use of the term "metaphor":

Metaphor is the application of a word that does not belong: either from the genus to the species, or from the species to the genus, or from the species to the species, or according to what is analogous. (Aristotle 1995, *Poetics* XXI, 1457b, trans. H. H. Lieb).[5]

Attributive use of the term "metaphor": Every word is either a standard term, loan word, metaphor... (Aristotle *Poetics* XXI, 1457b, trans. S. Halliwell)

The first quote exemplifies the relational concept of metaphor (metaphor is xyz); the second one exemplifies the attributive concept of metaphor (xyz is a metaphor). The second quote predicates metaphoricity over a subject; the first one predicates the properties of the concept of metaphor. Or, in more informal terms, it expresses what a metaphor is supposed to be.

It is clear that the attributive concept of metaphor depends upon the relational concept of metaphor. In other words, when we identify metaphors in a given text (which implies the second structure "xyz is a metaphor"), we apply to specific lexemes or expressions what has already been declared to be the structure of metaphor (which presupposes having filled in the missing predication in the proposition "metaphor is xyz"). And it is precisely this missing predication in the proposition with which we will be concerned in the remaining part of this section. What are its historical constants, and what are its variants?

The issue of how to determine the structure of metaphors (mostly verbal metaphors) has been and continues to be controversial. Although at first sight our account may seem like a further repetition of what have become the standard surveys of theories of metaphor, Lieb's differentiations indicate two important issues: first, they reveal that there is less variation among the various concepts of metaphor than the huge amount of literature and the lack of systematic reflection upon concepts of metaphor would suggest; second, they document that some kind of assumption regarding the structure of metaphors is unavoidable but often remains implicit.

I believe that avoiding the discussion, and a critical reflection upon it, undermines the scientific basis of any analysis of metaphor. To my profound surprise, most of the contemporary inquiries into metaphor (be they empirical or theoretical) do not devote much energy to a reflection upon this issue, which leads to a lack of reliability as to what is considered to be a metaphor at all. This problem is evident both on the level of metaphor identification in texts and on the level of metaphor theory. If we do not clarify our concept of metaphor, we simply do not know what our theories or what our research is concerned with. Recent research on metaphor identification, on metonymy, and on other tropes indicates a growing recognition of the complexity of this issue and the necessity of methodological and terminological rigor (Barcelona 2000; Gibbs 1994; Panther and Radden 1999).

To begin with, a discursive and nontechnical presentation of Lieb's formal reconstruction of the historical concepts of metaphors will be provided. Lieb's study revealed fourteen different concepts of metaphor from antiquity to the present. In this chapter, I shall focus on four versions of Lieb's analysis, which, in many respects, are the fundamental ones. All are variants of the relational concept of metaphor (metaphor is xyz): two are variants of the wider sense of metaphor, and two of the narrower sense. As we will see, the order in which they are presented is significant.[6]

The first one (1rw), the relational concept of metaphor in a wider sense (metaphor in a wider sense is xyz), documents the structure of Aristotle's concept of metaphor as it is presented in the first half of the famous sentence quoted above: "Metaphor is the application of a word that does not belong: either from the genus to the species, or from the species to the genus, or from

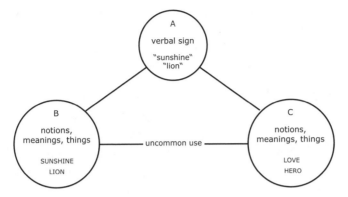

Fig. 24. The triadic structure of the historically and logically basic concept of metaphor in a wider sense, or Lieb's (1996) relational concept of metaphor in a wider sense, 1rw (metaphor is xyz).

the species to the species, or according to what is analogous" (Aristotle *Poetics* XXI, 1457b). As mentioned in chapter 1, Lieb characterizes this fundamental concept of metaphor as a set of ordered triples (Gegenstandsdreiheiten). Consider the diagram in figure 24 for a visualization of the structure that constitutes the basis of all Western concepts of metaphor.

Obviously, this very much resembles the triadic structure introduced in chapter 1. This means that, at the heart of Western concepts of metaphor, we find a triadic structure. However, Lieb's reconstruction makes explicit assumptions regarding the relata of the triangle (as opposed to the proposal of unspecified relata in chapter 1). For the historically and logically basic concept of metaphor in a wider sense or Lieb's (1996, 346–7) relational concept of metaphor in a wider sense, 1rw, (metaphor is xyz), this means that A is a linguistic sign that relates to B and C as two sets of nonlinguistic entities (concepts, meanings, or things). The assumed relation is one of uncommon use or of transfer. Hence, B is transferred to C or used such that it denotes C.

> The linguistic sign, which should be, according to most definitions an expression-in-the-language, normally a single word, means the first but not the second "concept" (has the first but not the second "meaning"), or else, refers to the first but not to the second class of "things". In addition, the expression-in-the-language has been "used", i.e. an expression-in-speech, similar in form has been produced; and this expression in speech refers, to the second "concept" or the second class of "things", respectively. (Lieb 1996, 346–7)

Two examples will help to illustrate Lieb's analyses, in a somewhat simplified manner: "You are the sunshine of my life" and "This man is a lion."[7] To begin with, consider the nontechnical paraphrase of the very core of Western concepts of metaphor:

- A linguistic sign is used and turns into a materialized sign: a spoken or written form. (The lexemes 'sunshine' and 'lion' are used.)
- The linguistic signs (in their spoken or written form) relate to two sets of nonlinguistic entities (concepts, meanings, or things). (The lexeme 'sunshine' relates to THE SHINING OF THE SUN and to LOVE; the lexeme 'lion' relates to THE ANIMAL and to HERO.)
- Between the two sets of nonlinguistic entities there exists a relation of uncommon usage or of transfer.
- The linguistic sign (in its spoken or written form) denotes the second set (LOVE, HERO) but not the first one (THE SHINING OF THE SUN, THE ANIMAL).

The ontology of the relata and the assumed relations between them constitute the critical differences between the varying concepts and theories of metaphor. We will see as we go along that the assumption of a triadic structure at the core of metaphor is the constant factor in historical concepts of metaphor.

The second version of the historical concept of metaphor reconstructed by Lieb is a special case of the first one. It is a relational concept of metaphor in a narrower sense (1rn) (Lieb 1996, 347), and it is expressed in the second part of Aristotle's famous passage quoted above: "Metaphor is the application of a word that does not belong: . . . , or according to what is analogous" (Aristotle *Poetics* XXI, 1457b). It shares the triadic structure of the wider concept of metaphor (1rw), but it is narrower in that it is restricted to those ordered triples that display an analogical relation between the two sets of nonlinguistic entities (concepts, meanings, or things).[8] Note that this is the rationale of the distinction between metaphor as an expression for any kind of trope and metaphor as a form of trope that contrasts with metonymy and synecdoche. Consider the diagram in figure 25 for an overview.

In other words, the historical concept of metaphor in the narrower sense assumes a relation of analogy between two sets of "concepts, meanings, or things." Accordingly, in our example sentences, there is a supposed analogical relation between SUNSHINE and LOVE and between LION and HERO.

The third version of the historical concept of metaphor has become widely known under the label of the "theory of substitution." Again, there is a wider and a narrower sense. We will begin with the wider sense (2rw) in

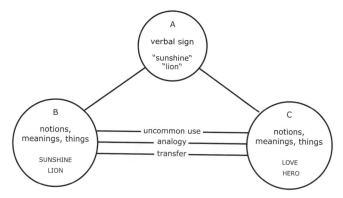

Fig. 25. The triadic structure of the historically and logically basic concept of metaphor in a narrower sense, or Lieb's (1996) relational concept of metaphor, 1rn (metaphor in a narrower sense is xyz).

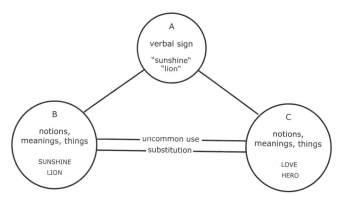

Fig. 26. The triadic structure of the theory of substitution, or the second kind of relational concept of metaphor in a wider sense (2rw).

which the first version (1rw) is elaborated by a further condition, namely, that the linguistic sign in its materialized (spoken or written) form (here, 'sunshine' and 'lion') substitutes another linguistic sign ('love' and 'hero,' respectively),[9] which is not materialized. The substitution theory goes back to Quintilian and has heavily influenced literary rhetorics.[10]

The substitution view has been widely challenged, and, as a closer look at the examples reveals, skepticism is justified here. Our examples show that it is only due to a fair amount of interpretation that we may find "literal" expressions that may be used to replace the metaphorical ones. Hence, assuming that in Stevie Wonder's lyrics "You are the sunshine of my life," "sunshine" replaces "love" and that in Lieb's rendition of Homer's verse

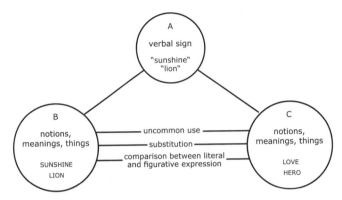

Fig. 27. The triadic structure of the theory of comparison, or the second kind of relational concept of metaphor in a narrower sense (2rn).

"Achilles was a lion" the lexeme 'lion' replaces the lexeme 'hero' presupposes a rather huge amount of interpretation. This points, of course, to the well-known phenomenon of so-called catachresis—lexemes filling lexical gaps in the lexicon of a language (cf. for instance Black 1962, 32–33; Ullmann 1967, 213). Catachreses, such as "the leg of a table," "the foot of a mountain," and "the arm of a chair," are a major source of language change, and, interestingly enough, they have not often been treated as cases of metaphor at all.[11]

In its narrower sense, this second variant (2rw) of the historical concept of metaphor has been called the theory of comparison. The comparison view of metaphor, or in Lieb's terms "the relational concept of metaphor in a narrower sense (2rn)," is mostly presented as a version of the substitution theory (2rw) (cf. Black 1962, 35–37, Black 1993, 20; Lieb 1964, 58–59, Lieb 1996, 347–8). The substituting linguistic sign is characterized as an abbreviated comparison, in which the substituted linguistic sign is called the "literal expression" or the "realized comparison." Hence, in our examples, this would mean that the linguistic signs 'sunshine' and 'lion' were being used in an uncommon way in that they establish a comparison between a literal and a figurative meaning (love is compared with sunshine, and a hero is compared with a lion); the compared elements sunshine and lion would be the ones that motivate the substitution. Consider the diagram in figure 27 for an illustration.

An overview and discussion of the comparison view are provided by Black (1962, 35–37), Lieb (1964, 58–59), Kurz (1982, 7–21), and Kurz and Pelster (1976, 7–28).

Here is a summary of the historical concept of metaphor sketched above:

- A linguistic sign is used and turns into a materialized sign: a spoken or written form. (The lexemes 'sunshine' and 'lion' are used.)
- This linguistic sign (in its spoken or written form) relates to two sets of nonlinguistic entities (concepts, meanings, or things). (The lexeme 'sunshine' relates to the SHINING OF THE SUN and to LOVE; 'lion' relates to THE ANIMAL and to HERO.)
- Between the two sets of nonlinguistic entities there exists a relation of uncommon use or of transfer. (SHINING OF THE SUN is used to denote LOVE; THE ANIMAL LION is used to denote HERO.)
- The linguistic sign (in its spoken or written form) denotes the second set of entities (LOVE and HERO) but not the first one (SHINING OF THE SUN, THE ANIMAL LION).

Some additional conditions apply:

- Analogy: The relation between the two sets of nonlinguistic entities (concepts, meanings, or things) is an analogical one.
- Substitution: The linguistic sign in its materialized (spoken or written) form (here, 'sunshine' and 'lion') substitutes another linguistic sign ('love' and 'hero,' respectively), which is not materialized.
- Comparison: the substituting linguistic sign ('love', 'hero') is characterized as an elliptic comparison (love is compared with sunshine; hero is compared with 'lion); the substituted linguistic sign is termed "literal expression" or "realized comparison" ('love', 'hero').

Note, however, that this concept of metaphor conceives of metaphor as single lexical entity: a metaphor is a word.

At the core of the historical concept of metaphor is a triadic structure, in which the relata are verbal or conceptual: A is a single word; B and C are concepts, meanings, or things. The use of A establishes a relation of transfer or uncommon use between B and C such that A denotes C and not B.

I will not go into the details of the attributive concepts of metaphor (metaphor is xyz) because they are derivations of the relational concepts of metaphor. In other words, what is identified as being a metaphor in a given text depends upon a preestablished relational concept of metaphor.

Instead, I shall invite you to pay closer attention to some contemporary versions of the concepts of metaphor outlined here that have become

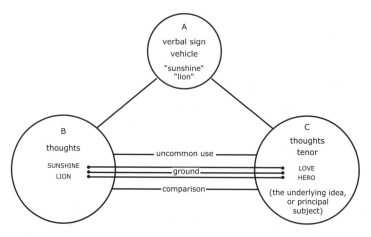

Fig. 28. Richards's elaborated theory of comparison.

very influential or even landmark accounts of the structure of metaphor: Richards's elaborate comparison view, Black's interaction view, and Searle's speech-act view. Finally, I shall briefly reconsider Lakoff and Johnson's conceptual metaphor view. This will provide further support for the purpose of this chapter, namely, to show that a triadic structure is at the core of historical and of contemporary concepts of metaphor and that the variations concern the ontology of the relata and the nature of their relations.

With Richards's introduction of the terms "vehicle," "tenor," and "ground," a more sophisticated and more explicit version of the comparison view of metaphor was developed. "Vehicle" refers to the materialized linguistic sign ('sunshine', 'lion'), and "tenor" refers to nonlinguistic entities (LOVE, HERO), or in Richards's terms, "the underlying idea or the principal subject" (Richards 1936, 96) of the metaphor; the term "ground" refers "to the common element underlying the transfer" (cf. also Ullmann 1967, 213). Thus, in terms of our two example sentences, the ground would consist of a range of similarities between the two sets of nonlinguistic entities (i.e., between SUNSHINE and LOVE or between LION and HERO), such as the source of life, warmth, and radiation, in the first case; and braveness, fierceness, force, and leadership, in the second case. By introducing the term "ground," Richards seeks to explicitly capture the common elements or the implied similarities between the two entities. Yet at the core of Richards's concept of metaphor, there is also—albeit implicitly—a triadic structure. The vehicle (linguistic sign) is the mediating element that establishes a duality of meaning.

It is noteworthy that both Richards and Ullmann continue to regard metaphor as something happening on the level of a single lexical item, a single thought or concept. And this is maintained even though Richards explicitly introduces what he calls the "context theory of meaning." His analyses of metaphor remain focused on words.

In contrast, Black's interaction view is the first to systematically include the role of the context into a concept of metaphor (Black 1962, 1993). He still develops a variant of the comparison theory, but it is significantly elaborated and remains the landmark account in contemporary stylistics and literary criticism for the analysis of verbal metaphors.[12]

Black's analysis of metaphor elaborates on that of Richards and introduces two important new aspects: metaphor as a specific kind of statement and the dependency of metaphor on the sentential context. The role of the verbal context here is to indicate the "duality of reference," which is characteristic of metaphor. Reconsider the passage quoted above: "The duality of reference is marked by the contrast between the metaphorical statement's *focus* (the word or words used non-literally) and the surrounding literal *frame*" (Black 1993, 27; emphases in the original). Thus, in our examples, the metaphorical focus would be the lexemes 'sunshine' and 'lion'; the remaining parts of the sentences are the literal frame. Duality of reference captures an aspect that Richards has only more or less implicitly accounted for (it is present in his idea of "having two thoughts at a time"); Black calls these two domains "secondary subject" (THE SHINING SUN, LION) and "primary subject" (LOVE, HERO). Furthermore, he adds that he conceives of the secondary subject, in particular, as "a system rather than an individual thing" (Black 1993, 27). In a metaphorical utterance, a set of features (an implicative complex) is projected from the secondary subject onto the primary subject. But this is not a unidirectional movement; rather, the projection implies the parallel construction of implicative complexes in both the primary and the secondary subjects. This is, of course, the reason why Black's account of metaphor has been called the interaction view of metaphor. Consider Black's summary of the interaction between the two subjects or domains of reference: "In the context of a particular metaphorical statement, the two subjects 'interact' in the following ways: (a) the presence of the primary subject incites the hearer to select some of the secondary subject's properties; and (b) invites him to construct a parallel implication-complex that can fit the primary subject; and (c) reciprocally induces parallel changes in the secondary subject" (Black 1993, 28). Hence, in the case of Stevie Wonder's song lyric, "You are the sunshine of my life," Black would assume that the primary

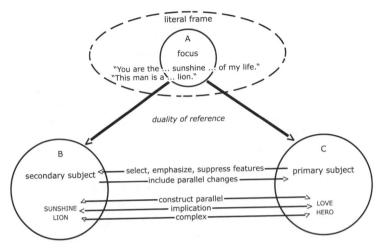

Fig. 29. Black's interaction theory of metaphor.

subject LOVE would be present first and inspire the hearer to find parallel properties in the secondary subject SUNSHINE, such as the source of life, warmth, and radiation. In the case of our classical example, "This man is a lion," this would mean that the primary subject HERO would incite the hearer to identify parallel properties in the secondary subject LION, such as braveness, force, and leadership. In this way, the primary subject would change the conception of the secondary subject in that it emphasizes certain aspects while suppressing others. Consider the diagram in figure 29 for an overview of Black's concept of metaphor.

Black's interaction view conceives of metaphors as the active constructions of a speaker/hearer that make use of cognitive operations, such as "selection, emphasis, and suppression," which, in turn, organize parallel sets of features in the two domains: "The maker of a metaphorical statement selects, emphasizes, suppresses, and organizes features of the primary subject by applying to it statements isomorphic with the members of the secondary subject's implicative complex" (Black 1993, 28). Note that Black introduces here a highly important facet of metaphors, and this property of metaphors has received considerable attention in CMT (cf. for instance Lakoff and Johnson 1980, 10–13). On the other hand, Black's interaction view contrasts with the unidirectionality view held in CMT, but it is in line with the interactive view developed by Fauconnier and Turner's blending theory (Fauconnier and Turner 2002). We will return to this point later and go into it in more detail.

For now, we may conclude that at the core of Black's view there is also an elaborate triadic structure: A focus (linguistic sign, A) mediates between or connects a primary subject (group of entities, C) and a secondary subject (group of entities, B). This triadic structure is specified regarding the ontology of the relata and regarding the relations they may form. The relata are specified: A is the focus, a linguistic sign within a literal frame; C is the primary subject; and B is the secondary subject. The relations they may form are as follows:

- Tension between metaphorical focus and literal frame,
- Duality of reference (A relates to B and C), and
- Construction of parallel implication complex (between C and B):
  - Selecting, emphasizing, suppressing features (in C and B), and
  - Inciting parallel changes in C and B

Note, moreover, that Black's systematic inclusion of the sentential context into his concept of metaphor extends the phenomenon from the word level to the sentence level.

Let me also briefly introduce another widely held account of the inherent structure of metaphor: John Searle's pragmatic concept of metaphor. The pragmatic views of metaphor informed by Grice (1975) and Searle (1993) rest upon a truth-conditional semantics. Yet Grice and Searle hold that metaphor is not part of what is asserted but of what is implied (Grice 1975) or intended (Searle 1993). The pragmatic view has become very influential and continues to be a topic of heated controversies in psycholinguistic research on metaphor comprehension.[13] Searle is interested in reconstructing the steps a given listener needs to go through in order to figure out what the speaker/writer intended. Metaphor is regarded as a form of utterance meaning. The hearer/reader constructs it by going through a contradictory proposition on the level of the literal meaning and progresses to a semantically related, noncontradictory proposition on the level of a figurative meaning.

> The best we can do in a paraphrase is reproduce the truth conditions of the metaphorical utterance, but the metaphorical utterance does more than just convey its truth conditions. It conveys its truth conditions by way of another semantic content, whose truth conditions are not part of the truth conditions of the utterance. The expressive power that we feel is part of good metaphors is largely a matter of two features. The hearer has to figure out what the speaker means—and he has to do that by going through another and related semantic content from the one which is

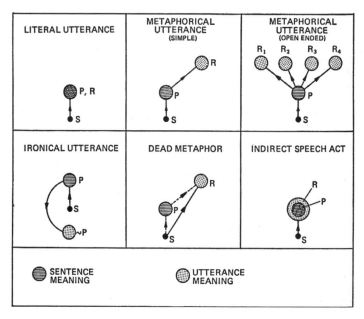

Fig. 30. Searle's diagram "Metaphorical Utterance" (simple). Searle (1993, 110).

communicated. And that, I take it, is what Dr. Johnson meant when he said metaphor gives us two ideas for one. (Searle 1993, 111)

Put another way, because a literal reading of a sentence like "You are the sunshine of my life" violates truth conditions (i.e., it cannot be literally true), the reader goes on to reconstruct a semantically related, figurative meaning that does not violate truth conditions (i.e., it may be figuratively true). The nature of this semantic relation is not further specified. Consider Searle's diagram given in figure 30, "Metaphorical Utterance" (simple).

In Searle's little diagram, the meaning structure of metaphorical utterances is represented in a rather interesting way. Searle explains the diagram as follows: "A speaker says S is P but means metaphorically that S is R. Utterance meaning is arrived at by going through literal sentence meaning" (Searle 1993, 110). Consequently, Searle regards metaphor as a matter of utterance meaning, not of the meaning of a word or a sentence, and he relates this to the older view of metaphor as giving two ideas or two thoughts to express one. Yet a very specific kind of duality of reference (or metaphorical utterance meaning) is established. Searle proposes that this meaning is achieved by indirectly proceeding from S to P to R. There is no direct relation between S and R as there is, for instance, in Black's concept of metaphor.

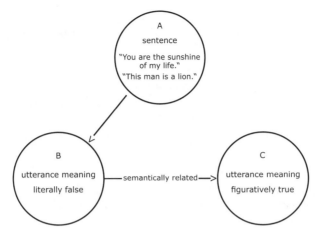

Fig. 31. Searle's diagram in terms of the basic triadic structure.

Considering Searle's view in terms of the basic triadic structure, we see that his concept of metaphor also implies a basic triadic structure but that it differs with respect to the relata and with regard to the assumed relations. The relata are the sentence (A), the literal utterance meaning (B), and the figurative utterance meaning (C). The assumed relation is from sentence (A) to literal utterance meaning (B) to figurative utterance meaning (C); the relation between literal and figurative meaning is semantically motivated. There is no direct relation from A to C. In the light of our two examples, this conception leads to the following accounts. The sentence "You are the sunshine of my life" is uttered (A); the literal meaning, "You are literally the sunshine of my life," (B) is rejected; and a semantically related, figurative meaning is constructed, "You are figuratively the sunshine of my life" (C). The same holds for "This man is a lion." Consider the diagram in for an illustration.[14]

Conceptual metaphor theory takes a radically different view on the nature of metaphor by regarding it as a general conceptual structure. I have repeatedly drawn attention to this point, and, more specifically in chapter 1, I have argued that Lakoff and Johnson's theory also conceives of metaphor in terms of a triadic structure. There is no need to recycle this argument here. Instead, we shall focus on the ontology of the three relata and the nature of the relations among them.

Let us begin with a characterization of the relata of this triadic structure in CMT. Recall that CMT claims that expressions such as "We may have to *go our separate ways*" or "Our relationship hit a *dead-end street*" are realizations of an underlying conceptual metaphor, in this case LOVE IS A

JOURNEY. According to Lakoff, a conceptual metaphor " . . . involves understanding one domain of experience, love, in terms of a very different domain
of experience, journeys" (1993, 206). Or, to put it more generally, as Kövecses
does in his introduction to (conceptual) metaphor, "A conceptual metaphor
consists of two conceptual domains, in which one domain is understood in
terms of another" (Kövecses 2002, 4). Lakoff regards conceptual metaphors
as cognitive structures that govern the ways in which humans—at least
partially—experience love relationships. Experiencing love relationships is
conceived of as the construction of a mental scenario in which roles, agents,
activities, entities, and inferences are transferred from one domain to another. This constructive view shows traces of Black's implicative complex,
although it is conceived of as uniquely unidirectional. Lakoff gives the following informal description of what he calls a "metaphorical scenario":

> The lovers are travelers on a journey together, with their common life
> goals, seen as destinations to be reached. The relationship is their ve-
> hicle, and it allows them to pursue those common goals together. The
> relationship is seen as fulfilling its purpose as long as it allows them to
> make progress toward their common goals. The journey isn't easy. There
> are impediments, and there are places (crossroads) where a decision has
> to be made about which direction to go in and whether to keep traveling
> together. (Lakoff 1993, 206)

The conceptual metaphor LOVE IS A JOURNEY establishes a name for a specific
interrelation between two conceptual domains: LOVE in terms of JOURNEY.
Therefore, the lovers are conceived of in terms of travelers, and therefore
there are expressions like "We may have to *go our separate ways*" and "Our
relationship hit a *dead-end street.*" In terms of the basic triadic structure
then, A would be the experience of love relationships as movement in space
and time, and B and C would be the conceptual domains JOURNEY and LOVE,
respectively. It remains rather vague how these experiences enter the conceptual systems of individual beings (via language or other cultural sign
systems or via individual experience) and to what degree are they still experientially grounded on an individual level. Note that the conception of
primary metaphors and the assumption of complex metaphors constitute
an effort to approach this issue more systematically. The assumption that
primary sensory experiences give rise to primary conceptual metaphors is
an explicit characterization of the third relatum (A) (cf. Grady 1999; Grady,
Taub, and Morgan 1996; Lakoff and Johnson 1999).[15]

Moreover, CMT is not the only account holding that B and C are conceptual structures of some kind, be they described in terms of mental models or as forms of linguistic or nonlinguistic thought (Bühler 1982; Black 1962; Searle 1993; Stählin 1914; Richards 1936; Weinrich 1976; Wundt 1922). However, these accounts ultimately ground metaphor in language (Aldrich's foregrounding of visual metaphor is an exception). In other words, the difference between linguistic and conceptual accounts of metaphor is not simply reducible to ontology—as statements such as "metaphor is a property of concepts and not of words" (Kövecses 2002, viii) tend to suggest. Why not? Because in both cases, the assumed domains are conceptual domains. Yet, whereas LMTs call upon a word, a sentence, an utterance, or a proposition to connect two disparate domains, CMT holds that, ultimately, experience is the motivating factor that brings them together. The argument goes as follows: because people experience love relationships as journeys in the sense sketched above, they create these verbal expressions. It is in this sense that verbal expressions are seen as the results of preceding experiences.

Another important difference relates to the nature of the conceptual domains, and here is the place where ontology does come into play: LMTs for the most part (we will return to one exception later) assume the primary existence of semantic (or verbal) domains of meaning; in contrast, CMT assumes the primary existence of experiential domains or, more precisely, of internalized cognitive models (ICMs; see Lakoff 1987), with lexical meaning being part and parcel of those experiential domains.

Regarding the assumed relations between the relata, CMT occupies a specific position in two respects: it does not specify the relation of A to B and C, but, conversely, it devotes considerable attention to characterizing the relations between B and C. These are quite specifically described as "mathematical mappings" or, in Lakoff's terms, as "a set of ontological correspondences" (Lakoff 1993, 207). Lakoff illustrates this with the following set of correspondences established between the source domain of JOURNEY and the target domain of LOVE:

THE LOVE-AS-JOURNEY MAPPING[16]
The lovers correspond to travelers.
The love relationship corresponds to the vehicle.
The lovers' common goals correspond to their common destinations on the journey.
Difficulties in the relationship correspond to impediments to travel.
(Lakoff 1993, 207)

The set of correspondences listed above is ontological in that it projects a certain ontology of the source domain of JOURNEYS onto the target domain of LOVE. These ontological correspondences are not conceived of as objective reflections of the world but as constructions of experience and knowledge about the world. The LOVE-AS-JOURNEY MAPPING reflects the culture-specific way of constructing the domain of love, since the ontological correspondences are actually epistemic correspondences, in that "knowledge about journeys is mapped onto knowledge of love" (Lakoff 1993, 207).

In this context, it is important to clarify that the names of these mappings should not be confused with the mapping itself; they are merely used as mnemonics for the set of ontological correspondences between the two conceptual domains (cf. also Lakoff and Johnson 1980). This is an important aside, because it clarifies that metaphors in Lakoff and Johnson's sense are not conceived of as propositional. Although the names of the mappings may resemble the structure of verbal metaphors, LOVE IS A JOURNEY (Lakoff and Johnson 1980, 44) and "The man is a lion" have a similar propositional structure. Yet the nature of conceptual metaphor is not propositional in the sense that the proposition would actually describe the nature of the mapping. Lakoff concludes, "metaphors are mappings, that is, sets of conceptual correspondences" (Lakoff 1993, 207).

Hence, it appears that Lakoff and Johnson's CMT shares with LMTs the assumption of a basic triadic structure of metaphors, while it differs from them regarding the nature and the role of the three relata that constitute that structure. Basically, the divergence concerns the question of whether metaphor is supposed to be a phenomenon of linguistic or of general cognitive organization. CMT holds that metaphors are first and foremost a principle of general cognition. The role of verbal metaphor is reduced to an instantiation of general cognitive principles. A specific level of linguistic organization is neither systematically integrated nor conceived of as necessary. Linguistic metaphor theories, on the other hand, lack a systematic account of nonlinguistic metaphors; and by focusing entirely on verbal metaphors, they overlook the possibility of a general cognitive principle and of general conceptual structures governing this truly ubiquitous trait of language, as well as social structures and works of art.

4.3 Conclusion: Activated Metaphors Establish a Triadic Structure

We have seen that, at the core of historical and contemporary concepts of metaphor, we do indeed find a triadic structure. This is the constant trait in the scholarly reflections upon the very nature of metaphor. The triadic structure is neutral with regard to the relata, and it only assumes a relation whereby A relates B and C such that C is seen in terms of B. As already argued in chapter 1, this rather abstract and general structure is taken to be the core of metaphoricity. Activating metaphoricity is activating a triadic structure of this kind, regardless of whether the relata for A are lexemes, expressions, sentences, utterances, pictures, sculptures, gestures, or simply the process of seeing-in-terms-of; or whether the relata for B and C are concepts, meanings, things, verbal or conceptual domains, conceptual metaphors, or sensory experiences.

One critical aside appears necessary: the assumptions of this abstract structure backgrounds at least one important facet of verbal and of conceptual metaphors. I am referring to the relation between the collective system and its individual use. Since Aristotle's treatment, metaphor has been conceived of as a phenomenon of use, yet how this relates to the system of language is a widely neglected topic. Lieb's distinction between "Sprachzeichen" (expression-in-the-language) and "Redezeichen" (expression-in-speech) seeks to capture this dimension (trans. H.-H. Lieb). Nevertheless, he departs from a triadic structure; furthermore, systematically including this relation would amount to assuming a four-place structure. Fauconnier and Turner's blending theory aims to capture more systematically the ad hoc construction of utterance, but exactly how the ad hoc constructed mental spaces relate to a stored system of language is not systematically discussed (Fauconnier and Turner 2002).

Stählin (1914) offered an important contribution to this debate in his account of the psychological characteristics of metaphor comprehension. His psychological perspective inspired a dynamic view of the process involved. Accordingly, he did not see metaphor as a static and binary quality of words in a lexicon. For him, the comprehension of verbal metaphors is based on an active process of integrating two domains of meaning, and in this process verbal metaphors may obtain different forms and degrees of metaphoricity. Metaphors in this view are not absolute but dynamic and gradable properties of verbal expressions that rest upon a duality of meaning.

The dynamic view proposed in this book adopts a similar perspective but it focuses on the production side of the process. And in this vein, the subsequent chapters are devoted to investigating more closely how metaphoricity is activated online during speaking and writing. I shall begin with an in-depth study of mixed metaphors. This will reveal instances of metaphor use that function in a way that is contrary to what we might expect, namely, that when a verbal metaphor is activated, both domains of meaning ought to be equally active too. We will see that this is not the case.

CHAPTER FIVE

Mixed Metaphors: Selective Activation of Meaning

Mixing metaphors is typically considered to be a consequence of *not* being aware of the metaphoricity of an expression, a result of not disposing of the double meaning of a metaphor. Reference books on style, rhetoric, and linguistics tend to assume that it occurs unwittingly and happens just because the literal meaning of an expression is not available to the conscious awareness of a given speaker or writer. Consider the following example taken from *The Oxford Companion to the English Language*:

ENGLISH: The butter mountain has been in the pipeline for some time.[1]

FIGURATIVE: "As a result of the overproduction of butter in the European Union, huge amounts of it have been awaiting distribution for some time."[2]

LITERAL: "A real mountain consisting of butter is stuck in a kind of oil pipeline."

In this example, the president of the Farmers' Union mixes two metaphors: "butter mountain" and "to be in the pipeline." These two metaphors work well together on the level of the figurative meaning but not on the level of the literal meaning. A butter mountain just does not fit into a pipeline of a normal size—it would have to be transformed into some kind of liquid or cream to be transportable through a pipeline. The *Oxford Companion* considers mixed metaphors as a commonplace feature of style and reports that "the practice is widely regarded as a stylistic flaw caused by unthinkingly mixing 'clichés'" (McArthur 1992, 663). Put another way—the mixing of metaphors is supposed to happen because speakers or writers have not activated metaphoricity and, therefore, combine metaphors from different and often contradictory domains. Considering the above example, the situation appears to be straightforward: the mixing of metaphors results from the non-activation of the literal meaning, which is not brought to the speaker's focal attention during speaking. In this chapter, I shall follow up this assumption in great detail. Much attention will be devoted to an in-depth analysis of the semantic and syntactic structures of mixed metaphors while pursuing a two-fold goal: first, a documentation of the semantic structures of mixed metaphors; and second, a documentation of the descriptive power of different approaches to the analysis of verbal metaphors from the perspective of language use and cognition. Together, these investigations will offer highly important insights into the nature of the cognitive activation of verbal metaphors that occurs online during speaking and writing.

The following questions will guide the presentation in this chapter: Do mixed metaphors in general have the structure outlined above? Or what other reasons could explain why mixed metaphors do not make sense? Is it possible that from some point of view they do make sense and that this is why they have been produced? What are the explanations for mixed metaphors provided in LMTs and CogMTs? What does an analysis in terms of Fauconnier and Turner's blending theory add to the CMT and the LMT accounts? And finally, what does all this reveal about the selective activation of metaphoricity online during speaking?

5.1 What Are Mixed Metaphors? How Linguistic and Conceptual Metaphor Theory Set the Stage

This kind of mixing of metaphors is a well-known and widely reported phenomenon in stylistics; English as well as German, Spanish, and French reference works criticize it as a stylistic fault. Linguistic encyclopedias, reference books on stylistics and rhetoric, and popular language critics[3] condemn it as an incorrect use of language. Students are warned that they should always be careful not to mix metaphors. Yet sometimes mixed metaphors are considered to be very funny and may even turn into poetic devices for creating strong images, as in the case of the oxymoron, where the mixing of images is pushed to the extreme.[4] On the other hand, they may even become lexicalized—as in expressions like the following ones:

English	French	Spanish	German
bitter-sweet	*doux-amer*	*agridulce*	*bittere Süße*
eloquent silence	*silence éloquent*	*silencio elocuente*	*beredtes Schweigen*
clear-obscure	*claire-obscur*	*claroscuro*	*helldunkel*

In German, mixed metaphors are termed "image breaks" (Bildbrüche), and in German rhetoric they are classified as a form of catachresis, that is, a misuse of a word (cf. Ueding 1998, 914). According to the *Oxford Companion*, this misuse is caused—as we have seen above—by "unthinkingly mixing 'clichés'" (McArthur 1992, 663), which is in line with Ludwig Reiners, who in his *Stilkunst* (Reiners 1976) describes the psychological background of image breaks as a use of clichés without truly imagining them.[5]

Note that the assumed causes of mixed metaphors appear to imply that, under normal circumstances, the linguistic knowledge necessary to avoid mixing or contaminating metaphors should be constantly available during speaking and writing. The typical explications even specify the kind of knowledge that should be available, namely, the literal meaning of a metaphorical expression. Hence, if the speaker had activated the literal meaning of "butter mountain" and "in the pipeline" while he was talking, he would have become aware of the emergent contradiction implied in combining two metaphors from distinct and even mutually exclusive source domains. And—to continue the speculation—this recognition would have presumably prevented him from combining these two metaphorical expressions in the way he did. Why? Because he was talking seriously. Bringing together metaphors from mutually exclusive source domains may have created a specific rhetorical effect that the president of the Farmers' Union most likely did not intend because it would have deeply affected the pragmatics of his utterance. A combination of the two metaphorical expressions as metaphors (!), that is, as expressions whose double meaning is activated at the moment of speaking, would have turned a serious statement about a political issue into a joke.

Put another way, once the focus of attention has shifted to the literal meaning of the expression, it is clear that mountains usually do not fit into pipelines. On the literal level, the logical contradiction is obvious, and it seems clear that a bit more attentiveness would have prevented the president of the Farmers' Union from bringing together these two metaphors in the way that he did. Yet this kind of explication carries a rather far-reaching implication because it suggests that a normally attentive speaker or writer should be aware of the literal meaning of a metaphor during online language production (be it spoken or written). On the other hand, conventionalized verbal metaphors are typically characterized as having lost the awareness of a double meaning when being used by a speaker and as gradually losing their vividness, sometimes up to the point of a complete loss of transparency.

The cited literature on this topic apparently departs from two contradictory assumptions: on the one hand, it is assumed that mixing noncompatible metaphors is a consequence of the fact that the metaphoricity (i.e., the literal and the figurative meaning) is not available during speech production. Speakers are blamed for being so inattentive and thoughtless that they combine metaphors that create contradictions on the literal level. Yet, on the other hand, LMTs have always taken for granted that conventionalized verbal metaphors have lost their metaphoricity and claim that the literal meaning of a metaphor is not available during speaking. So, if this were true—if conventionalized verbal metaphors of ordinary language had indeed lost all their metaphoric quality—then nobody would have to bother about mixing metaphors.

It therefore seems to be the case that LMTs want an aspect of meaning to be present when those "dead" verbal metaphors are used—an aspect that they claim is *not* normally present, namely, the literal meaning of a conventionalized verbal metaphor. This is a kind of logical contradiction that appears to have bypassed reflections on the consciousness of metaphoricity in LMTs.

Furthermore, all conventionalized metaphors are equally regarded as dead metaphors, and for Black the situation is clear—a dead metaphor is dead because it has lost its metaphoricity, that is, it is used without awareness of metaphoricity: "A so-called dead metaphor is not a metaphor at all, but merely an expression that no longer has a pregnant metaphorical use" (Black 1993, 25). Black's opinion continues to express a widely shared, almost canonical, view on conventionalized metaphors. A view that Gibbs in his *The Poetics of Mind* critically comments on:

> Even though many instances of contemporary speech have obvious figurative roots, most scholars assume that idiomatic language may once have been metaphorical but has lost its metaphoricity over time and now exists in the mental lexicon as a set of stock formulas or as dead metaphors. Just as speakers no longer view *leg of table* as metaphoric, few people recognize phrases such as *spill the beans, blow your stack, off the wall, in the pits,* or *a rolling stone gathers no moss* as being particularly creative or metaphoric. After all, metaphors are lively, creative, and resistant to paraphrase, whereas idioms, clichés, and proverbs are hackneyed expressions that are equivalent in meaning to simple literal phrases. To classify some utterance or phrase as "idiomatic," "slang," or "proverbial" is tantamount to a theoretical explanation in itself, given the widely held view that such phrases are dead metaphors that belong in the wastebasket of formulas and phrases that are separate from the generative component of a grammar. (Gibbs 1994, 267–8; emphases in the original)

Yet, if Black and the scholars sharing his assumption are right, how can we account for the mixing of metaphors if they are not metaphors at all, if they have indeed lost all their metaphoricity—and with it the presence of a double meaning—and have indeed turned into purely nonmetaphorical expressions? Why then is it problematic to combine conventionalized, supposedly dead metaphors with different literal roots, if those roots have been cut off?

The answer that CMT would presumably give here is that conventionalized metaphors are normally conceived and processed as metaphors—albeit at a different level of consciousness. Recall that for CMT, lexical meaning is always conceptual meaning—and more specifically—verbal metaphors are supposed to be processed and understood through the activation of underlying conceptual metaphors. That is, language users are expected to process the metaphoricity of lexicalized metaphors, not on the level of conscious awareness, but on the level of nonconscious processes, namely, by activating conventionalized and deeply entrenched mappings between conceptual metaphors. Thus, conventionalized verbal metaphors are taken to be the products of active and vital conceptual metaphors and to be processed on the same level of consciousness as most structural linguistic knowledge. Hence, Lakoff states that "The system of conventional conceptual metaphor is mostly unconscious, automatic, and used with no noticeable effort, just like our linguistic system and the rest of our conceptual system" (Lakoff 1993, 245). That is, the metaphoricity of verbal and of conceptual metaphor is expected to be awake and active just as much as the linguistic and the conceptual system is when we use language: "Our system of conventional metaphor is 'alive' in the same sense that our system of grammatical and phonological rules is alive; namely, it is constantly in use, automatically, and below the level of consciousness"[6] (Lakoff 1993, 245). In other words, the processing of linguistic metaphoricity is supposedly mediated through the activation of conceptual metaphors. Though this information is not consciously perceived, it should still be active and guiding the construction of sentences that include metaphors. This would explain why it might indeed be problematic to combine conventionalized verbal metaphors with contradictory literal roots; namely, because the literal sources of the metaphors are active, their combination creates a contradictory conceptualization. Now, while CMT provides us with a possible explanation as to why conflicting literal meanings in lexicalized metaphors do not combine well, it does not explain why speakers nevertheless mix metaphors in the way we have seen above. If the fundamental assumption of the CMT holds true, that is, if indeed the source concepts or source domains of a conceptual metaphor are always active during metaphor production and comprehension, why should the system allow for the mixing of metaphors that create contradictory scenes—when taken literally (i.e., when their mappings between source and target are active)? Why does the conceptual system not block the combination of those metaphors and impede sentences like "The butter mountain has been in the pipeline for some time"?

There is no brief answer to this question. Moreover, it addresses an aspect of CMT that has been under discussion since the early days of its formulation. I am referring to the notions of consistency and coherence across conceptual metaphors, which are of fundamental importance in systems of conceptual metaphors. Mixed metaphors are only discussed within this context, and they are characterized as impermissible combinations of the underlying conceptual metaphors. In more technical terms—they are described as lacking shared entailments (Lakoff and Johnson 1980, 87–105).[7]

Conceptual metaphor theory does not expect to find consistency across metaphors frequently; instead, it is proposed that we mostly find coherence when metaphors combine. Coherence operates on partial overlaps between conceptual metaphors. More specifically, coherence is based on "shared entailments" (Lakoff and Johnson 1980, 92). Thus, even though two metaphors may be inconsistent in that they do not create a single image, they may still be coherent in that they share at least one entailment (Lakoff and Johnson 1980, 94); this happens when they address the same aspect of a concept or follow the same purpose. In these cases, the conceptual metaphors involved share at least one epistemic correspondence (Lakoff and Kövecses 1987, 201). If two combined metaphors share an entailment, are coherent, and do not produce contradictory scenes, then they combine well.

Lakoff and Johnson (1980, 92–95) illustrate such a coherent combination of metaphors with two conceptual metaphors: AN ARGUMENT IS A JOURNEY and AN ARGUMENT IS A CONTAINER. These metaphors are claimed to underlie verbal metaphors such as "If we keep *going the way we're going*" and "We'll *fit all the facts in.*"[8] See the following examples taken from Lakoff and Johnson (1980, 92) for further combinations of verbal realizations of these two conceptual metaphors within one sentence:

At this point our argument doesn't have *much content.*
In what we've done *so far,* we have provided the *core* of our argument.
If we keep *going the way we're going,* we'll *fit all the facts in.*

The authors suggest that there is a shared entailment, a common property of the two source domains: as we proceed—either moving along a path

(AN ARGUMENT IS A JOURNEY and A JOURNEY DEFINES A PATH), or building a container (AN ARGUMENT IS A CONTAINER)—more surface is created. In other words, as we make an argument, more of a surface is created: "The overlap between the two metaphors is the progressive creation of a surface. As the argument covers more ground (via the journey surface), it gets more content (via the container surface). What characterizes this overlap is a shared entailment . . . " (Lakoff and Johnson 1980, 93). Combinations of verbal metaphors addressing the same aspect of the two conceptual metaphors in play are called "permissible" mixed metaphors. However, when two metaphors highlight different aspects of one concept, their combinations may also be "impermissible." Lakoff and Johnson (1980, 95) give the following examples for impermissible metaphors:

> We can now follow the *path* of the *core* of the argument.
> I am disturbed by the *vacuous path* of your argument.

Again, these are linguistic instances of the two conceptual metaphors used to structure the concept ARGUMENT: AN ARGUMENT IS A JOURNEY and AN ARGUMENT IS A CONTAINER. The elements that are supposed to conflict are "direction" and "content." "Path" is an aspect of a journey that does not fit together with information about the content of a container, such as the "core," or the "vacuity" of a container.

On the basis of this analysis, Lakoff and Johnson argue that the two conceptual metaphors introduced above are not fully consistent, because "there is no 'single image' that completely fits both metaphors" (Lakoff and Johnson 1980, 94). AN ARGUMENT IS A JOURNEY and AN ARGUMENT IS A CONTAINER mainly highlight different aspects of the same target concept, and, therefore, they are largely inconsistent. The diagram in figure 32, which is an extended version of Lakoff and Johnson's (1980, 94) diagram, visualizes this structure of coherence between the two conceptual metaphors AN ARGUMENT IS A JOURNEY and AN ARGUMENT IS A CONTAINER.

What this diagram nicely documents is an important trait of the issue of combining metaphors in general, namely, that metaphors might combine well with regard to certain aspects, while being inconsistent with regard to others. Trying to break down the analysis and to determine the specific elements that participate in metaphorical mappings is a highly important contribution of CMT to the problem of mixed metaphors—regardless of whether we analyze them on the conceptual or on the verbal level. Hence, I shall use this as one starting point in our further analysis of mixed metaphor.

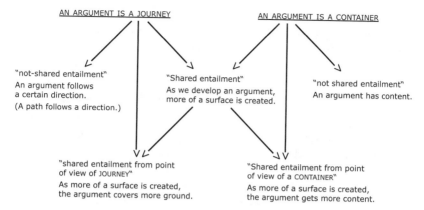

Fig. 32. Coherence between two conceptual metaphors as shared entailment. This is an extended version of Lakoff and Johnson's (1980, 94) diagram.

This little example indicates once more that a refined analysis of mixed metaphors is needed—defining the problem as a contradiction on the literal level of meaning simply does not account sufficiently for the actual semantic structure of mixed metaphors.

It appears noteworthy, however, that in the extended discussion of coherence across conceptual metaphors, the problem of impermissible mixed metaphors has not received much further attention. Instead, the discussion has been centered around the related question of how coherence within the system of conceptual metaphors works, that is, for instance, the combination of metaphors sharing a target domain. This is a fundamental topic within CMT because the theory needs to account for the fact that coherence has to be maintained when concepts that may be understood in terms of many sources are combined. Take, for example, the abstract concept of ARGUMENT, which is conceptualized via the source concepts of JOURNEY, CONTAINER, BUILDING, WAR, and probably even many more (Lakoff and Johnson 1980, 87–105). As these metaphors combine, they must cohere: "When a concept is structured by more than one metaphor, the different metaphorical structurings usually fit together in a coherent fashion" (Lakoff and Johnson 1980, 86). Coherence is, as we have seen above, explained in terms of shared entailments. In other words, coherence and consistency in CMT are primarily analyzed as being within metaphor coherence. This is a corollary of the fact that CMT addresses systems of conceptual metaphors and that one target concept or one target domain is often characterized by a variety of source domains. Thus, Kövecses (2002, 36) states, "By coherence we simply mean that target concepts tend to be conceptualized in a uniform manner." Moreover, this structuring of target domains is supposed to provide a coherent structuring of how we experience the respective target domains. Lakoff and Johnson illustrate this with the complex domain of rational argument.

> Understanding a conversation as being an argument involves being able to superimpose the multidimensional structure of part of the concept WAR upon the corresponding structure CONVERSATION. Such multidimensional structures characterize *experiential gestalts,* which are ways of organizing experience into *structured wholes.* . . . Structuring our experience in terms of such multidimensional gestalts is what makes our experience *coherent.* We experience a conversation as an argument when the war gestalt fits our perceptions and actions in the conversation. (Lakoff and Johnson 1980, 81; emphases in the original)

This brief aside brings another specificity of the CMT account of mixed metaphors to our attention: the fact that mixed metaphors are regarded only either as subsets of two conceptual metaphors sharing one target, as in the above case of ARGUMENT, or as duals, that is, two mutually exclusive perspectives realized in one lexeme. In so-called duals, two perspectives are inconsistent subsets of one metaphor. Note that these metaphors cannot be physically mixed in one sentence because they are mutually exclusive perspectives realized in one and the same lexeme (cf. Lakoff 1993, 216).

To sum up, it turns out that CMT provides a rather specific view on the problem of mixed metaphors. And while providing us with important hints as to how to proceed in the analysis of mixed metaphors in general (regarding the notions of "coherence," "consistency," and "shared entailments"), it does not significantly advance our understanding of how the combination of two metaphors with different targets (on the literal as well as on the conceptual level) works. Furthermore, it does not provide us with a straightforward explanation of why certain metaphors with different targets combine well and others do not. Accordingly, it does not show us a straightforward road to follow when we are seeking to conceive of mixed metaphors on the verbal level, such as the ones we have encountered in the "butter-mountain" example.

Still, I shall attempt to account for the butter-mountain example in CMT terms. This will give us a chance to determine more clearly what kind of insights a CMT approach to cross-metaphorical "noncoherence" can deliver and which of these insights may indicate a useful strategy toward providing a more differentiated account of mixed metaphors—with regard to both their semantic structure (verbal and conceptual level) and the cognitive mechanism that triggers impermissible metaphors.

5.1.1 The "Butter-Mountain" Example from a Conceptual Metaphor Theory Point of View

We know now that CMT locates the problem of mixing metaphors on the conceptual level and that so-called impermissible mixed conceptual metaphors are supposed to lack shared entailments. We therefore need to determine the conceptual metaphors underlying the verbal metaphors "butter mountain" and "in the pipeline" in our initially discussed sentence, "The butter mountain has been in the pipeline for some time." Without being in a position to carry out a systematic corpus-based analysis of the two verbal metaphors, my analyses in terms of conceptual metaphors must remain preliminary. But they rely, at least partially, on relatively well-established findings of research into conceptual metaphors. Thus, "butter mountain" appears to be an instantiation of the well-known orientational metaphor MORE IS UP (cf. Lakoff and Johnson 1980, 14–21; Kövecses 2002, 35–36). Further verbal realizations of this metaphor are as follows:

> This is a *highly* interesting case.
> The number of books printed each year keeps going *up*.
> She has a *high* income.
> His income *fell* last year.
> He faces a *mountain* of work this term.
> The problem of Europe's *butter mountain*.

In contrast, "in the pipeline" is not an instantiation of a similarly well-established conceptual metaphor. But it seems plausible to assume that it is based on the generic-level metaphor PHYSICAL MOTION IS ABSTRACT MOTION (Kövecses 2002, 37–38). Verbalizations of this metaphor would be as follows:

> The *flow* of goods to the countryside is bad.
> The *flow* of information is well organized.
> The letters must be *passed* on to the secretary.
> The Euro is in the *pipeline*.

To begin with, the two conceptual metaphors MORE IS UP and ABSTRACT MOTION IS PHYSICAL MOTION may cohere when combined in a sentence. Hence, we may encounter sentences such as the following one: "He just *passed* on those *mountains of work* to his student assistants." Thus, the noncoherence cannot be based on the mere combination of the two conceptual metaphors. Whether it is based on entailments of these two metaphors is hard to decide because the notion of entailments has hitherto—at least as far as I know—not been applied to generic-level metaphors, and it is not evident which entailments they would carry. Therefore, it appears to be worthwhile taking a closer look at the mappings on the verbal level of the two metaphors. Notice that this is an analytic step that CMT does not make. Verbal metaphors tend not to receive close semantic analysis on the lexical level; they are basically analyzed as realizations or instantiations of conceptual metaphors. This may make some sense when the focus of investigation is on conceptual metaphors, but it is still methodologically problematic.[9] Analyzing the mixing of metaphors appears to make a closer analysis of the metaphorical processes on the verbal level look like a promising step toward identifying the interfering elements of meaning. Thus, we will use the strategy applied to analyzing coherence within conceptual metaphors to the analysis across verbal metaphors.[10]

First, we should recall that each of the two metaphors is built on "within" mappings. In the case of "butter mountain," "mountain" is mapped onto the target domain of quantification and, hence, serves to express a large quantity of butter in this compound. In the case of "in the pipeline," "pipeline" maps onto the domain of transport (specifying a means of steady distribution), and "in" locates a specific substance in the pipeline (here, news or information). Now, in the cross-metaphorical mapping, the butter mountain (i.e., the large amount of a specific substance) is mapped onto a specific means of transportation—a pipeline. And, as I shall argue, the mixing takes place on the level of the verbal realms of the metaphor, not on the level of the conceptual metaphor. The combination of the two verbal metaphors does not make sense because their source domains or image-offering fields are active (probably supported by the active, conceptual source domain MORE IS UP). The "up" element interferes with an entailment of the pipeline metaphor, namely, that it is long and narrow. The verbal instantiation "mountain" of the conceptual metaphor MORE IS UP interferes with a further entailment of the pipeline metaphor, namely, that it transports liquids or gas but not solid objects. For the pipeline metaphor, there is no indication that the conceptual metaphor was active, that is, the motion aspect does not appear to play a role in this cross-metaphorical mapping. What does not interfere is the idea of a pipeline as a means of steady distribution. What does interfere, instead, are some other specific properties of the verbal metaphor "to be in the pipeline,"

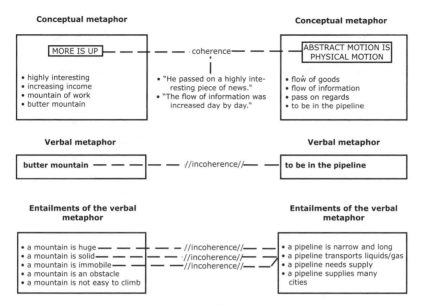

Conceptual metaphor   **Conceptual metaphor**

| MORE IS UP | — — — coherence — — — | ABSTRACT MOTION IS PHYSICAL MOTION |

- highly interesting
- increasing income
- mountain of work
- butter mountain

- "He passed on a highly interesting piece of news."
- "The flow of information was increased day by day."

- flow of goods
- flow of information
- pass on regards
- to be in the pipeline

Verbal metaphor   **Verbal metaphor**

| butter mountain | — — — //incoherence// — — | to be in the pipeline |

Entailments of the verbal metaphor   **Entailments of the verbal metaphor**

- a mountain is huge — — — //incoherence// —
- a mountain is solid — — — //incoherence// —
- a mountain is immobile — — //incoherence// —
- a mountain is an obstacle
- a mountain is not easy to climb

- a pipeline is narrow and long
- a pipeline transports liquids/gas
- a pipeline needs supply
- a pipeline supplies many cities

Fig. 33. "The butter mountain has been in the pipeline for some time." A conceptual metaphor analysis.

namely, its shape and the transported substance. Hence, the mixed metaphor does not make sense because the shape (high) and the substance (solid) of mountains interferes with the shape of (narrow) and the substance that is transported in pipelines (liquid).

If, however, we suppress the source domains and focus on the target domains, then the combination does not interfere. Consider a possible paraphrase: "A specific political issue has been continuously and widely distributed." Hence, there is a sense in which the combination of the two metaphors does appear to make sense. Consider the diagram in for an overview of the analysis of the butter-mountain example from a CMT point of view.

5.1.2 Discussion

The analysis of the butter-mountain example in terms of CMT shows that reducing the problem of mixing metaphors to the level of conceptual metaphors does not capture the problematic issues sufficiently. Only the consideration of the level of rich verbal metaphoricity made it possible to uncover the rationale of both the inconsistent and the consistent aspects of this mixed metaphor.

The focus on the analysis of coherence within systems of conceptual metaphors is in line with the collective-mind view, which dominates Lakoff and Johnson's writings. It appears noteworthy to mention that they share this perspective with the traditional, stylistic views on mixed metaphor. Moreover, and quite surprisingly, Lakoff and Johnson, at least as far as their 1980 publication is concerned, adopt a basically normative view on this issue. Recall that Lakoff and Johnson distinguished two types of mixed metaphors: permissible and impermissible ones. First of all, in doing this they extended the traditional notion of mixed metaphors as an incorrect combination of metaphors that do not fit on the level of their literal meaning into a combination of metaphors in general. Second, they base their distinction on a normative judgment. Although permissibility and impermissibility are presumably thought to reflect the conventionalized and, therefore, default readings of possible combinations of metaphors, the terms still have a normative flavor.

Yet, while providing a more differentiated account of why some metaphors combine well whereas others do not, CMT does not give us a satisfactory account of the cognitive underpinnings of why people actually produce mixed metaphors. If the conceptual system underlying lexical metaphors is indeed active and alive all the time during language production, it should hinder speakers from combining inconsistent aspects of conceptual metaphors. Since this is obviously not the case—on the contrary, speakers appear to produce mixed metaphors quite frequently (cf. Cienki and Swan 2001)—the mixing of metaphors could be taken as an argument against this fundamental assumption of CMT. We will return to this point later in this chapter.

This lack of clarification causes Lakoff and Johnson to miss the cognitive linguistic commitment to "make one's account of human language accord with what is generally known about the mind and the brain, from other disciplines as well as our own" (Lakoff 1990, 40). As mentioned before, Lakoff formulated this commitment ten years after the first formulation of the CMT; in the meantime, empirical investigations into the psychological reality of conceptual metaphors have become a field of central importance in cognitive linguistics.[11] However, Lakoff and Johnson have developed their theory as a theory of the collective mind, and it is this perspective that presumably leads them to formulate this normative characterization of mixed metaphors; a normative view implies a collective perspective on language, since it aims at regulating language use with regard to an established system of a conventionalized set of rules. How metaphors relate to the individual mind and how the architecture and the structures of consciousness influence the processing of metaphors are not yet sufficiently accounted for. Since in this book I strictly follow this perspective, later in this chapter I will try to give an answer to the question of why people actually produce mixed metaphors. For now, it is sufficient to be aware of the different perspectives involved in the discussion of mixed metaphors. This is important because these perspectives are for the most part not separated from each other, let alone analyzed distinctly, which they should be. I am referring to the perspective of the linguistic expert (the collective-mind view) and the perspective of the individual who produced the mix (the individual-mind view). The linguistic experts analyze the use of mixed metaphors from a normative stance and claim that they are nonacceptable or nonpermissible expressions. This nonacceptability or nonpermissibility implies that there is a certain common sense way of combining metaphors and that this has been violated. Note, however, that this judgment is not based on empirical investigations of how recipients react to mixed metaphors; it is based on the linguistic and stylistic competence of language experts. Occasionally, the expert's perspective is supplemented by a side-glance at the individual mind, the perspective of the person who produces these metaphors. Typically, this happens when speculations about the causes of mixed metaphors (thinking flaws, inattentiveness) are promoted. The examination of this phenomenon offered here aims at changing this established way of analyzing mixed metaphors and intends to rehabilitate the perspective of the producer of mixed metaphors. The phenomenon of mixing metaphors is a highly revelatory form of metaphor use in discourse, for it allows us to reconstruct how language users experience and process metaphoricity in conventionalized verbal metaphors when they speak or write. Studying mixed metaphors from the perspective of the language user enables us to describe more specifically which elements of meaning are activated and which ones are suppressed or disregarded during speaking or writing. Mixed metaphors are frozen creations of new meaning, a frame grab of the mind while processing metaphors.

Quite unexpectedly, the well-known phenomenon of combining metaphors in a nonnormative way turns out to be more complicated but doubtlessly also more interesting than it appears at first sight—giving us sufficient reasons for taking a closer look at the linguistic and cognitive aspects of mixing metaphors during discourse.

5.2 Why Mixed Metaphors Don't Make Sense! "Thinking Flaws" and Semantic Inconsistency

Mixing metaphors is problematic because it produces a kind of semantic inconsistency. As we have seen above, LMTs assume quite clearly that this inconsistency is located on the level of the literal meaning of metaphoric expressions and is caused by inattentiveness. Conceptual metaphor theory does not give us comparable causal explanations for the mixing of metaphors, but it does suggest that the problem of mixed metaphors is not reasonably characterized by such general statements; moreover, it shows that the phenomenon of mixed metaphors deserves systematic attention and is related to the rather complex issue of cross-metaphorical coherence on the conceptual level. Although the CMT's tendency to locate it uniquely on the level of conceptual metaphors does not seem plausible, what is clear is that we must seek to determine precisely the elements of meaning and the specific mappings that provoke the semantic inconsistency. Therefore, a much more fine-grained semantic analysis is needed than those that have been provided by more traditional linguistic and stylistic accounts of this phenomenon.

Let us now turn to a more systematic analysis of the semantic structure of three cases of mixed metaphor and see if we can arrive at a more precise account of why mixed metaphors do not make sense. The examples to be considered are taken from textbooks and reference books on stylistics and linguistics. The discussion of mixed metaphors, therefore, relies on examples that reference works consider as instances of mixed metaphor. In other words, the decision of whether or not these examples are indeed cases of mixed metaphor is not mine. This methodological procedure opens up the possibility of doing two things at once: analyzing the semantic structure of these examples and confronting this analysis with the line of argumentation held by the linguistic and the conceptual views on metaphor. This methodological procedure enables us to uncover shortcomings of the views held so far, and it provides grounds for enhancing our understanding of the semantic and cognitive properties that characterize the mixing of metaphors.

In the discussion, we will concentrate on examples in which at least one metaphorical idiom is involved.[12] It is noteworthy to mention that this reflects the structure of most of the cases of mixed metaphors provided by the selected literature. Most of them happen to contain one or even more metaphorical idioms.

5.2.1 The Rope Example

The first example is taken from one of the canonical German reference books on linguistics,[13] and it has been circulating in German works on style for many years.[14]

Example 7: "Wenn alle Stricke reißen, hänge ich mich auf" *(If all else fails, I'll give up)*

GERMAN: Wenn alle Stricke reißen, hänge ich mich auf.
FIGURATIVE: If all else fails, I'll give up.[15]
LITERAL: If all ropes break, I'll hang myself up.

Interlocutors tend to appreciate this mixed metaphor quite a lot—but it often stimulates laughter rather than disapproval. It thus tends to be primarily criticized by experts on style. But, however this sentence is assessed, it is always treated as a formulation that is somehow deviant. Therefore, let us consider more closely in exactly which sense it is deviant.

It is clear that the sentence is semantically inconsistent regarding the literal meaning of the two idioms.[16] It combines two idioms that, when taken literally, produce a logical contradiction: with a broken rope, it is hard to hang oneself.

This incongruence is strengthened by the semantic implications of the conditional construction. The conditional structure sets up a temporal and often causal relation between two events or actions, such that the first event comes first and provides the necessary conditions for the second event to take place.[17] See the following example for a temporal and causal relation between event one and two:

Example 8: "Wenn der Kuchen fertig ist . . . " *(If/when the cake is ready . . .)*

GERMAN: Wenn der Kuchen fertig ist, können wir ihn zum
           Nachtisch essen.
ENGLISH: If/when the cake is ready, we can eat it for des-
           sert.
GERMAN: *Wenn der Kuchen fertig ist, können wir die Eier in
           den Teig rühren.
ENGLISH: *If/when the cake is ready, we can put the eggs into
           the dough. (trans. CM)

Thus, once the cake is ready, it makes no sense, and it is even impossible, to add eggs to its dough. The rope example shows a similar kind of contradiction. Once the ropes are broken, they are no longer usable for hanging anything up. The conditions set up by the first idiom make the action referred to in the second idiom impossible, and this interferes with the semantic implications of the conditional clause. Hence, already on the level of the literal meaning of the idioms, there is more than an image break, more than a combination of two contradictory images or source domains. It is not just that they do not fit together well—on the contrary, one could argue that these two metaphors work with experiential domains that are somehow related, both having something to do with ropes. The incongruence we observe here is, therefore, not just a matter of wrongly combining two verbal images from different domains. What happens in this example is that the semantic inconsistency is reinforced, if not produced, by the semantic implications of the conditional clause. Thus, the characterization of this mixed metaphor as an image break appears to simplify the actual semantic structure.

Furthermore—and this aspect also remains unnoticed in the reference works that present this example—the sentence is also semantically inconsistent on the level of the figurative meaning. This is true, because the protasis, "Wenn alle Stricke reißen" (if all else fails) implies a positive turn in the dependent clause, yet the apodosis brings in a negative turn "hänge ich mich auf" (I will give up). Consider the following set of examples, in all of which a positive consequence of the protasis is described in the apodosis:

> *Example 9:* "Wenn alle Stricke reißen... " *(If all else fails...)*
> GERMAN: Wenn alle Stricke reißen...nehmen wir ein Taxi.
> ENGLISH: If all else fails...we take a taxi.
> GERMAN: Wenn alle Stricke reißen...nehme ich den OH Projektor.
> ENGLISH: If all else fails...I will use the OH projector.
> GERMAN: Wenn alle Stricke reiben...lasse ich das Mittagessen ausfallen.
> ENGLISH: If all else fails...I will drop lunch.

In all three cases, the actions described in the apodosis formulate some kind of positive solution to a problematic situation that is referred to in the protasis. The pragmatic implications of the apodosis can be paraphrased as follows: "If all else fails...I will find a solution that will solve the problem or save the situation." Hence, it seems quite clear that the first idiom of the rope example, when taken figuratively, combines well with positive events in the second clause.

This view gains further support from the fact that the idiom in the protasis "Wenn alle Stricke reißen" (if all else fails) does not, at least not by default, go with a negation in the apodosis. See the following examples:

Example 10: "*Wenn alle Stricke reißen..." (**If all else fails...*)

GERMAN: *Wenn alle Stricke reißen...kann ich nicht mit der
          U-Bahn nach Hause fahren.

ENGLISH: *If all else fails...I cannot take the subway back
          home.

GERMAN: *Wenn alle Stricke reißen...kann ich den Vortrag
          nicht halten.

ENGLISH: *If all else fails...I cannot give the talk.

GERMAN: *Wenn alle Stricke reißen...vergesse ich alles
          was ich sagen wollte.

ENGLISH: *If all else fails...I will forget everything I
          wanted to say.

None of these sentences makes sense, with the exception of cases in which the negation is interpreted as a positive solution to the frame of reference established in the first clause. Thus, take the first illustration in example 10. Here, it only works if not taking the subway back home does not matter; if it matters, the clause with the negation is not adequate. The same holds for the second illustration in example 10: only if not giving the talk is unproblematic—does the sentence work the way it is. If not, it is semantically inconsistent. This is also true for the last illustration listed in example 10. Here we encounter a similar structure, although there is no overt negation. Instead, the negative outcome of a situation is directly expressed: "I will forget everything I wanted to say" is, in a default reading of the sentence, only an acceptable continuation of the protasis, if forgetting everything does not matter. If it matters, the two clauses are semantically inconsistent.

Now remember that in the rope example, the idiom in the apodosis also expressed a negative solution to some kind of problem: "Wenn alle Stricke reißen, hänge ich mich auf" (If all ropes break, I'll hang myself up). As we have seen, this may be paraphrased as "If all else fails, I'll give up." Unfortunately, the English translation does not render the idiomatic meaning very well; what is lost is the affective connotation of "giving up in desperation."

Finally, it turns out that the second idiom in this mixed metaphor comes with certain presuppositions that are also violated in the rope example. As the following set of examples indicates, typically, "hänge ich mich auf" (I'll hang myself up; giving up) is preceded by repeatedly unsuccessful trials of the same kind.

Example 11: "...hänge ich mich auf" (... I'll give up desperately)

GERMAN: Wenn der Nagel jetzt nicht in die Wand geht...hänge
          ich mich auf.

ENGLISH: If the nail does not enter the wall ...I'll give up
          desperately.

GERMAN: Wenn das Auto jetzt nicht anspringt...hänge ich
          mich auf.

ENGLISH: If the car does not start up now...I'll give up
          desperately.

A nail that does not enter the wall or a car that does not start are repetitions of the same activity. Yet, this is not what is described in the protasis of the rope example. "Wenn alle Stricke reißen, hänge ich mich auf" (If all ropes break, I'll hang myself up; If all else fails, I'll give up) refers to various possible ways of solving a problem. "Wenn alle Stricke reißen" (If all ropes break; If all else fails) figuratively expresses different forms of solutions, not the repetition of one activity.

It is striking, but apparently, this is a third contradictory aspect in this mixed metaphor. Thus, to account for this kind of mixed metaphor as an image break appears to be at least a rather superficial, if not completely misleading, analysis of this example.

It is clear now that the contradictions in the rope example are manifold and not simply explainable as broken images. More correctly, they should be accounted for as different forms of semantic inconsistencies:

- On the literal level, regarding the semantic implications of the elements of the conditional construction (i.e., the condition set out in the protasis interferes with the consequence in the apodosis: with broken ropes, it is impossible to hang oneself up).
- On the figurative level, there are two forms of semantic inconsistencies: one regarding the implications of the protasis (i.e., the protasis implies a positive turn in the apodosis; instead, the apodosis describes a negative turn: "I'll hang myself up," "I'll give up"); and another one regarding the presuppositions of the apodosis (i.e., the apodosis presupposes repeated trials of the same kind of action in the protasis; instead, the apodosis describes repeated unsuccessful trials of different kinds of activity).

Obviously, this mixed metaphor does not just show semantic inconsistencies on the literal level. Describing mixed metaphors as image breaks on the literal level appears to overlook the semantic contradictions on the figurative level of this example and, therefore, must be regarded as an over-simplification.

This detailed analysis of the rope example has, I think, revealed that it is necessary to take a much closer look at mixed metaphors than is commonly done, which we will be doing in the subsequent sections. Doing this will enable us to achieve a more sophisticated and more adequate understanding of what kind of linguistic phenomenon the mixing of metaphors appears to be. Only then can we proceed and work out a well-founded explanation of the cognitive underpinnings of mixing metaphors in discourse.

Given this background, it is possible to describe in a much more precise way what the speaker or writer actually disregarded when formulating this mixed metaphor. He disregarded the semantic implications of the conditional construction, both on the literal and the figurative level, as well as the specific semantic implications and presuppositions of the figurative meaning of both metaphorical idioms. Hence, the speaker disregarded not only aspects of the literal meaning of the metaphor but also aspects of its figurative meaning that were related to the semantic structure of the conditional clauses. Thus, in producing this mixed metaphor, he seems to have had a very restricted focus of attention on the semantic and syntactic structure of the utterance. Apparently, he was only focused on the core figurative meaning, while disregarding semantic implications and presuppositions. Therefore, what he most probably intended to say could be paraphrased in the following way: "In the worst case, I will give up."

This observation reveals that the mixing of metaphors is not sufficiently characterized as a flaw of thinking—as a kind of thinking error. Instead, it turns out that, apparently, during speaking, some aspects of meaning have not been accessed; they were not in the focus of attention and, hence, could not influence the construction of the sentence. It could be that the cognitive processes responsible for the mixing of metaphors that we observe here might be generally at work during speech production. This example of a mixed metaphor indicates that the focal attention responsible for selecting and combining semantic and syntactic information may be very restricted and selective and may suppress all kinds of aspects of meaning—not just the literal meaning of a metaphor. This is a highly relevant aspect that has been brought to light by the analysis of the rope example; it indicates that the mechanisms of consciousness during speech production, especially regarding the information management online, need to be taken into closer consideration if we want to achieve a better understanding of the cognitive mechanisms underlying the production of mixed metaphors.

Let us now turn to some further cases of mixed metaphor given in the selected literature—all of which are characterized as image breaks— to see what kind of inconsistencies they show and what these tell us about the ways in which varying aspects of meaning are activated online during speaking or writing.

5.2.2 The Put-on-the-Last Example

The next example illustrates a case in which two metaphors are conflated.

Example 12: "Der bürokratische Staat schert alles über einen Leisten" *(The bureaucratic state lumps everything together)*

GERMAN: Der bürokratische Staat schert alles über einen Leisten. (Wustmann 1943, 242).

FIGURATIVE: The bureaucratic state lumps everything together.

LITERAL: The bureaucratic state tars everything on the last.

This is an interesting case because it is not—as in the example discussed above—a combination of two fully verbalized idioms; here two metaphoric idioms are syntactically conflated, meaning that they have merged into one single construction. The two idioms are given separately below:

Example 13: "Über einen Leisten schlagen" *(treat all alike);* "Über einen Kamm scheren" *(treat or judge all/everything alike)*

GERMAN: Über einen Leisten schlagen.

FIGURATIVE: Treat all alike.

LITERAL: Put on the last.

GERMAN: Über einen Kamm scheren.

FIGURATIVE: Treat or judge (all) everything alike.

LITERAL: Tar with the same brush.

"Über einen Leisten schlagen" is derived from the realm of the work of shoemakers. It literally means "to put on the last"; a last is a shoemaker's model for shaping or repairing a shoe or boot. Figuratively, it expresses that someone or something is treated alike. "Über einen Kamm scheren" is in turn derived from the realm of barber's work and literally means "to tar with the same brush." Its figurative meaning can be paraphrased as treating or judging everybody or everything alike. Both German idioms originated in medieval times and describe cultural techniques that at the time were very common and part of a widely distributed cultural body of knowledge. Nowadays, these techniques have become less current and presumably less present. In addition, the wording has preserved a specific historical meaning and syntactic structure since it represents a way of speaking that is no longer common in contemporary German.

The mixing of the two metaphoric idioms in this example is, in fact, a syntactic conflation. Instead of saying "Der bürokratische Staat *schlägt* alles über einen Leisten" [The bureaucratic state *puts everything on* the last], the author inserts the verb *scheren* (to tar) from the idiom "über einen Kamm scheren" (to tar with the same brush), which results in "Der bürokratische Staat *schert* alles über einen Leisten" [The bureaucratic state *tars* everything on the last]. In this example, the fixed formal structure of one idiom has been violated through the inclusion of a foreign element.

It is obvious that on the level of the literal meaning the two idioms cannot conflate with or merge into each other because they create a semantically inconsistent scene. In this respect, they are somewhat comparable to the examples discussed above. But the situation differs profoundly with regard to the level of the figurative meaning of the two idioms. The English translations taken from Cassell's dictionary (1987) reveal this in a nice way, for they give basically similar paraphrases of the two idioms. Both are translated as "treat all alike," and this is the general, abstract, figurative meaning that both idioms express in German: "many things or people are treated alike." Note, furthermore, that there are even more idioms sharing this figurative meaning:

Example 14: "Etwas nach Schema F erledigen" *(to do something according to rule, and without discrimination);* "Nach der Schablone arbeiten" *(to work according to a routine)*

GERMAN:	Etwas nach Schema F erledigen.
FIGURATIVE:	To do something according to rule, and without discrimination.
LITERAL:	To do something according to model F.
GERMAN:	Nach der Schablone arbeiten.
FIGURATIVE:	To work according to a routine.
LITERAL:	To work according to the pattern.

In other words, they are taken from a cluster of idioms expressing a similar figurative meaning using a variety of different literal meanings. Thus, on the literal level, these idioms are incompatible, whereas on the level of the figurative meaning, they are compatible. And this is, presumably, one of the reasons why the author of the expression has conflated the two idioms in the example above.

Let us summarize. Quite surprisingly, the two idioms are inconsistent on the literal level but semantically consistent on the figurative level. They are synonymous expressions on the figurative level. The problem here is that they cannot merge into each other because this would destroy the fixed phraseological structure of the idioms. Thus, although their figurative meaning is consistent, mixing is not possible because it violates the fixed phraseological structure. Again—and in this respect the example is comparable to the rope example—inconsistencies inherent in mixed metaphors are not reduced to the literal level (as the literature suggests); there is also some kind of violation on the figurative level. Yet this violation only concerns the syntactic structure and not the figurative meaning of the mixed metaphors that are conflated. This crucially differentiates it from the rope example. Whereas in the rope example, implications and presuppositions related to the figurative meaning and the syntactic structure of the combined metaphoric idioms were disregarded, in the put-on-the-last example only the fixed phraseological form was violated.

Also, from the point of view of cognition in language use, this is a further interesting case for it shows even more clearly than the rope example that the speaker must have focused all his attention on the figurative meaning of the idioms. This focus very likely supported or even triggered the mixing of the two metaphors in the way it happened, because, on the level of the figurative meaning, these two metaphors are congruent or even synonymous. Thus, in this case of mixed metaphor, the speaker seems to have focused his attention solely on the figurative meaning, while disregarding the phraseological structure as well as the literal meaning of the two idioms.

This analysis should be taken as a further indication of the rather limited explanatory power of concepts like "image break" or "thinking errors" that have been used hitherto to explain the semantic structure and the cognitive backgrounds of mixed metaphors in the German and the English research literature. It also indicates that the problem of mixing metaphors cannot be sufficiently explained by noncoherence on the level of conceptual metaphors. It is obvious that the semantic inconsistencies identified above are located on the level of rich-image semantic structure of lexemes as well as of syntactic structures. Thus, even if we assume that there is a general level of metaphorical concepts, then these cases point to an important level of language-internal, meaningful structure. Concepts like "information management" or "selective activation of meaning" appear to account more adequately for the cognitive backgrounds of this phenomenon than noncoherence or thinking flaws. It seems that there are limited and varying aspects of meaning activated in speech production. Note that this point can only be made because of the more fine-grained semantic analysis of the mixed metaphors that we have carried out here. Otherwise, we would only have been able to rather generally state that the literal meaning was not activated during the process of formulating these utterances. Yet a closer semantic analysis has revealed that it is not a question of moving literal meaning to focal awareness in speaking or writing, but that focal awareness is a mechanism that may suppress all kinds of aspects of meaning inherent in a given utterance.

5.2.3 The Molting River Example

A third form of mixed metaphors will throw further light on which elements of meaning may remain nonactivated during the production of a mixed metaphor. The next example to be considered will add further critical mass for a different understanding of mixed metaphors. It will show once more that the traditional accounts have incorrectly reduced mixed metaphors to a semantic inconsistency on the literal level. As we will see, there are mixed metaphors that do not show any kind of contradiction on the literal level:

Example 15: "Die Isar soll sich ... mausern also offenbar mit neuen Federn schmücken" (the Isar is supposed to convert itself... hence apparently adorn itself with a new outfit)

GERMAN: Die Isar soll sich wieder zu einem Wildwasser Fluß *mausern* also offenbar *mit neuen Federn schmücken*. (Schneider 1999, 237)

FIGURATIVE: The Isar is supposed *to convert* itself into a torrent and hence apparently adorn itself with a *new outfit*.

LITERAL: The Isar is supposed to *be molting* itself into a torrent and hence apparently adorn itself with *new feathers*.

Here is a sentence that makes perfect sense when focusing entirely on the literal meaning: somebody is molting, that is, is shedding his old plumage and adorning himself with a new and nicer one. The experiential source domains of the two idioms are nicely congruent. It could be argued that the author elaborates the verbal metaphor "sich mausern" (to take a turn for the better, to molt) by using an idiom that also refers to changing feathers. All this would make perfect sense. Yet the example is treated as a mixed metaphor, or in German terms as a broken image. Why is this?

One reason is that the sentence carries a semantic inconsistency on the level of the figurative meaning. This inconsistency emerges because the two idioms—in spite of being derived from a similar source domain (changing feathers)—express different figurative meanings. Even though the figurative meaning of the second idiom "sich mit neuen Federn schmücken" (to adorn oneself with a new outfit, to adorn oneself with new feathers) appears at first glance to fit well with the figurative meaning of the first idiomatic metaphor "sich mausern" (to take a turn for the better, to molt)—a closer look at it reveals that this is not the case. It turns out that the idiom is contaminated, that, a free lexical unit has been inserted into a fixed phraseological unit. Here is the correct version of the contaminated idiom:

Example 16: "sich mit fremden Federn schmücken" *(to deck oneself out in borrowed plumes)*

GERMAN: sich mit fremden Federn schmücken
FIGURATIVE: to deck oneself out in borrowed plumes
LITERAL: to adorn oneself with foreign feathers

In his utterance, the speaker has replaced "fremde Federn" (foreign feathers) with "neue Federn" (new feathers). Now, "sich mit fremden Federn schmücken" (to deck oneself out in borrowed plumes, to adorn oneself with foreign feathers) carries a negative connotation because it means that somebody adorns himself with feathers that are not his own. It is, hence, a stolen merit. Apparently, this negatively connotated, figurative meaning is present in the idiom, despite the fact that the author has contaminated it in a way that would make it semantically appropriate as a positively connotated elaboration of the first idiomatic metaphor "sich mausern" (to molt)—only if we disregard its phraseological or figurative meaning.

We may conclude, therefore, that the elaboration of the metaphor introduced by the first idiom fails because the contaminated metaphoric idiom continues to carry its original figurative sense. It is in this sense that it interferes with the figurative sense of the first metaphor. From a cognitive point of view—this type of mixed metaphor shows that the focal attention during speaking may also activate the literal meaning by suppressing the figurative meaning and by disregarding fixed phraseological structures. Hence, once again, focal attention during discourse appears to be highly mobile and context-dependent and not simply always focused on the same kind of aspects of meaning—be it the figurative or the core ones (as the general tendency to lose literal meaning in conventional metaphors tends to suggest). On the contrary, the first metaphor "sich mausern" (to molt) has activated the source domain of CHANGING FEATHERS IN BIRDS, and this specific context has presumably not only triggered the second idiomatic metaphor but has also motivated the contamination of it, for the contamination of the second metaphor turned the negative connotation of it into a positive one and, thus, made it an adequate elaboration of the first metaphor. Focal attention on the source domain of this idiomatic metaphor has opened up a creative elaboration that violated the figurative meaning and the phraseological structure of a second idiomatic metaphor. Put another way, the speaker's or the writer's focal attention on the source domain or on the literal meaning created the context for a violation of the figurative meaning and the formal structure of the second idiom.

This last form of mixed metaphors to be considered here shows, I believe, rather convincingly, that the analysis of mixed metaphors as broken images or as contradictory imagistic expressions is profoundly misleading. What, in contrast, appears to be at stake in the process of mixing metaphors is a mobile or shifting focus of attention during speaking: a focus of attention that can shift back and forth between the literal and the figurative meaning and/or between presuppositions and implications of the literal and/or the figurative meaning.

In conclusion, the analysis presented in this section has revealed that there are objective reasons for mixed metaphors not to make sense. Although these reasons are not reducible to semantic inconsistencies on the literal level of meaning, there are good grounds for judging mixed metaphors to be somewhat contradictory expressions: these contradictions may occur on various levels of meaning (figurative and literal), both with regard to different aspects of meaning (implications, presuppositions) and to the formal structure (contamination of fixed forms) of expressions. Therefore, mixed metaphors appear to be more convincingly characterized as semantic and syntactic inconsistencies rather than as broken images or thinking flaws.

Let me now return to the contradictory argumentation found in explanations of the mixing of metaphors addressed at the beginning of this chapter. In this section, we gained some rational support for the widespread assumption that grounds mixed metaphors in thinking flaws or in inattentiveness. But I have also offered an alternative, less normative assessment of this process, namely, the selective activation of meaning. In mixed metaphors, certain aspects of meaning appear to be more actively processed than others.

Note that "more actively" refers here to their potential semantic productivity. So far, I have demonstrated why a selection of mixed metaphors does
not make sense, but we have also seen that they do seem to make sense in
some sense. And this is presumably why a speaker or writer produced them.
Here is the question I shall address in the next section. Why can mixed
metaphors make sense and make no sense at the same time?

5.3 Why Mixed Metaphors Make Sense! Blending and Salience

There seems to be one way in which mixed metaphors do make sense; we
have seen that this is true for the examples discussed above, but apparently this is a property that most—if not all—mixed metaphors show. Gibbs
in his brief discussion of mixed metaphors also adopts this viewpoint. He
points out that "we understand what the original speakers must have intended with each of these examples" (Gibbs 1994, 4). Gibbs's assumption is
straightforward and intuitively plausible, and it is further strengthened by
the fact that in everyday conversation participants typically do not seem to
react to these kinds of semantic inconsistencies; rather, they seem to have
no difficulties—at least no overt ones—in making sense of utterances containing mixed metaphors. This is supported by a study on metaphors, coherence, and blending conducted by Cienki and Swan (2001). In this study, they
analyzed metaphoric expressions that were spontaneously produced when
two students were engaged in a conversation about honesty in taking ex-
ams. Cienki and Swan found that speakers and addressees did not show any
overt difficulties in producing and understanding noncoherent metaphoric
expressions:

> But we observed in the data examined here that multi-part metaphoric
> expressions with non-coherent entailments did not appear problematic
> for either the speakers or listeners. Even when the speakers in our data
> constructed blends which did not cohere syntactically or conceptually,
> addressees did not let this deter from the flow of conversation, *but made
> sense out of the given phrase in some way*, as evidenced by their contin-
> uation of the topic rather than asking for clarification. (Cienki and Swan
> 2001, 28–29; emphasis CM)

How is it possible that we as analysts of and as participants in conversational interaction can make sense of mixed metaphors? What kind of
sense is it? Are they systematic misconceptions or digressions from a correct reading, or are they plainly unsystematic errors? If we depart from the

assumptions that experts in style who adhere to LMT make, then the answer is relatively simple: mixed metaphors should always make sense on the figurative level. This is so because mixing metaphors is supposed to be a consequence of disregarding the literal meaning of the metaphors in play. Or, in terms of CMT, because their source domains do not have overlapping entailments.

Yet, as we have seen above, the situation is not as clear as the experts in metaphor and style have hitherto assumed. Sometimes, mixed metaphors may make perfect sense on the literal level but not on the figurative one. Their source domains may then show coherent entailments, but the target domains may differ. Hence, the question arises as to what are the cognitive processes that could account for this unconventional but creative way of using language, or, in other words, what could explain this form of online meaning construction.

A theoretical framework that explicitly addresses processes of online meaning construction is blending theory (Fauconnier and Turner 2002; Turner and Fauconnier 1995). Blending theory provides a means of describing the elements of meaning construction and of reconstructing the processes leading to the emergence of new meaningful structures. If mixed metaphors do indeed make sense, blending analysis should provide us with the means to specifically account for the creative processes that create such new structures of meaning.

5.3.1 Metaphor, Blending, and Conceptual Integration: The Butcher Example

Conventionalized dead verbal and conceptual metaphors belong to the static aspects of language and thought, whereas blending theory addresses their dynamic aspects. It seeks to document the dynamics of online meaning construction. According to blending theory, this situated meaning construction is based on two or more conceptual input spaces. From these input spaces, some elements are projected into the blended space, where they interact and create new meaningful structures. I will illustrate the format that blending theory uses to describe these processes with an example taken from an excellent comparative discussion of CMT and blending theory by Joseph Grady, Todd Oakley, and Seana Coulson (1999).

5.3.1.1 GRADY, OAKLEY, AND COULSON'S ANALYSIS OF "THIS SURGEON IS A BUTCHER" Somebody characterizes a surgeon as a butcher. In terms of metaphor theory (be it linguistic or conceptual), we would either assume two fields of meaning or two conceptual domains—but not more than two (the third relatum of the metaphoric structure tends not to be considered systematically). One of these would be the source (the butcher), and the other one would be the target (the surgeon). Properties from the source would be mapped onto the target; there would be no projection back to the source domain. The idea of a metaphorical mapping does not imply an interaction between the two domains involved, even though it does imply a projection from source to target, and, in this sense, it is an active process. Because, as we have seen above, metaphoricity presupposes the activation of source and target, it is not assumed that this leads to a third verbal domain of sense or a third conceptual domain. Here is where blending theory develops a different conceptualization of the process. Blending theory starts from the idea that elements from source and target domains are projected into a third domain, which is created ad hoc. In this blended conceptual space, the elements interact, and in this way new aspects of meaning may be created. Aspects of meaning that were not present, either in the source domain or in the target domain, may emerge in the blended space. For instance, certain kinds of inferences can only be drawn on the basis of the interaction of these different and often contrasting aspects of meaning. Thus, in the butcher example above, the inference that the surgeon is incompetent—which, of course, is the inference to be drawn from this sentence—cannot be explained as the straightforward consequence of a projection from the source domain (BUTCHERY) to the target domain (SURGERY). Why not? Because a butcher as a butcher is not typically an incompetent person; rather, butchers may be more or less skillful in their business, but this does not imply that incompetence is a typical trait of a butcher. Therefore, the fact that characterizing the surgeon as a butcher prompts this kind of inference must be explained in other terms. And here is where the interaction of elements of meaning in a third conceptual space comes into play. In this blended space, the means-end relationship of a butcher's work contradicts the means-end relationship of a surgeon's work. Whereas a butcher's goal is to prepare a dead animal for consumption, a surgeon's goal is to heal people, keep them alive, put their broken limbs together, and sew up their wounds. Therefore, it is not that the means-end structure of the butcher's domain is directly mapped onto the target domain, for this would result in a characterization of the surgeon as somebody who actually kills people in order to prepare them for consumption; this would turn the surgeon into somebody performing a cannibal ritual. What appears to take place instead is an interaction between the two means-end structures, such that it remains clear that the surgeon does not aim to kill his patients and that his operating technique does not lead to the actual carving up of his patient. The projection from the surgeon's means-end to the butcher's means-end results in a moderation of the butcher's means-end structure, such that it is now converted into the expression of an unskillful surgeon: somebody operating on some other living being in such a way that it does not really kill him but does not really heal him either. As a result of the interaction between the surgeon's and the butcher's means-end structure, an inference emerges that was presumably the driving force behind this metaphoric expression: the characterization of a specific surgeon as an incompetent person.[18] Consider the diagram in figure 34 by Grady, Oakley, and Coulson, which documents the blending process (the solid lines in figure 34 depict the cross-space correspondences, which constitute the mapping between the input spaces; the dotted lines depict the projections between spaces; and the dashed lines in figure 34 document the fusion of the butcher role and the surgeon role).

Blending theory claims that these integrational processes are not reduced to metaphor; rather, metaphor is conceived of as a specific form of blending (Fauconnier and Turner 2002, 155–6).

Conceptual integration is ultimately an attempt at describing human creativity in all realms of cognitive activity, not just in language. Fauconnier and Turner provide explanations ranging from a Buddhist riddle to counterfactuals and the construction of possible worlds. All of these cognitive constructions of meaning are supposed to follow what I would like to term a "four-space" mechanism: two input spaces, a generic space, and a blended space. The generic space accounts for the rationale behind the blending process. It documents the commonalities or the shared aspects of the two input spaces (specific semantic roles, or a scenario) on a higher level of abstraction. The two input spaces provide the material that fills out this general structure, which is projected into the blended space. In the blended space, principles that determine the composition of elements of meaning, the completion of structural patterns, and their elaboration trigger the emergence of new meaning.[19]

Multiple blends are possible; they must even be considered as the default in ordinary, everyday processes of meaning construction. Projection between spaces is selective, and conceptual blending is ultimately based on three processes: recognizing identity, conceptual integration, and imagination. Blending theory seeks to capture modality-independent and dynamic processes of meaning construction, and as such it is in harmony with the dynamic view of metaphor proposed in this book.

Therefore, in the remainder of the chapter we shall revisit the examples discussed above from a blending theory viewpoint and see whether this

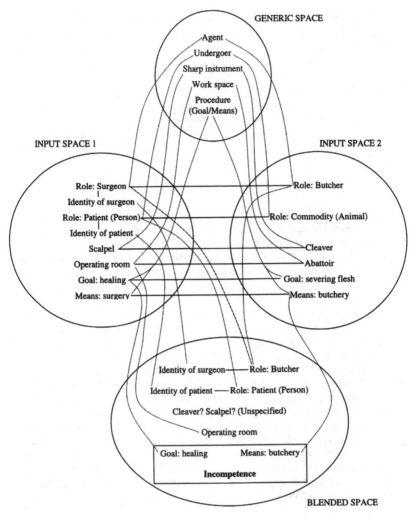

Fig. 34. Conceptual blending: "butcher as surgeon." Grady, Oakley, and Coulson
(1999, 105).

reveals more specifically the ways in which they make sense for a given
speaker or writer during language production.

5.3.1.2 THE BUTTER MOUNTAIN IN THE PIPELINE EXAMPLE REVISITED   The
first example of mixed metaphors considered above turned out to be a "classical" case of mixed metaphor. Our analysis in more traditional semantic

terms confirmed the expectations motivated by the traditional view by showing that the mixing of metaphors was basically due to inconsistencies on the literal level of the two metaphoric expressions involved. The sentence did not make sense if the literal meaning was taken into account; but it did make sense if the figurative meaning was considered just on its own.

Let us reexamine the example taken from *The Oxford Companion to the English Language* and recall that it was presented as a prototypical form of mixed metaphor caused by "unthinkingly mixing 'clichés'" (McArthur 1992, 663):

ENGLISH: The butter mountain has been in the pipeline for some time.

FIGURATIVE: As a result of the overproduction of butter in the European Union, huge amounts of it have been awaiting distribution for some time.

LITERAL: A real mountain consisting of butter is stuck in a kind of oil pipeline.

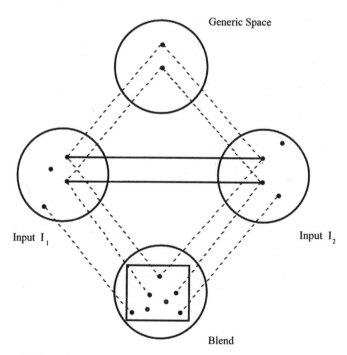

Fig. 35. The basic diagram of conceptual blending. Fauconnier and Turner (2002, 46).

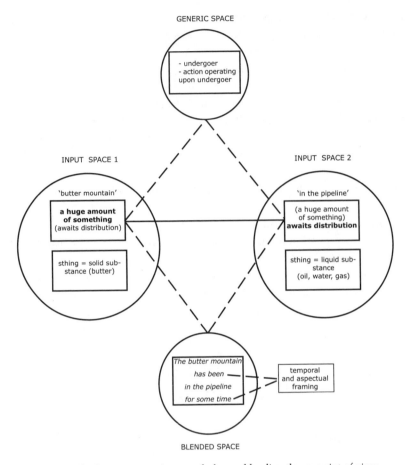

Fig. 36. The butter mountain example from a blending theory point of view.

In terms of blending theory, the example could be analyzed in the following way (figure 36): there are two input spaces that go into the blend—one that includes "butter mountain as the European Union stock of butter" and a second one that includes the idiomatic expression "to be in the pipeline" referring to abstract entities waiting for distribution or to the ongoing discussion of a specific issue. In other words, input space 2, "to be in the pipeline," comes with at least two readings.

Note that input space 1, "butter mountain," carries a set of associated inferences, such as the problem of subventions and prices, the farmers' situation in the European Union (EU), international competition, and butter waiting for distribution. In the process of online meaning construction—or in the blending procedure—only a few elements from the two input spaces are projected into the blend (dashed lines in figure 36). From input space 1, two elements are projected: "butter mountain" as the EU stock of butter and the inference that this is something that is awaiting distribution among EU citizens. From input space 2, only one element seems to be projected: the notion of something awaiting distribution. The temporal ("has been") and aspectual ("for some time") framing of the process as an enduring one further reinforces this element of meaning. This also reinforces the inference that is projected from input space 1, namely, the fact that the butter mountain is waiting for distribution. Furthermore, this is precisely the element of meaning that the two input spaces seem to share: the idea of something waiting for distribution (this is represented in the generic space). These are the elements in the two input spaces that show a cross-space mapping (the solid lines in figure 36). In the process of blending, they have been selected as the meaningful elements that go into the blend. They are mapped onto each other and selected for projection into the blended space. Thus, the blend operates on the general idea that there is some kind of entity that has been awaiting distribution for a long period of time.

The blending analysis has enabled us to locate more precisely the elements of meaning that motivated the mixing of the two metaphors, namely, the idea of something awaiting distribution. This is what goes into the generic space, this is what both input spaces share, and this is why this mixed metaphor does make sense—in some sense. The blending analysis provides a descriptive means not only of identifying and describing the actual elements of meaning that triggered the mix, but it also accounts for the procedure of the meaning construction that was involved in its production: elements of meaning were mapped from one input space onto another one and projected into a blended space where they combined, interacted, and produced new meaningful structures. It is noteworthy, even crucial, that the elements of meaning selected by the speaker represent an "uncommon" usage of the two metaphors, because it is this uncommon form of combining metaphors that reveals that the salience of elements of meaning may depend upon the specific choice a speaker makes, be it a specific viewpoint that he or she adopts or a specific intention to be fulfilled. The salience structures of the elements of meaning that go into metaphoric expressions may apparently be created ad hoc; they may be independent of normative, entrenched understandings of metaphoric expressions. The salient elements of meaning go into the blend, where they are conceptually integrated to form a new "unconventional" sense.[20]

5.3.1.3 THE ROPE EXAMPLE REVISITED   The analysis of the rope example revealed semantic inconsistencies on various levels of meaning: first, like the butter mountain example, it turned out to be semantically inconsistent on the level of the literal meaning (the structure of the meaning of the conditional sentence was contradicted by the content of the protasis and the apodosis, when understood literally); second, and in this respect the example differed from the butter mountain, it appeared to be semantically inconsistent on the level of the figurative meaning from two points of view: (1) the pragmatic implications of the protasis were contradicted by the apodosis, and (2) presuppositions of the apodosis were contradicted by the protasis. Regarding the question about the way in which it *did* make sense, we stated that the speaker/writer had presumably only focused on the core aspects of the figurative meaning by disregarding implications and presuppositions.

> GERMAN: Wenn alle Stricke reißen, hänge ich mich auf.
> FIGURATIVE: If all else fails, I'll give up.
> LITERAL: If all ropes break, I'll hang myself up.

By conducting a blending analysis, we can formulate more precisely why this example of a mixed metaphor makes sense. Figure 37 shows that the blend operates on very few projections. The generic space documents the underlying logic of the blend: what is being projected and then conceptually integrated is the conditional structure (if-then). Input space 1 shows that the protasis comes with a specific event structure: "If all activity options have been tried without success . . . "; the event structure of the apodosis, " . . . no further activities will be realized," is projected into input space 2. So, what is projected into the blend, or in other words, what the speaker/writer conceptually integrated when the sentence was formulated, is basically the conditional structure and two interrelated event structures. What are not projected are the implicatures and presuppositions that are associated with the protasis and the apodosis.

The blending diagram below provides us with an elegant way of describing the connections between the different elements of the semantic and syntactic structures that motivated a specific linguistic form combining two metaphors in one sentence. It reveals quite neatly why this mixed metaphor did make sense to the person who produced it, because it documents specifically which projections and mappings between spaces were activated when this piece of discourse was produced and which were disregarded. Again, this analysis appears to be a useful supplement to our initial examination of the reasons why this mixed metaphor did not make sense.

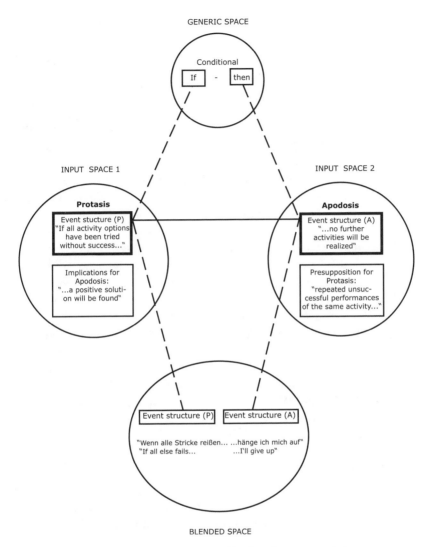

Fig. 37. The rope example from a blending theory point of view.

Note that, with this kind of analysis, we have shifted from the perspective of the expert in stylistics who assumes that this combination of two metaphors produces semantic inconsistencies and is, therefore, from the normative point of view an unacceptable form of language use, to a reconstruction of the cognitive processes of meaning construction that underlie the production of this mixed metaphor in a given speaker at a given moment in time.

5.3.1.4 THE PUT-ON-THE-LAST EXAMPLE REVISITED   The analyses carried out in the first section of this chapter have already described the rationale behind the conflation of the two idiomaticized metaphors in a relatively straightforward way: the two idioms "über einen Kamm scheren" (to put on the last) und "über einen Leisten schlagen" (to tar with the same brush) share a figurative meaning; in other words, they are synonymous. Presumably, this is why the contaminated metaphorical idiom made sense for a given speaker at a given moment in time.

GERMAN:	Der burokratische Staat schert alles über einen Leisten
FIGURATIVE:	The bureaucratic state lumps everything together.
LITERAL:	The bureaucratic state tars everything on the last.

Furthermore, an analysis in terms of blending reveals that the triggering force behind the conflation of these two metaphoric idioms is a complete homology of the syntactic and semantic structure of the two idioms.

The generic space accounts for this because it is made up of the full syntactic and semantic structure of the two idioms: "agent acts upon the undergoer, and his action displays a specific quality." Accordingly, in the cross-space mappings between the two input spaces in play, we see a one-to-one mapping of the elements that instantiate the generic structure. These elements are all projected into the blend "somebody treats different things alike"—and, obviously, they do not interact or trigger aspects of new meaning because they are homologous. Note that there are no mappings to the literal meaning of the metaphors in the two inputs, and this might be the reason why this formal blend did not produce any interferences at the moment of its production. Without activation, the source domains of the two conflated idioms were not processed during the creation of this mixed metaphor. This is why the conflation of the two idioms does make perfect sense on the level of figurative content, and it seems evident that these are the meaningful elements that were salient at the moment of speaking. Apparently, the speaker/writer chose the syntactic and semantic structure of the figurative meaning as salient meaningful elements by disregarding the fixed formal structure of the idioms involved and both source domains. In other words, the formal blend did not result in a conceptual blend because the conflated idioms share the same figurative meaning and syntactic structure.[21]

This raises the general issue of how to conceptualize the cognitive structures underlying idiomatic expressions that function as synonyms. Consider again the examples mentioned above: "etwas nach Schema F erledigen" (to

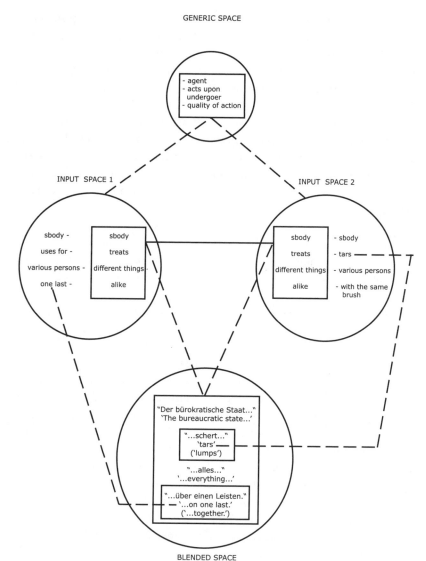

Fig. 38. The put-on-the-last example from a blending theory point of view.

do something according to rule, and without discrimination, to do something according to model F), and "nach der Schablone arbeiten" (to work according to a routine, to work according to the pattern). They both follow the same structural principle that is captured in the generic space described above: "agent acts upon the undergoer according to the same principle." This raises the question as to what kind of status the generic space has in this case. It could be that these kinds of generic meaning structures are conventionalized as abstract structures and that they are productive and so continue to generate new instantiations.

5.3.1.5 THE MOLTING RIVER EXAMPLE REVISITED   The molting river example is a complex and particularly interesting example of how a truly unconventional form of combining two idiomaticized metaphors may still make sense. Here the activated source domain of the first metaphor triggered a very specific activation of the source domain of the subsequently produced metaphor.

GERMAN: Die Isar soll sich wieder zu einem Wildwasser Fluß
            mausern also offenbar *mit neuen Federn schmücken.*
FIGURATIVE: The Isar is supposed *to convert* itself into a torrent and
            hence apparently adorn itself with a *new outfit.*
LITERAL: The Isar is supposed to *be molting* itself into a torrent and
            hence apparently adorn itself with *new feathers.*

We observe here a rather complex conceptual integration of two highly conventionalized metaphoric expressions: "sich mausern" (to molt, to convert) and "mit fremden Federn schmücken (to adorn oneself with foreign feathers [with borrowed feather], to adorn oneself with a foreign outfit), in which the second idiom is formally and conceptually contaminated. "New" has been inserted into the idiom in place of "foreign" and has led to a change in meaning. In the analysis provided above, I argued that the insertion of a new lexical unit into a formally fixed expression was triggered by an active source domain (BIRDS CHANGING FEATHERS). Again, an analysis in terms of blending theory provides us with a formalism to describe more specifically what triggered the combination of these two metaphors and what motivated the violation of the formal and semantic structure of the second idiom. To begin with, consider the diagram in figure 39:

The conceptual integration of these two highly entrenched metaphors is based on a rather simple semantic structure, which is captured in the generic space: an agent and a self-reflexive action with a specific quality. What is projected from input space 1 to input space 2 is the idea that something is being embellished or is embellishing itself. This is what both metaphoric expressions share, and in this regard their combination in the above-cited sentence makes perfect sense.

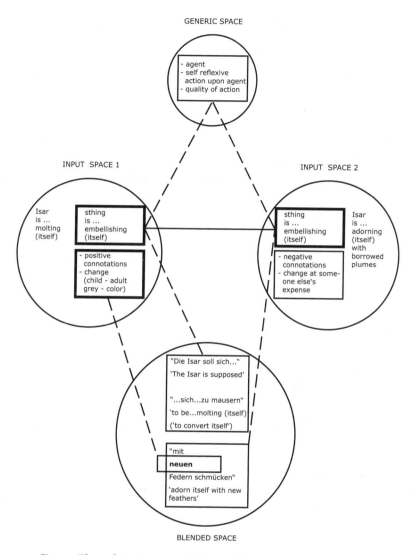

Fig. 39. The molting river example from a blending theory point of view.

Yet we still need to explain how the new lexical unit entered the blend hence why the speaker used "adorn itself with new feathers" instead of "adorn itself with borrowed feathers." Although both input spaces involved in the blending procedure share the idea of changing feathers, the most plausible source of it seems to be input space 1 not input space 2. Why? The meaning element 'new' is at best implicitly present in the idiom "sich mit

fremden Federn schmücken" (to adorn oneself with foreign feathers, borrowed plumes); although the expression somehow implies that foreign feathers are new ones, this reading does feel very ambitious and somehow forced.
On the other hand, this element of meaning seems more readily implied
in the first metaphoric expression "sich mausern" (to molt): "to molt" is directly and positively associated with an exchange of old feathers for new ones
when birds mature. Therefore, it appears more plausible to assume that the
newly inserted lexical unit has been projected from input space 1. Note that
this is the input space that contains the first metaphor to be produced in this
sentence and not input space 2, which contains the idiomatic expression.
Apparently, only a part of the form and a partial meaning structure were projected from input space 2 into the blended space. This partial meaning structure was presumably triggered by a cross-space mapping from input space 1
to input space 2. The mapping connected the shared elements ("something is
embellishing itself"), while at the same time it suppressed parts of the form
and elements of the meaning of the idiomatic expression in input space 2.
The mapping suppressed or deactivated the negative connotation of input
space 2 and replaced it with a positive connotation that came from input
space 1 and was realized in the inserted lexical element 'new.'

     This is a highly interesting fact. It shows that a mapping may produce
salience effects of meaning structures that run counter to the entrenched
ones. Furthermore, it points to the effects that the salience structure of a
previously established blend (input space 1 went into the first part of the sentence and was hence produced first) may have on subsequent ones. Apparently, the entrenched salience structures of the metaphor that was produced
first in the sentence ("sich mausern": to molt) attracted the focal attention of
the writer to such a degree that it altered the salience structure of the source
concept of the metaphoric idiom so that its conventional form and meaning
were ignored.

     We encounter here an intriguing case of new emergent meaning: pre-
ceding salience structures motivating new salience structures in innovative
metaphors. This example thus documents beautifully that conceptual integration is a procedural enterprise, most probably including the activation
of networks of meaning structures, which, in turn, may foreshadow subsequent ones. It is in this way that activated source domains may create new
senses, and these new senses may stand in contrast to the conventionalized
ones. This is why this mixed metaphor did make perfect sense for the writer
as he was formulating his thoughts.

     Let us conclude. The question of how speakers or writers may make
sense of mixed metaphors can now be answered more precisely: they select

specific elements of meaning for projection and activate or deactivate entrenched mappings between spaces. This selection process results in a novel salience structure of the conventionalized metaphor, typically, one that contrasts with the entrenched one. Within the process of conceptual integration, this salience structure may become the context for a subsequent process of meaning construction and, in this way, motivate further salience structures (as in the case of the molting river, where the salience of the literal meaning of the first metaphor activated a highly uncommon literal reading of the second metaphor, resulting ultimately in the contamination of its formal structure).

5.4 Conclusion: Dead Metaphors Are Available for Conceptual Integration

We have seen that mixed metaphors offer a range of highly interesting new insights into the nature of the cognitive activation of metaphoricity online during language production.

To begin with, the analyses carried out in this chapter clearly show that the traditional accounts of mixed metaphors are reductionist if not profoundly inadequate. Hence, Black's claim that conventional metaphors are dead because they do not show a pregnant metaphorical use is once again refuted. While in chapter 3 we saw that supposedly dead verbal metaphors may display active metaphoricity both on the conceptual and verbal levels, the inquiry into mixed metaphors conducted in this chapter has revealed that dead metaphors may be activated selectively and still be semantically productive. Recall that, according to the view of LMT, the mixing of metaphors happens because the literal meaning is not actively processed. Accordingly, a mixed metaphor that is based on a congruent literal meaning, while suppressing the inconsistent figurative meaning, should not exist. Yet as we have seen, this may indeed occur. In addition, the CMT stance of grounding the mixing of metaphors on the level of noncoherent entailments of conceptual metaphors does not capture the phenomenon of mixed verbal metaphors sufficiently: as we have seen, mixed verbal metaphors may be grounded in coherent conceptual metaphors with incoherence being located on the level of verbal metaphors and their entailments. All the mixed metaphors we have considered in this chapter show a highly active level of verbal metaphoricity, which was selectively and creatively activated.

We are now in a position to characterize mixed metaphors more specifically in terms of semantic inconsistency between various elements of meaning (be they figurative or literal, explicit or implicit). Our closer linguistic analysis has suggested that the nature of mixed metaphors or of image breaks is not sufficiently characterized as a simple neglect of the literal level of meaning caused by a flaw in one's thinking; rather, what seems to be the rationale behind these "errors" is that meaning is selectively activated on-line during language production. Apparently, different bits and parts of semantic and syntactic information during discourse are more or less actively processed. Importantly, there is no simple and constant way to characterize the kinds of elements of meaning that are cognitively active during speaking and writing. Clearly, it is not only the deactivation of the literal meanings of metaphors that explains why mixed metaphors do not make sense. Moreover, we have seen that, in some respect, the mixed metaphors we have analyzed do make sense. In all cases, it is possible to at least suspect what the speaker might have intended to say, which means that we do have an idea about which aspects of the meaning were the focus of attention of the writers or speakers when they were producing these mixed metaphors.

The ways in which mixed metaphors do make sense uncover a creative part of language production. They show that language production is always a process of online meaning construction, which may counter conventional uses of metaphors and still make sense. Blending theory provides a theoretical framework and a descriptive means that enable us to account for these kinds of creative processes. Even though the diagrams look like the static representations of a meaning structure, what they actually depict are often successive steps in a process of meaning construction.

The blending diagrams provided us with a means of documenting the specific selections—in terms of activated projections and mappings—that the producer of the respective mixed metaphor had made. They offered a means of identifying and describing the elements of meaning and the projections that were salient for a given speaker at the very moment of processing a meaning construction. It appears, therefore, that the reanalyses of the mixed metaphor examples from a blending theory viewpoint significantly altered our understanding of the semantic processes. They made it possible to document the dynamic process of meaning construction and, in this way, they complemented the analyses in CMT as well as in more traditional linguistic terms.

What is selected from input spaces depends on the context, on the salience of certain aspects of meaning, and presumably also on the focus of attention during discourse. In any case, it is a specific choice. And what is salient is the focus of attention. Put differently, the focus of attention chooses certain salient aspects of meaning in the process of language production, and these may be located on the figurative or on the literal level of meaning. Here is where cognitive processing mechanisms and meaning construction come together. And this is where the sense of mixed metaphors emerges.

But why do mixed metaphors may make sense and no sense at the same time? This relates to the analytic viewpoint: they make no sense from the perspective of language experts (this is a post hoc perspective), whereas they do (did) make sense from the viewpoint of the speaker/writer at the moment of speaking (this is the here-and-now perspective of the discourse situation). It seems as if, at least insofar as spoken discourse is concerned, the recipients tend to follow the viewpoint of the speaker and make sense of the mixed metaphors too. This, finally, brings in a crucial methodological issue, namely, what are the empirical grounds for claiming that these mixed metaphors are involved in the cognitive processes of meaning selection that have been outlined above? I think, once again, that adopting an interactive perspective provides a well-founded approach that is based on a reasonable assumption, that is, what is interactively salient, or what from an interactive perspective in a certain context appears as salient, presumably was salient internally for the speaker. Briefly, examining the reasons why mixed metaphors make sense offers good empirically verified grounds for gaining insights into the spontaneous cognitive processes of meaning construction.

Mixed metaphors offer a very interesting field of research for inquiring into cognitive processes. They are probably as revelatory for cognitive linguists as speech errors are for psycholinguists, and, last but not least, they are highly vital witnesses of the vitality of supposedly dead metaphors.

CHAPTER SIX

Sleeping and Waking Metaphors:
Degrees of Metaphoricity

This chapter on sleeping and waking metaphors brings us back to the onset of the book and to the last facet of its key issue: the refutation of the dead versus alive distinction in verbal metaphors. As I have argued in the introduction, these are the two commonly distinguished categories of metaphors. It is notable that the critical evaluation of this classification has not been a central issue in metaphor theories.[1] As we can see in the complete quote from Black that I gave in the introduction, it turns out that he is not just rather critical of this classification but that he claims that dead metaphors are not metaphors at all: "For the only entrenched classification is grounded in the trite opposition (itself expressed metaphorically) between 'dead' and 'live' metaphors. This is no more helpful than, say, treating a corpse as a special case of a person: A so-called dead metaphor is not a metaphor at all ... " (Black 1993, 25).

Black's argumentative stance is representative for LMTs and is explicitly challenged by CMT with the argument that it is precisely that which is deeply entrenched that is the most active in the conceptual systems of language users. In other words, the issue of these two categories is not one of terminological purism but one that affects the very subject of metaphor theories.

Black proposes a slightly more differentiated distinction, to which we will return later in this chapter. For now, it is sufficient to bear in mind that the status of those two categories is one of the most, if not the most, controversial issue in the debate about the discrepancies between LMTs and CMTs.

6.1 The Dead versus Alive Distinction: A Critical Evaluation

How a theory of metaphor accounts for dead and live or vital metaphors defines the dividing line between LMTs and CMT. The issue under discussion is the status of dead metaphors. Linguistic accounts of metaphor tend to assume that a critical feature of metaphor is what has generally been termed the "vitality of a metaphor."[2] Thus, for contemporary speakers of German, "Kummer" (sorrow or grief) is a dead metaphor because its historical roots in the Indo-Germanic root *bher (carry) and Gallo-Latin comboros (what is collected), which resulted in the Middle High German kumber, meaning (debris, pile of rubble), are opaque. Since 1200, kumber has been common as an expression for carrying an emotional load ("eine seelische Last tragen"), and similar expressions are observed in Old French and Old Provençal.[3] In contrast, expressions like "die Tänzerin" (the dancer) in "Du bist die Tänzerin im Sturm" (you are the dancer in the storm; cf. chapter 2) are regarded as vital metaphors.

At first sight, this looks very much like a straightforward distinction, but a closer look reveals that the notion of vitality incorporates two or maybe three different properties of metaphor: conventionalization, conscious awareness, and transparency. LMTs assume that all dead metaphors lack vitality, and they make no distinction between dead metaphors that are opaque and those that are transparent. Hence, conventionalized metaphorical expressions, such as "gebrochenes Herz" (broken heart), are regarded to be as equally dead as expressions such as "Kummer" (sorrow). The foremost reason why they are considered to be dead is an aspect of vitality that is for the most part not explicitly addressed: awareness of metaphoricity. Opaque as well as transparent "dead" metaphors are supposed to lack awareness of metaphoricity. Usually, this psychological criterion is not recognized as an individual criterion but rather as a collective one, and we find characterizations of this aspect of metaphors that go right back to the beginning of historical linguistics. Take as an example a quote from one of the earliest monographic treatments of metaphor by Friedrich Brinkmann: "We will have the opportunity later to talk about the uninterrupted process whereby metaphors become hackneyed during the lifetime of a language as they lose more and more of their original colour and fade, and many of which completely die as pictures and degenerate into stark verbal sounds that immediately call to mind the designated thing without reminding us in the slightest of the picture" (Brinkmann 1878, 17). The conventionalization of metaphors is supposed to lead automatically and instantaneously to a loss of transparency and of awareness of metaphoricity.[4] As a consequence, all conventional metaphors are regarded as dead, and since they are dead, LMTs tend not to address them, at least not systematically.

To put it another way, both kinds of conventionalized metaphors are regarded as dead because it is supposed that they are not used metaphorically.

Consider once again Black: "A so-called dead metaphor is not a metaphor at all, but merely an expression that no longer has a pregnant metaphorical use. A competent reader is not expected to recognize such a familiar expression as 'falling in love' as a metaphor, to be taken *au grand sérieux*. Indeed it is doubtful whether that expression was ever more than a case of catachresis (using an idiom to fill a gap in the lexicon)" (Black 1993, 25). It seems clear that novel metaphors are most likely to have this pregnant metaphorical use and are consciously used as linguistic expressions with an activated metaphoricity. There is also little doubt that the frequent use of a verbal metaphor leads to some kind of loss in the vividness of its metaphoricity. Yet, what exactly vividness is for LMTs is not a self-evident issue. Intuitively, the distinction between novel metaphors ("du bist die Tänzerin im Sturm" [you are the dancer in the storm]) and conventionalized ones ("gebrochenes Herz" [broken heart]) is clear. While making sense of the first example implies that metaphoricity is newly created, in the case of the second example, this is not necessary because metaphoricity is already conventionally established.

In the quote above, Black characterizes vitality as "pregnant metaphorical use," which does not add much precision. He does not explicate what it means for a speaker "to recognize . . . a familiar expression . . . as a metaphor" (Black 1993, 25). Yet it seems that recognizing a metaphor as a metaphor implies the conscious awareness or at least the consciousness of metaphoricity. The way in which Black characterizes the dead versus alive distinction is representative of metaphor theories in general. We shall therefore now consider it in more detail.

It is significant that Black bases his distinction both on the collective level of common usage within a language community ("an expression that no longer has a pregnant metaphorical use") and on the individual process of comprehending metaphor ("a competent reader is not expected to recognize"). In other words, in one sentence he moves from the collective level of usage to the individual level of "a competent reader." With the next argumentative step, he shifts back to the collective level (the linguistic system) by speculating "whether that expression was ever more than a case of catachresis (using an idiom to fill a gap in the lexicon)." This back and forth between the individual and the collective level of language is a characteristic trait that, to my knowledge, crosscuts all accounts that have sought to categorize metaphors along the lines of vitality. I believe that this problem is rooted in the notion of vitality (Lebendigkeit); vitality typically relates to the process of the comprehension of metaphor, and comprehending metaphor is first of all an individual process. This holds true even if we assume an idealized reader of some fictive literary text; recognizing and comprehending metaphor remains an individual cognitive process, not a property of any kind of collective system. As Black says, a metaphor is vital only if it is perceived as a metaphor; once this perception is gone, it ceases to be vital and slowly dies.

To account for the reasons for its slow death (its loss of vitality), it is again necessary to shift back to the collective level: the dying of metaphors is caused by processes of conventionalization, of frequent and common usage. But, to complete the argument, a further shift back to the individual level is necessary because it is only on the individual level of metaphor recognition that we can decide whether formerly vital metaphors that underwent this process of conventionalization, and presumably are stored in the warehouse of the lexicon as "literal entries," are indeed no longer perceived as metaphors. These kinds of argumentative shifts between the collective and the individual level characterize most existing accounts of this dichotomic categorization, and I shall propose an alternative conceptualization later in this section. To do this, we need to take a further look at the parameters under discussion.

Two parameters are of critical importance in how linguistic and conceptual metaphor theories conceive of "dead" verbal metaphors: vitality of metaphoricity and conventionalization. LMTs assume that the category of dead metaphors is to be excluded from a theory of metaphor because those conventionalized metaphoric expressions are no longer perceived as metaphors. Conceptual metaphor theory takes the opposite approach: because so-called dead metaphors are highly entrenched and conventionalized, they are an active and influential means of conceptualization.[5] See Kövecses in his critique of the so-called dead metaphor account: "The 'dead metaphor' account misses an important point; namely, that what is deeply entrenched, hardly noticed, and thus effortlessly used is most active in our thought. The metaphors above may be highly conventional and effortlessly used, but this does not mean that they have lost their vigor in thought and that they are dead. On the contrary, they are 'alive' in the most important sense—they govern our thought—they are "metaphors we live by" (Kövecses 2002, ix). Kövecses addresses exactly the type of metaphors that Black characterizes as dead. Hence, the controversy is about familiar phraseological expressions, such as *"falling* in love," *"driving* someone crazy," *"bursting* with joy," "being deeply *moved,"* and *"burning* to do something," but it is also about lexemes that are used metaphorically, such as "He *went* crazy," "She is *hungry* for knowledge," "The jacket I saw in the shop window *pulled* me into the store," and "Time *flies"* (Black 1993, 25; Kövecses 2002, 20–22). These expressions are supposed to be highly active as metaphors because they are instantiations of active conceptual metaphors and highly entrenched (Lakoff 1993, 245). This understanding of conventional metaphors goes hand in hand with the assumption that metaphor is pervasive in everyday language and not just a specific feature of poetic uses of language. Clearly, regarding the status of dead metaphors, the dividing line between the LMTs and CMT is deep—if not mutually exclusive. It appears to be as if both define their object of interest in a mutually exclusive way. While LMTs mostly disregard dead metaphors, CMT considers them to be their main field of interest (because they provide evidence for the existence of conceptual metaphors and because what is highly entrenched is highly influential). But there is more to this dichotomy than that: not only do both views attribute a categorically different status to the group of dead metaphors, but LMTs also do not want to consider dead metaphors as an interesting or important phenomenon in any way whatsoever, which is why they do not subclassify them further. For LMTs, the category "dead metaphors" merely serves to exclude a group of phenomena that they do not address. Accordingly, no attention is paid to the difference between opaque and transparent dead metaphors, a distinction that is well established in phraseology and historical linguistics (cf. Burger, Buhofer, and Sialm 1982; Burger 1996, 1998, 1999, 2004; Häcki-Buhofer 2003; Häcki-Buhofer and Burger 1992, 1994; Röhrich and Mieder 1977; Paul 1937; and Ullmann 1967) and that roughly parallels what Lakoff and Turner (1989) have called "historical and conventional" metaphors: "One reason that some theorists have not come to grips with the fact that ordinary everyday language is inescapably metaphoric is that they hold the belief that all metaphors that are conventional are 'dead'—they are not metaphors any longer, though they once might have been. This position, which fails to distinguish between conventional metaphors, which are part of our live conceptual system, and historical metaphors that have long since died out, constitutes the Dead Metaphor Theory" (Lakoff and Turner 1989, 129). Thus, whereas "Kummer" (grief, sorrow) is an opaque metaphor for contemporary speakers of German, "gebrochenes Herz" (broken heart) is a transparent metaphor, despite the fact that it is a conventionalized expression. As we have seen above, transparent metaphors that are conventionalized may be activated, for example, when they are accompanied by an image that depicts their source domain, in this case, a broken heart.

Because transparent as well as opaque metaphors that are conventionalized are supposed to be used without any consciousness of metaphoricity, LMTs consider them to be dead, if they consider them to be metaphors at all—as Black (see the quote in the first paragraph of this chapter) believes.

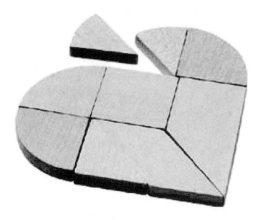

Fig. 40. Broken heart puzzle. Activated metaphoricity in a transparent and
conventionalized metaphor.

This view appears restrictive, at least if one is to account for metaphor
in all its facets and not only as a poetic device. Moreover, we have seen in
this book that conventionalized metaphors may also become poetic ones.[6]
The dynamic view proposed in this book does not allow for this kind of pre
hoc exclusion; it demands that the possible forms of consciousness of all
kinds of metaphors be examined neutrally. Therefore, I propose to follow the
distinctions established by Lakoff and Turner, as well as in phraseology and
historical linguistics, and further divide the group of dead metaphors into
those that are dead and opaque and those that are conventional and transparent. Conceptual metaphor theory bases the distinction between historical
and conventional metaphors explicitly on different forms of consciousness
and implicitly on their transparency. Historical metaphors are not conscious
and therefore dead; they cannot become conscious because they are opaque
(etymologists would exclude themselves from this judgment). In contrast,
conventional metaphors are transparent and dead but are perceived unconsciously. It should be noted, however, that the distinction between the not-
conscious and the unconscious perception of metaphors is fundamental for
CMT and brings in, once more, the notion of entrenchment, a rather important concept in cognitive linguistics. Conceptual metaphor theory regards
conventional metaphors as deeply entrenched metaphors. Since they are
grounded in highly active conceptual metaphors, they are an unconscious
but highly potent means of organizing thought and experience. Lakoff and

Turner (1989) put forward a radically different theory of what has pervasively been regarded as a core-defining feature of metaphor, namely, its
consciousness of metaphoricity (which is one important facet of its vitality). Instead of considering those metaphors that are consciously used as the
prototypical cases, the metaphors that are unconsciously used are regarded
as prototypical cases, as the most potent ones, the ones that tacitly guide the
language user's conceptualization of experience, that lead his or her inference and structure his or her activities. They are instantiations of a system
of conventional conceptual metaphors that is comparable to the system of
phonological and grammatical rules: "The system of conventional conceptual metaphor is mostly *unconscious, automatic,* and used with no noticeable effort, just like our linguistic system and the rest of our conceptual system. Our system of conventional metaphor is 'alive' in the same sense that
our system of grammatical and phonological rules is alive; namely, it is constantly in use, automatically, and *below the level of consciousness*" (Lakoff
1993, 245; emphases CM).This quote documents nicely that Lakoff has developed a radically different notion of the "aliveness" of metaphor, which is
based on a different understanding of the role that conscious, unconscious,
and nonconscious processes play in the structuring of human conceptualization, perception, and experience. I shall return to this point in more detail
later.

Less controversy exists regarding the status of vital or live metaphors.
They are the poetic and creative ones that constitute the primary field of
interest in LMTs; CMT considers them to be a specific, creative way of re-
alizing a conceptual metaphor, but they are supposed to be as much alive
as their conventional companions because they are similarly grounded in
active and vital conceptual metaphors. They are considered to be noncon-
ventional, transparent, and consciously used metaphors.

Distinctive criteria of the dead versus alive distinction are summa-
rized in table 2. The table documents that the dead versus alive dichotomy
is based on the criteria of language use and vitality. The notion of vitality
incorporates the criteria of conventionalization, consciousness, and transparency. Vitality figures as a general criterion governing the distinction
between dead and alive. Conventionalization distinguishes novel from conventionalized metaphors. Consciousness distinguishes not-conscious (dead)
from conscious (live/vital) metaphors in LMTs; but in CMT it distinguishes
between not-conscious (historical and dead), unconscious (conventionalized, entrenched and live), and conscious (novel and live) metaphors. Transparency distinguishes two kinds of conventionalized metaphors in CMT:
opaque (historical and dead) and transparent (entrenched and live) ones; the

Table 2. Distinctive criteria of the dead versus alive metaphor classification in linguistic metaphor theories (LMTs) and conceptual metaphor theory (CMT)

	Examples		
	Kummer (sorrow/grief)	*Gebrochenes Herz* (broken heart)	*Du bist die Tänzerin im Sturm, du bist ein Kind auf dünnem Eis* (you are a dancer in the storm, you are a child on thin ice)
Language use:			
LMT	Ordinary language	Ordinary language	Poetic language
CMT	Ordinary language	Ordinary language	Poetic language
Vitality:			
LMT	Dead	Dead	Alive/vital
CMT	Dead	Alive	Alive
Conventionalization:			
LMT	Conventionalized	Conventionalized	Novel
CMT	Conventionalized (historical)	Conventionalized (entrenched)	Novel
Consciousness:			
LMT	Not conscious	Not conscious	Conscious
CMT	Not conscious (historical)	Unconscious (entrenched)	Conscious
Transparency:			
LMT			
CMT	Opaque (historical)	Transparent (entrenched)	Transparent

transparency of novel metaphors is self-evident, and presumably for this reason it does not receive further attention. And in LMTs, transparency is apparently not a guiding criterion in this dead versus alive classification.[7]

Finally, the distinction between dead and vital metaphors appears to be historically motivated by the interest of rhetoric in investigating the poetic and artful forms of language usage; and it is this specific historical focus that presumably stimulated LMTs to concentrate on the right-hand side of the listed categories, that is, on those verbal metaphors that are alive, transparent, conscious, and novel creations in poetic language. Those are the ones that are a specific feature of poetic language, and, therefore, interest in these forms of language use appears to have fueled a historical motivation for the long-standing, twofold classification of metaphors into dead or alive.

The controversial category is the gray one: the question of whether conventional metaphors are dead or alive, of whether they are not conscious or unconscious, is at the core of the controversy about linguistic and conceptual metaphor theories. Furthermore, the criterion under discussion concerns the kind of consciousness attributed to conventional metaphors and entails implications regarding cognition or processes of conceptualization: are conventional metaphors the most or the least potent ones? Are they processed as metaphors or as literal expressions? Are they instances of conceptual metaphors or just extinct metaphors stored in the mental lexicon as literal expressions?[8]

Psycholinguistic research has been able to answer at least some of the above questions, providing ample support for the view that metaphor processing is just as effortless as literal language processing, a view that challenges some linguistic and philosophical assumptions (cf. Gibbs 1994; Katz 1998).[9] Gibbs, one of the main protagonists in this psychological enterprise, summarizes these findings as follows:

> Despite my conclusion that literal meanings are not well defined, it was important to consider whether figurative language requires special cognitive processes in order to be understood. The evidence on this question is overwhelming: Similar cognitive mechanisms drive our understanding of both literal and figurative speech. This does not mean that figurative language is always understood in exactly the same way as nonfigurative language or that all types of figurative language are processed similarly. There may be many occasions when we encounter figurative discourse, especially in reading literary texts, that require additional mental effort to be understood. But the experimental evidence shows that people need not recognize figurative utterances as violating communicative norms or maxims in order to understand what these expressions figuratively mean. (Gibbs 1994, 435)

Gibbs furthermore holds that figurative language processing implies access to conceptual metaphors—at least in cases where the metaphoric expressions are not novel, ad hoc creations (1994, 262). This conceptual structure view has been challenged by Glucksberg (2001) and Keysar et al. (2000), who argue for a single level of verbal metaphor processing.

Note that one inherent problem of the controversy in research and theory is the lack of terminological rigor. Given that vitality is used as a distinctive criterion in the evaluation of whether a metaphor is dead or alive, and given that the notion of vitality as such is not discussed, the discussion cannot be carried out on an adequate level. I have shown that the notion of vitality implies the notions of consciousness, conventionalization, and transparency; yet because they are only implied, they do not receive much explicit attention. An exception is probably the criterion of conventionalization, which tends to be more explicitly addressed in this controversy. LMTs assume it to cause loss of consciousness and transparency. Hence, LMTs assume that conventionalization leads to a loss in the perception of metaphors as metaphors. But is it true that loss of metaphoricity is a necessary and inevitable property of conventionalization? Yes and no, I would suggest. Yes, because as testified by processes of language change it may happen, and indeed it is often the case, that a metaphor loses metaphoricity at some point in its "life." But I would like to counter here that this is only one ultimate fate of a conventionalized metaphorical expression. And this fate necessarily goes hand in hand with the loss of transparency. A second possible fate is that it may survive as a transparent and conventionalized metaphor. This is a facet of the process that to my knowledge largely escapes LMTs.

Conceptual metaphor theory holds the opposing view, namely, that conventionalization is a testimony of pervasive usages and of common forms of conceptualization, leading to entrenchment and hence to an unconscious but highly influential "life" of verbal metaphors.

One of the positive consequences of the controversy regarding the status of dead and transparent (in LMT terms) or entrenched (in CMT terms) metaphors is that this third category of metaphors has become an issue in theories of and research on metaphor at all. It is astonishing that this phenomenon has so far received comparably little attention from linguistics proper. Traditional introductory works on the study of semantics tend not to devote an entire chapter to it (cf. for instance Lyons 1977; Ullman 1967). As already mentioned, conventionalized metaphors have typically been regarded as an important feature of language change, of the processes of lexicalization and grammaticalization, as well as a major topic in phraseology. It is to Lakoff and Johnson's credit that this recognizably pervasive feature of human language has become a major focus in the research of metaphor.

Unfortunately, a critical reflection on the criteria underlying the dead versus alive distinction is lacking. This is unfortunate because a discussion of these issues is a prerequisite for sorting out some of the controversial issues, or at least to clarifying some of the background assumptions, that stimulate the differing foci of interest in linguistic and conceptual metaphor theories. A critical discussion of these underlying criteria would reveal that they suffer from being incompatibly mixed. Once again, the distinction between the collective level of the linguistic system and the individual level of use is not made, and this creates terminological and notional difficulties. Specifying the criterion "consciousness of metaphoricity" is crucial. Consciousness of metaphoricity is only detectable on the individual level of a speaker or listener, of a writer or reader. Conventionalization and transparency are criteria that both apply to the level of a linguistic system. For conventionalization, this is self-evident, but not for transparency. Yet I think that transparency can and must be defined on the level of the linguistic system, and there is an easy and straightforward possibility that accounts for it: if a conventionalized metaphoric expression has a "literal" companion in the lexicon of a language, then it is transparent. Hence, metaphors such as "gebrochenes Herz" (broken heart), "kochen vor Wut" (boiling with rage), or "Tischbein" ("leg of a table") are transparent not because I as a writer conceive of them as transparent but because they have a literal companion that is still a part of the lexicon of the language. In the following section, I shall return to this distinction in more detail because it will be exploited as a rational criterion for a more straightforward and rather elegant way of classifying verbal metaphors.

6.2 The Dead and Alive Assumption: A New Proposal

The new proposal for the classification of verbal metaphors elaborates on the threefold classifications that are common in phraseology and historical linguistics. Especially in historical analyses of language (cf. for instance Brinkmann 1878; Closs-Traugott 1985), this distinction is fairly well established, but not so much in metaphor theories.[10]

In section 6.1, we saw that Lakoff and Turner (1989) propose such a threefold categorization (historical, entrenched, and novel), which is most likely informed by Black's (1993; first published in 1979) distinction among extinct, dormant, and active metaphors, which is based on their "actuality." Note that his notion of actuality is static and binary in that it refers to fixed properties of a lexical item and not to its use. In other words, an expression is either active *or* dormant *or* extinct; it cannot be dormant in one context and active in another one. However, Black is convinced that "not much is to be expected of this schema or any more finely tuned substitute" (Black 1993, 25). Accordingly, he focuses his reflections on the category that has traditionally attracted the interest of scholars of metaphor: "I shall be concerned hereafter only with metaphors needing no artificial respiration, recognized by speaker and hearer as authentically 'vital' or 'active'" (Black 1993, 25). However, talking of "artificial respiration" suggests that Black was aware of the possibility of revitalizing a sleeping metaphor (again revitalization is a notion which is well-known in phraseology and in historical studies of language) but that he simply did not consider it to be an interesting aspect of metaphor.

Suggesting that metaphors may be revitalized indicates that the dead versus alive distinction is not tenable, at least not insofar as one systematically takes into consideration metaphors in use. As I have pointed out in chapter 1, Romantic philosophers and poets were very aware of the potential vitality of ordinary everyday metaphors. But this property of conventionalized verbal metaphors did not really influence theories of metaphor until Lakoff and Johnson's proposal of a CMT, with the notable shortcoming that Lakoff and Johnson do not devote much energy to the analysis of the verbal level of conventionalized metaphors. But they do make the point that these seemingly dead metaphors display active metaphorical conceptualizations and hence are not dead at all.

Recently, more and more scholars of metaphor have come to devote their energy to this dynamic aspect of verbal metaphors, among them Sakis Kyratzis (2003), who puts forward the quite radical proposal to give up on these classifications altogether and to conceive of the notion of (verbal) metaphor as a single dynamic category.[11] Yet, within this category, he continues to use a variant of Black's and of Lakoff and Turner's distinction, which he terms "frozen and fresh" instead of "dormant and active" (Black) or "entrenched and novel" (Lakoff and Turner). Kyratzis's argumentation is highly interesting, not only because it once again underlines the shortcomings of the bipolar classification into dead and alive metaphors, but also because he bases his argument on empirical analyses of metaphor usage in discourse. This is important, because, as I have repeatedly pointed out, consciousness of metaphoricity is a property of the processing of metaphors, that is, a property of the individual mind. As such, it needs to be related to individual minds. It simply cannot be a feature of a lexical item per se. Consciousness of metaphoricity is first and foremost a matter of individual speakers and hearers. Traditionally, what has been done is to assume an idealized speaker or hearer (which in most cases was identical to the

personal intuition of the respective scholar) and to simply hypothesize that
this verbal metaphor was conceived consciously, whereas another one was
not. In the era of corpus linguistics, of discourse analysis, and of experimental psycholinguistics, it is clear that this cannot be considered to be a
valid scientific foundation for a theory. If we use a criterion that intrinsi-
cally relates to individual processes of metaphor understanding (production
and comprehension), then we need to investigate how individual speakers
process metaphors.

Looking at how people use metaphor very readily uncovers that the
twofold distinction does not hold and, even more so, that the static notion
of metaphor that attributes either metaphoricity or literality to a lexical
item is not supported empirically. Rather, it appears that lexical items may
show different forms of metaphoricity and that they may be more or less
active during language production.[12] Kyratzis's research supports this view.
Building upon empirical work by Stibbe (1996), he shows that metaphors in
context "can become more metaphorically active in certain contexts, i.e.,
become deautomatized" (Kyratzis 2003). Stibbe and Kyratzis have identified an interesting range of verbal strategies that function as what I shall
term "activation indicators" (in Stibbe's terms, "metaphorical activation";
in Kyratzis's terms, "deautomatization"; and in traditional terms, "revitalization"). Goatly's (1997) work offers a similar view, although he constantly
refers to the "revitalization" of inactive metaphors. I prefer to avoid this
term because it presupposes that conventionalized metaphors are characterized by nonvitality or, in Goatly's terms, "inactivity." In spite of the
very broad range of facets he touches upon and his basically similar stance
toward the dead-alive distinction, I consider his conflation of the systems
and the use perspective in his analysis to be problematic. Goatly (1997) proposes similar activation devices. Among them are repetition, diversification,
modification, extension, mixing, compounding of metaphors, literalization
of vehicles, and overdescription. The point is that metaphoricity may be
more or less active in a given verbal metaphor and that these degrees of
metaphoricity depend upon specific verbal contexts as well as on specific
forms of use. They function as verbal activation devices of metaphoricity.
Kyratzis gives the following list of verbal activation devices:

> *Adverbial modification*: When adverbs such as *actually, really, truly,
> literally* are used in conjunction with a metaphor "the source domain
> is made more salient and the expression more metaphorically active"
> (Stibbe 1996, 72): "... the State will introduce laws that will literally
> squeeze the juice out of the working people."

Repetition: Repeating metaphorical expressions may activate metaphoricity: "It's *fighting* the disease and *fighting* in your bones . . ." (Stibbe 1996, 72; Kyratzis 2003).

Change of word class: In the case of the lexeme 'combat,' the use of it as a verb appears to be frequent, and compared with the relatively infrequent use of "combat" as a noun, its metaphoricity seems less active in the verb than in the noun. Stibbe (1996, 73) gives the following examples: "the white cells are the things which you need to combat infection . . ." and " . . . the white cells are the things which go into combat against the infection . . ."

Explicit mappings: These are a kind of elaboration on the source domain of a metaphor (Stibbe 1996). Kyratzis (2003) gives the following example: " . . . of the State, a well-known dynast, who asks everything for himself, demands everything from the Greeks, and offers scantily."

Composing: Kyratzis distinguishes two different ways of composing: one is the clustering of metaphors from the same source domain, and the other is a metaphorical-literal juxtaposition. Here are the examples:

1. Clustering of source domain expressions: "Mr. President, ladies and gentlemen Members of Parliament, I am certain that tonight's discussion unites the Greek people against a new common enemy, namely the dangerous invasion of drugs in the Greek society, an enemy that threatens today every advanced society and one that no society has managed to defeat no matter how many weapons it has used."
2. Metaphorical-literal juxtaposition as in "Education, along with our army, is our national defense."

Elaborating: New or formerly backgrounded aspects of the metaphor are foregrounded. Consider the following example: "And there are quite a few University lecturers who, if they were free to speak or, when they do speak freely, if their voice could be heard everywhere, they would tell us that they have become beggars in the corridors of the European Community. Beggars. They are looking to see through which window they can get some funding not for research that our country needs, but for research that others need, companies and individuals, and maybe there will be something left to patch up the holes of public Education, which in this way ceases to be public."

Accumulation: The elaboration of a source metaphor on the text level, from talking about drug policies to talking about a declaration of war.

The fact that verbal metaphors may be activated in the ways described by Stibbe and Kyratzis clearly supports the view that metaphoricity is a dynamic not a static property of a lexical item. The activation of a verbal metaphor critically depends on its context. It is only within and with respect to a certain context that we can not only decide whether a given expression is a metaphor or not (does the sentence "Thomas ist ein Kind" [Thomas is a child] refer to an adult or a child?) but also to what degree metaphoricity is activated. Notice that speaking of the activation of metaphoricity implies what has formerly been termed the "consciousness" of metaphor. The old criterion for distinguishing between dead and live metaphors returns in the form of the "actuality" and "activation" of metaphoricity. Kyratzis notes that the activation of metaphoricity is a matter concerning the individual speaker: "Moreover I believe that the choice of the word literally by the speaker to do that reveals that (a) the speaker is *aware* that the expression is a metaphor, (b) she is also aware of the fact that it is a *conventional* metaphor, and (c) in order to make her point stronger by exploiting the metaphor, she feels that she has to expose the expression's (long forgotten) metaphoricity with the aid of a word such as *literally*" (Kyratzis 2003; emphases in the original). In spite of seeing that the activation of metaphoricity is an individual matter, Kyratzis continues to think collectively. The way in which he speculates about the "(long forgotten) metaphoricity" of an expression indicates that he takes the speaker's intuition about something as a measure of the average or commonly attributed degree of metaphoricity in a specific expression. Because this expression is conventional, it is commonly "frozen" and needs deautomatization to become more active. It is in this line of thinking that he proposes a dynamic notion of metaphor. The dynamics of metaphor are not equated with the activation of metaphoricity in one and the same verbal metaphor produced by a given speaker in a given context but with the dynamics of a category of metaphorical expressions; and within this category different members show varying degrees of metaphoricity, that is, they are more or less frozen. Here Kyratzis applies the concept of radial categories from prototype theory to metaphors. Unfortunately, he does not give an example of such a category on the verbal level. Instead, we are confronted with examples of conceptual metaphors (TIME IS A MOVING OBJECT, TIME IS MONEY, and TIME IS A THIEF). Throughout his article, the relation between verbal and conceptual metaphors is not clear, and while he speaks most of the time about verbal metaphors (most of his examples are verbal

Table 3. Distinctive criteria of threefold classifications of verbal metaphors: vitality, degrees of metaphoricity, and conventionalization (transparency implied)

	Examples		
	Kummer (sorrow/grief)	*Gebrochenes Herz* (broken heart)	*Du bist die Tänzerin im Sturm, du bist ein Kind auf dünnem Eis* (you are a dancer in the storm, you are a child on thin ice)
Black (vitality) Lakoff and Turner (conventionalization and transparency)	Extinct Historical	Dormant Conventional entrenched	Active Novel
Kyratzis (degrees of metaphoricity)	(Dead?)	→More or less frozen→	→More or less fresh→

metaphors), conceptual metaphors are sometimes mentioned and treated as if they were treatable on the same level of analysis. This lack of distinction is particularly unfortunate because empirical observations suggest a view of the dynamics of verbal metaphor that is extremely important but that seems to go unnoticed, because of the ultimate orientation toward the collective level of a system of conceptual metaphors.

In sum, Kyratzis's dynamic notion of metaphor also appears to concern at least a reconceptualization of the categories of frozen and fresh verbal metaphors in terms of one graded category. In this sense, metaphors are not either frozen or fresh, either dead or alive, but more or less frozen and more or less alive. Table 3 below shows how the existing threefold classifications relate to each other and shows that they are based on three different criteria. Black's distinction is based on vitality, Lakoff and Turner's is based on conventionalization and transparency, and Kyratzis's is based on the degree of metaphoricity.

Kyratzis's classification is inspired by Black's, Closs-Traugott's (1985), and Mooij's (1976) parameters of metaphoricity. These parameters function as measures for establishing the degrees of metaphoricity that different metaphors may have, and they explicate what metaphoricity is conceived to be. Kyratzis proposes four parameters: conventionalization, basicness, conceptualization, and reference. Again, these parameters shift between the linguistic and the conceptual level of metaphors: basicness and conceptualization refer to indispensability in and a restructuring of the conceptual system, whereby reference covers the link to a "literal equivalent" and conventionalization captures processes on the verbal and conceptual levels. Kyratzis contrasts this notion of metaphoricity with the one that is based on the perception of metaphoricity (which we have encountered in Black's approach): "In the theory of metaphor so far, metaphors were categorised into dead, conventional, and vital according to their level of metaphoric activity, that is, according to whether their metaphorical mappings were still perceived as such. This was taken to be the metaphoricity of each metaphor. Within the framework I am proposing, where no such boundaries exist and where metaphors perform functions in discourse, metaphoricity can no longer be seen as such a simple notion" (Kyratzis 2003, 4).

I agree with Kyratzis's analysis here, and I think the perception of metaphoricity is indeed neither a simple nor a dispensable facet of verbal metaphors. It just needs to be accounted for in the right locus of a category and a theory of metaphor. As I have argued in the preceding section, the perception of metaphoricity relates to the concept of consciousness of metaphoricity, and this in turn points to the factor of the individual processing of metaphoricity as a distinctive criterion for evaluating metaphors. Eventually, also in Kyratzis's proposal, it tacitly enters arguments where it is converted, for instance, into a variant of Mooij's (1976) and Closs-Traugott's (1985) reference parameter. Closs-Traugott herself quite explicitly relates the reference parameter to the individual level of perceiving metaphoricity. She says, "The parameter of reference. Here the consideration is how strongly an expression *is felt to be* metaphorical, that is, how strongly a metaphorical expression is linked to its literal extension; for example, *block of ice* in *Mary is a block of ice* has a strong reference to its literal extension, whereas *before* in *Mary left before Jane* does not, and indeed *most people do not think of it* as a spatial term; in other words, *block of ice* has a high reference value, while *before* has a low reference value" (Closs-Traugott 1985, 22; my emphases).

On the other hand, the parameter is also for Closs-Traugott a parameter that distinguishes lexemes on the collective level of the linguistic system. The opposition between "block of ice" and "before" is an opposition that is supposed to be psychologically real (with respect to people's feelings about metaphoricity), but the psychological reality merely serves to testify to and mirror the structures of the linguistic system. This is methodologically highly problematic. If we were to use the mental processing of metaphoricity as a well-grounded argument for a linguistic account of metaphors (be they verbal or conceptual), then we would need to either base our theories on corpus-linguistic analyses of metaphors in discourse, or on experimental studies of metaphor processing covering a representative sample of subjects, or on qualitative studies that reconstruct in detail the metaphoricity of lexical units based on verbal, pictorial, and gestural indicators of metaphoricity. The latter is the strategy that I have adopted in this book. To make a long story short, the perception of metaphoricity continues to play, albeit implicitly, an important role in accounting for metaphoricity and for degrees of metaphoricity.

Kyratzis conflates in a characteristic manner four facets of verbal metaphors: the verbal and the conceptual level and the individual and the collective level. He inherits this mixture from CMT and from historical linguists (such as Closs-Traugott) who employ a notion of reference that is implicitly based on the cognitive processes that determine the degrees of availability pertaining to the literal counterparts of metaphoric expressions.

I propose a relatively simple and straightforward way out of this confusion, namely, two categories of verbal metaphors: one that characterizes the forms of verbal metaphors with regard to the linguistic system, that is, the lexicon of a given language, and another that accounts for verbal metaphors with regard to their use. The first one addresses the collective level, and the second one addresses the individual level of verbal metaphors. How these relate to conceptual metaphors is another question, which needs to be modeled. How conceptual metaphors may be categorized is a different issue, which needs separate investigation. It would raise questions such as, can a conceptual metaphor newly arise in one individual, and if yes (as is suggested to be the case in primary metaphors), how are these individual conceptual metaphors related to the collective ones and how are they related to language as a collective system?

Hence, I am not proposing a new all-encompassing dynamic category of metaphor, but a dynamic classification of verbal metaphors (how this might relate to conceptual metaphors as systems of entrenched mappings is another topic, which for the time being must await more detailed consideration). This classification entails the definition of one dynamic category that covers a spectrum ranging from sleeping to waking metaphors. It is based on the activation of metaphoricity (the establishment of a triadic structure) in a given speaker/listener or writer/reader at a given moment in time. In sleeping metaphors, the activation of metaphoricity is low; in waking metaphors, it is high. This proposal follows a line of thought similar to Lynne Cameron's (1999b, 2007) in respect to her distinction between linguistic and process metaphors and to Steen's (1994) in respect of his concept of linguistic metaphors:

> *Process metaphors:* linguistic expressions that are processed metaphorically by language users; empirical phenomena that would be evidenced by neurological activity in a discourse participant on a particular occasion;

> *Linguistic metaphors:* linguistic expressions with the potential to be interpreted metaphorically; lexical and textual phenomena evidenced by discourse data and through logical argument, and that may or may not be processed metaphorically by language users. (Cameron 1999b, 108)

These proposals differ from the dynamic category suggested here in that they do not terminologically distinguish between forms of metaphors on the level of the linguistic system and those on the level of use. This holds, as far as I can see also for Steen's (2007b) work, despite the fact that he strongly argues for such a systematic distinction and for differentiation between approaches to symbolic structures and to behavior. I suggest that systematically introducing categories that are operational during language use distinguishes more clearly between the individual processing of metaphors (comprehension, understanding, and production) and the collective, sedimented forms of metaphor that are found in grammar, in the lexicon, and in quantitative studies of metaphor usage in large corpora. All these stances disregard individual processing and highlight collective processes of metaphor usage, that is, they focus on collective processes that lead to the conventionalization of metaphors in language.

The dynamic category ranging from sleeping to waking metaphors specifies a facet that remains implicit in Cameron's concept of process metaphor: "The category of process metaphor contains those instances of language processed analogically across distinct domains, also labelled 'psychological metaphors' . . . and 'novel metaphors'. . . . It will contain linguistic metaphors which have not only been identified as having *potential* for metaphorical processing, but which have actually *realised* this potential, by being interpreted, in real time, through an active process of analogical reasoning across two distinct concept domains" (Cameron 1999b, 109; emphases in the original).[13]

Sleeping metaphors are metaphors that are realized in an utterance or written text and have metaphoric potential (determined from the analyst's point of view); waking metaphors are metaphors whose metaphoric potential is activated online during speaking (determined from the user's point of view through activation indicators, i.e., activation is empirically observable through elaboration, specification, and a metaphoricity that crosscuts modalities). The point that I wish to make is that the category of process metaphors is actually a dynamic one—ranging from sleeping to waking metaphors.

There are no clear-cut boundaries between sleeping and waking metaphors; rather, I conceive of them as two endpoints on a scale of activated metaphoricity. Activated metaphoricity refers to the cognitive activity of establishing or using a tripartite structure or to the process of active conceptual integration. It does not matter if this construction follows established paths, as in entrenched metaphors, or if it creates a new path, a new mapping between concepts. The crucial and core point is that a tripartite structure is activated.

The concept of activated metaphoricity is consonant with constructivist views of the ad hoc construction of meaning and of dynamic concept activation (Rose 1993; Schank 1982; Barsalou 1987; see Cameron for an overview of this work 1999a, 10f). I wish to underline only two core parallels of the neurophysiological concept of activation with the dynamic concept proposed here. Cameron puts forward that the connectionist model might offer important suggestions for an applied framework of metaphor research because it suggests specific properties inherent in the activation of concepts that might import on the activation of metaphoricity:

- Activation of mental representations will *spread* through various types of motivated links (e.g. sound resemblance, exemplar memory, sensory memory, contextual information).
- Because of spreading activation, the mind can successfully process partial information.
- Gradability is inherent in the activation, because pathways can be differentially strengthened through multiple links. (Cameron 1999a, 19)

The spreading of activation through motivated links is what I think we see in multimodal metaphors. If a metaphor is expressed in speech and gesture at the same moment in time, or if a verbo-pictorial metaphor is constructed by a writer, then this is very likely based on the activation of a mental representation spreading through some of the links suggested above.

The processing of partial information is what supposedly underlies the production of mixed metaphors, as presented in chapter 5. Mixed metaphors are products of a speaker/writer's focusing on unusual aspects of meaning while suppressing the processing of common meaning elements in a given entrenched metaphoric expression.

Gradability is at the core of the dynamic view proposed in this book. Metaphors in actual instances of language use range from sleeping to waking, and this implies that they might show different degrees of metaphoricity. Verbal metaphors may be activated to different degrees—depending on the context and on an individual speaker/listener's focus of interest or background knowledge. Yet their activation does not automatically follow the logic of novelty or entrenchment. Both entrenched and novel metaphors may show varying degrees of activated metaphoricity. This means that the degree of metaphoricity is not a fixed property of a specific metaphoric expression (as suggested by Kyratzis) but a flexible, dynamic category that applies to all transparent verbal metaphors—because one and the same metaphoric expression can be more or less activated depending on its context of use, that is, it can be sleeping in one context and waking in another. In one context, metaphoricity may be slightly activated; in another context, it may be highly active and become an object of focused attention or even of metalinguistic awareness.

Note that I relate the notion of activation to the amount of activation indicators, not to consciousness. Consciousness is an extremely difficult issue, and we can perhaps only assess it empirically via indirect indications. Therefore, I prefer to ground this distinction in empirically observable indicators, be they verbal, gestural, or pictorial. Sleeping metaphors are singular uses of a verbal metaphor that are not elaborated by verbal, gestural, or pictorial means. Put differently, a sleeping metaphor is a metaphor whose metaphoricity is potentially available to an average speaker/listener, writer/reader because it is transparent, but there are no empirical indications of activated metaphoricity. Hence it relates to Cameron's concept of linguistic metaphors, but it differs in that I suggest that the metaphorical potential is not only available for the analyst but also given for the speaker (transparency guarantees this potential). In contrast, waking metaphors are surrounded by metaphoricity indicators, such as verbal elaboration, specification, semantic opposition, syntactic integration, or coexpressions of metaphor in a cooccurring modality such as gesture or pictures. And the more metaphoricity indicators surround such a metaphor, the more it is waking.

Metaphoricity indicators address the notoriously difficult issue of how to empirically detect activated metaphoricity online during discourse. Cameron points out very clearly how difficult it is to identify "process

Table 4. New proposal of a dynamic category of verbal metaphors based on the degree of activated metaphoricity (perspective of language use)

		Examples
		Du bist die Tänzerin im Sturm, du bist ein Kind auf dünnem Eis (you are a dancer in the storm, you are a child on thin ice)
	Die Tänzerin im Sturm (dancer in the storm)	
	Gebrochenes Herz (broken heart)	*Gebrochenes Herz* (broken heart) and picture
Dynamic category: (Language use)	Sleeping	Waking
Criterion: Activation of metaphoricity	Low	High

metaphors" (waking metaphors) in an actual discourse event: "The identification of 'process metaphor' is clearly an empirical matter, and a very different operation from the identification of linguistic metaphor. The category is constructed anew for each individual during each discourse event, and there is a major problem in finding observable behaviours from which metaphorical processing can be reliably inferred (see, for example, Steen, 1994, on the use of Think-Aloud techniques)" (Cameron 1999b, 109).

I suggest that activation indicators are an empirical solution of this dilemma ma because they allow insights into online processes during speaking and writing. In contrast to post hoc thinking-aloud techniques, they allow us to infer some aspects of online activation through empirically observable indicators.

Waking metaphors may be conventional or novel verbal metaphors. Note that this concept of the activation of metaphoricity captures the phenomenon that has traditionally been subsumed under the terms "consciousness" or "awareness of metaphoricity" but that applies it in a fundamentally different way. Consider table 4 for an overview of the new proposal of a dynamic category of verbal metaphors.

Since I suggest that the degree of activation of metaphoricity is always context dependent and does not automatically follow from conventionalization, it cannot not function as a viable criterion for distinguishing so-called dead from so-called alive metaphors. Dead and alive metaphors are active in that their metaphoric structure may be equally more or less activated during speaking or listening, writing or reading. This also means that the approach advocated in this book does not take poetic metaphor to be the prototypical case of metaphor. Poetic metaphors, vital, novel, or creative metaphors, are in this respect just a specific variant of metaphors with a high degree of activated metaphoricity. Black lucidly opens up the path to reconceptualizing the core of a theory of metaphor: "Although I am on the side of the appreciators [of metaphors as an "omnipresent principle of language" (Richards 1936, 92); quote from Black 1993, 20;—CM], who dwell upon what Empson and Ricœur call 'vital' metaphors, I think their opponents (typically philosophers, scientists, mathematicians, and logicians) are right in asking for less 'vital' or less 'creative' metaphors to be considered. It may well be a mistaken strategy to treat profound metaphors as paradigms" (Black 1993, 21).

The dynamic view proposed in this book indicates a way out of this established dichotomy. By regarding the activation of metaphoricity as a core property of metaphor, the poetic/ordinary distinction turns into a random quality. Focusing on the level of language use and on individual processes of the cognitive activation of metaphoricity reveals that metaphoricity is not dependent upon poetic or ordinary language uses.

In order to capture the scope of the phenomenon of verbal metaphor, it appears necessary to complement this dynamic classification with a separate static classification. This static classification is located on the level of the language system, and it is based on the criteria of conventionalization and transparency.

Dead metaphors are dead because they are opaque. Their metaphoricity is no longer available to an average speaker or listener, writer or reader. It is self-evident that they are conventionalized. Often, but not always, conventionalization leads to opacity. Following Lakoff and Turner's terminology, I term these verbal metaphors "historical metaphors." In contrast to LMTs, I do not consider conventionalized metaphors that are transparent to be dead. They are not dead because they may be highly activated, which is why I prefer to use the term "entrenched" for them and why this section is entitled the Dead *and* Alive Assumption. Entrenched verbal metaphors are dead and alive at the same time. Recall, however, that transparency is not defined with regard to a specific individual speaker or listener but with regard to the parallel availability of a literal expression in the lexicon of a given language (hence my notion of transparency shows some parallels with Closs-Traugott's notion of reference parameter). Novel verbal metaphors are

Table 5. New proposal for a static classification of verbal metaphors based on the criteria of transparency and conventionalization (perspective of language system)

	Examples		
	Kummer (sorrow/grief)	*Gebrochenes Herz* (broken heart)	*Du bist die Tänzerin im Sturm, du bist ein Kind auf dünnem Eis* (you are a dancer in the storm, you are a child on thin ice)
Static categories:			
Language system	Historical	Entrenched	Novel
Criteria:			
Conventionalization	High	High	None
Transparency	None	Given	Given

transparent and not conventionalized. Table 5 gives a summary of this new proposal for a static classification of verbal metaphors.

6.3 Degrees of Metaphoricity and Salience

Kyratzis's as well as Goatly's studies have documented a fairly wide variety of verbal indicators of activated metaphoricity, yet they did not introduce a criterion or empirical indications for determining different degrees of activation. I think that, when taking into account some of the modalities in which language is embedded, such indicators quite naturally appear on stage. For spoken language, the issue is relatively clear—the spoken word is always embodied. It is part and parcel of a multimodal ensemble of gesture, posture, gaze, and facial expression. For written language, it is not as clear. However, especially in public forms of written discourse (newspapers, magazines, advertisements, and billboards), the written word is often accompanied by pictures. But how does this relate to degrees of metaphoricity, salience, and foregrounding? Here is the point I wish to make: the more instantiations of a source domain or image-offering field, the higher the degree of activation

of metaphoricity in a given speaker at a given moment in time. My methodological argument is straightforward and based on three parameters: iconicity, salience, and interaction. The more "material" is used to express metaphoricity, the more salient this metaphor is for a listener or reader—and hence
the more active it is for a speaker/writer. Verbal metaphors that inspire elaborations, specifications, and/or multimodal expressions are more salient—
and hence must have been highly activated in the producer—than metaphors
without such a semantic uptake. The rationale underlying this argument is
inspired by a fundamental insight provided by ethnomethodology and conversation analysis: coparticipants in an interaction reciprocally display what
is pertinent to them at the very moment of speaking. I therefore suggest that
a metaphoric expression that is *made* salient *by* a speaker or writer *for* a co-
participant must be somehow salient for the speaker herself too. Put another
way, what is constructed as interactively (or interpersonally) salient can be
regarded as intrapersonally salient (and such a salience implies activation
of the salient concepts in the speaker). I shall illustrate this argument with
three exemplary analyses that show that the gradability of metaphoricity is
observable on the verbal level only but that it may be significantly altered
by combining words and visual modalities, such as pictures and gestures.

6.3.1 Verbal Level Only

Take a look at the following excerpt from a local Berlin newspaper:

> Punches below the belt
> Some of the speeches delivered on Ash Wednesday really hit below
> the belt of the political opposition.
> Verbal attacks are a part of politics. That has once again been demon-
> strated over the last few days. But the Ash Wednesday speeches also
> raise the following question: where does insult actually begin?[14] (*Der
> Tagesspiegel*, March 2, 2001)

This short text characterizes the political debates of Aschermittwoch (Ash
Wednesday). Every year, on the last day of the German carnival season, the
political parties gather, each in their own camp, for a big meeting with the
foremost aim of sharply criticizing their respective political opponents. This
ritual probably goes back to the political roots of carnival in Germany. Nowadays, it is a famous ritual of German political culture, and the leaders use it
to increase their recognition within their own party. The sharper the verbal
attacks, the more fun for the audience, and the more points for the speaker.

In this short piece of text, we find three verbal metaphors that are cases of the famous ARGUMENT IS WAR conceptual metaphor identified by Lakoff and Johnson (1980): "Tiefschläge" (low punches), "unter die Gürtellinie" (below the belt), and "Redebeiträge" (speeches) and "verbale Attacken" (verbal attacks). The first two may be considered metaphoric synonyms sharing the same verbal imagery (physical fighting) and verbal-image receiver (aggressive verbal contribution); the third one, "verbal attack," may be regarded as a more general facet of physical fighting. Taken together, they support each other and foreground the source domain of "war" or, more specifically, the image-offering field of physical fighting. Why do they foreground it? Because the threefold mentioning of the same image field in a short piece of text is a form of metaphorical elaboration. This elaboration indicates that metaphoricity was activated for the writer as he was composing these lines. But a verbal metaphor can be further elaborated by combining it with a picture that instantiates the source domain. This is what we will consider in the next section.

6.3.2 Verbo-pictorial Metaphors

Take a look at figure 41, which accompanies the above lines (or vice versa). The photo shows a close-up shot of two boxers with the focus on the lower part of their trunks. The boxer on the right-hand side hits his opponent in the lower part of the abdomen. In other words, the photo provides a visual representation of the image-offering field (physical attacks) or the source domain of the verbal metaphor. Together, the three verbal metaphors and the photo are an elaboration of the same image-offering field or source domain, which points to a rather high degree of cognitive activation of metaphoricity for the image-offering and the image-receiving field or for source and target domain. Metaphors therefore display a higher degree of activation because the mapping between source and target was able to trigger a cluster of metaphorical products and because it crosscuts modalities.

This amounts to a compound structure of metaphor: word and picture merge and constitute verbo-pictorial metaphors. Both word and picture refer to the same image-offering field or source domain (physical fighting) and the same image-receiving field or target domain (verbal contributions) on the verbal level. There is no empirical evidence that these two rich image fields (source and target) are to be taken as indicators of the activated conceptual metaphor ARGUMENT IS WAR, let alone that the verbal and pictorial elaboration could be taken as an indication of active conceptual metaphors. I think that there are not enough empirical grounds for this argumentation

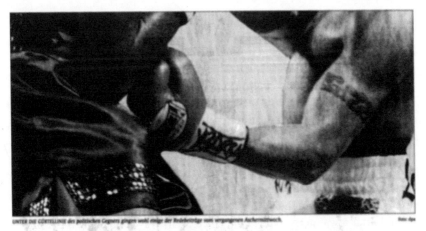

Fig. 41. "Tiefschläge" (low punches). Verbo-pictorial metaphors indicate a higher degree of metaphoricity. *Der Tagesspiegel*, March 2, 2001. Photograph by John Gerzinski/Getty Images.

because we can sufficiently account for the empirical facts without assuming a general level of active conceptual metaphor here. Therefore, it appears preferable to be more cautious here and just take these observations as an indication of the highly activated metaphoricity of a verbal level, with the picture being a part of the verbal level of metaphoricity because it directly depicts the imagery given in the verbal metaphors. The diagram in figure 42, shows the structure of the metaphoricity of this verbo-pictorial metaphor.

Having documented that the activation of metaphoricity may vary in degree while writing or composing a unit of text and image, we will now discuss the gradability of metaphoricity in spoken language and gesture.

6.3.3 Verbo-gestural Metaphors

We will begin with an intriguing case of a high degree of activated metaphoricity that is visible in words, gestures, and gaze. In the following short sequence, a woman characterizes the course of her first love relationship as a kind of relative experience with its ups and downs and with a permanent tendency downhill. Before going further into the details of this excerpt, please take a look at the drawings and the transcript (example 17):

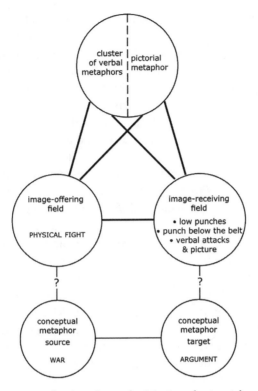

Fig. 42. Structure of activated metaphoricity in verbopictorial metaphors.

Example 17: "Auf und ab" (*up and down*)

<pre>
                                    rh Hand holding glass
                                    moves right and down
</pre>

1   JA es war eben ein relatives auf und ab [**mit der= mit
     der**
     Yes it was just a relative up and down with the= with the

2   **der ständigen tendenz bergAB** \] (.hh) [aber es ging= | |
     the permanent tendency downhill (--)   but it went

<pre>
        lh index finger drawing sinuous line reducing size
        of amplitudes and overall downward movement; gaze
        follows finger
</pre>

3   ne **es startete SO und flachte dann so (—) weiter ab**]
     right it began like this and flattened then like this
     continuosly out

Here gestures enact and specify aspects of the literal meaning of verbal metaphors: "auf und ab mit der ständigen Tendenz bergab" (up and down with a steady tendency downwards). In this metaphorical characterization of the speaker's first love relationship, speech and gesture work tightly together. To begin with, the gestures indicate that the metaphoricity of these seemingly dead metaphors is quite active.

Note, however, that when she uses the verbal metaphor "auf und ab," no gesture is produced concurrently. Instead, the speaker begins to perform gestures when she further specifies the ups and downs of her relationship: it was not just a permanent up and down, but an up and down with a permanent tendency downhill. With a glass in her hand, she performs a downward movement with her right hand, and in this way she enacts this constant downward tendency of her relationship. This manual gesture is doubled by a head movement that performs, in temporal synchrony, a similar downward movement to the right-hand side.

As she continues, she further elaborates this description. Now it is the gesture alone—with the free left hand—that draws a kind of graph with high amplitudes at the beginning and smaller amplitudes at the end, characterizing in one gesture the ideas that verbally had to be pronounced separately: the ups and downs and the permanent tendency downward. Note that in this part of the utterance, the main communicative burden lies on the gestural description.

Gesture carries the entire communicative information regarding the ups and downs and the overall downward tendency of the relationship. Verbally, she only mentions that it flattened out: "but it went, well it began like this and flattened then like this steadily downward." By using the German phoric particle "so" (like this), she syntactically integrates the gesture into the utterance and directs the attention of the listener to it. The phoric particle "so" (like this) points to the gesture, and it integrates the gesture syntactically into the ongoing utterance. Note that it is only through gesture that the nature of this relationship is once again characterized, namely, as a graph with high amplitudes at the beginning, lower amplitudes toward the end, and an overall tendency downward. Furthermore, she gesturally specifies the ups and downs in her first love relationship. She shows that at the beginning the amplitudes were larger than at the end. This adds a further aspect to her characterization of this relationship. It was not just a steady downward movement, but one that contained larger ups and downs at the beginning than at the end. In addition, these gestures are made interactively meaningful objects of attention because they receive the speaker's gaze, they are performed in the center of the visual field of both communication partners, and they are verbally indicated. Hence, three factors draw the recipient's attention to the speaker's gestures (Streeck 1988, 1993).

The coordination of speech, gesture, and gaze indicates a high degree of activated metaphoricity. Note that while the speaker is describing her first love relationship in terms of an up-and-down movement, she does not use gesture or any other additional means to express this metaphor. We may therefore assume that metaphoricity was not highly activated at that moment of speaking. Yet it was not completely deactivated either (as the dead metaphor assumption would hold) because it was able to trigger further elaboration: both on the verbal and on the bodily level. On the other hand, it was clearly more activated as the verbo-gestural elaboration ("with a steady tendency downhill" together with the right hand and the head moving downward to the right) was being produced. Pushing the argument yet one step further, we suggest that it was even more activated, as the gesture was replacing the verbal metaphor syntactically *and* receiving the gaze *and* being performed in the center of visual attention *and* being performed with the free left hand.

In this short sequence of speech and bodily expression, I think that we can see in a nutshell that metaphoricity is subject to varying degrees of activation. On the other hand, it is clear that it is permanently available in conventionalized and transparent verbal metaphors. And that is why I conceive of them as sleeping. They sleep, and they may become more or less awake depending on the speaker's focus of attention and the affordances of interaction.

Let us summarize our excursion into verbal metaphors, their multimodal embedding, and what this reveals about the salience of metaphoricity. First of all, we have found that the metaphoricity of verbal metaphors is indeed dynamic in that it varies in degrees of activation. These degrees of activation are detectable from the contextual indications, with "context" being used here in a very broad sense: it may incorporate textual, pictorial, or gestural elaborations of the verbal metaphor as well as foregrounding devices such as gaze direction, size, duration, and locus of gesture performance. The important point is that the verbal metaphor was able to trigger further elaborations, regardless of the modality in which they were materialized. Apparently, verbal metaphoricity is the point of anchorage because, in all the cases we have examined, the elaborations were quite closely related to the rich image of the verbal metaphor. Moreover, no clear evidence for the concurrent activation of conceptual metaphors can be provided. If the elaborations are explainable in terms of the imagery of the verbal metaphor, then there is no empirical indication that a level of general cognition or a level of conceptual metaphor is necessarily involved in triggering all—verbal, pictorial, gestural, verbo-pictorial, and verbo-gestural—metaphors. Therefore, in figure 42, the lines connecting the level of verbal metaphor with the level of conceptual metaphor are interrupted by question marks. Even though conceptual metaphors may be active during the processing of verbal metaphors, these kinds of data do not reveal the activation of metaphoricity on the level of general cognition. The situation was different in the example "depressive," which I presented in chapter 3 as evidence of the activation of a general conceptual metaphor, SAD IS DOWN. In that case, the speaker did not use a transparent verbal metaphor together with the gestural downward motion, and, hence, no verbal metaphor could have motivated the imagery of the gesture.

Put another way, we do have clear indicators that verbal metaphoricity is gradable, and we do have further support for our claim that these so-called dead metaphors are not dead but highly vital. They can just be more or less sleeping or waking depending on the contextual and interactive affordances. They seem to be more sleeping when they are not motivating elaborations at all than when they are motivating a few elaborations on the verbal or gestural level. But when metaphors in words and gestures are foregrounded through verbal or visual deixis, through syntactic integration, and through a gesture's spatial and temporal properties, then the online activation of metaphoricity is high, and they are salient for a listener and waking for a speaker.

6.4 Conclusion: Dead Metaphors Vary in Activation and Salience

We have seen that the dead versus alive distinction is highly problematic because it uncritically mixes incompatible criteria. Hence, the notion of vitality in fact implies very different aspects of metaphors: conventionalization, transparency, and consciousness. The first two aspects refer to properties of metaphors as members of a linguistic system, and the third refers to the cognitive activation of metaphors in an individual speaker. Moreover, it turns out that the dichotomous classification conceals the fact that different kinds of dead metaphors exist, namely, ones that are transparent and ones that are opaque. This distinction has been captured in threefold classifications proposed by historical linguistics and phraseology and by Lakoff and Turner. But the threefold classifications all suffered from the same lack of terminological explicitness as the twofold distinction. One major reason for this confusion is that they do not systematically distinguish between the individual and the collective level of metaphors. Metaphors are members of a linguistic system *and* they are used by individual speakers and writers and comprehended by individual listeners and readers. Hence, it appears to make perfect sense to also terminologically distinguish between these two forms of metaphoric life. And this is what I have done in proposing two classifications of verbal metaphors, a static one that captures three kinds of verbal metaphors based on the criteria of transparency and conventionalization (historical, entrenched, and novel) and a dynamic one based on the degree of activated metaphoricity (from sleeping to waking) in a given speaker or writer at a given moment in time.

In the brief discussion of three examples, a methodological and an empirical argument were put forward. From the point of view of methodology, I have argued that when metaphoricity is *inter*personally salient, that is, when it shows up in various modalities, triggers verbal elaborations, and/or is foregrounded indexically, then it is also *intra*personally active. In other words—*salience is the observable indicator of activated metaphoricity.* I was then able to make the empirically supported point that we have instances in which the metaphoricity of a verbal metaphor is more salient and, hence, more activated than in others. In contrast, when a verbal metaphor is used without any kind of further elaboration, then it is presumably not very active at that moment for the speaker or writer. Let us now conclude this chapter with our major finding. Metaphoricity appears to be dynamic with regard to language use, and it is in this sense that dead (and transparent) metaphors may be very much alive for a given speaker or writer at a given moment in time.

CHAPTER SEVEN

The Refutation of the Dead versus Alive Distinction:
A New Approach and Some of Its Implications

W hy take a new approach? And what exactly is new? The dynamic view proposed here is new in that it exploits a cognitive perspective for gaining insights into a controversial issue pertinent to linguistic theory: the categories of dead versus alive metaphors. In a nutshell, it enables us to conduct in-depth studies of instances of the spontaneous use of language, to make inferences about the psychologically real categories of verbal metaphors that orient speakers and writers, and to investigate the cognitive semantic properties of such metaphors. It throws light upon exactly how metaphoric meaning is retrieved, accessed, activated, and extended and how it must be structured in order to be processed as metaphoric meaning.

This kind of approach appears necessary because the phenomenon we are confronted with—metaphoric language—is a multifaceted phenomenon. A phenomenon that, as I have argued throughout the book, has at least a collective and an individual side. And even though these different facets interact constantly when language is used, they need separate treatment, which accounts for their respective specific properties. Only in a separate step can use and system be convincingly related to each other. So far, metaphor research (and most of linguistics including pragmatics too) has focused either on the systems level or has tended to conflate individual and collective properties, as in the case of the criterion "consciousness of metaphoricity." As frequently mentioned throughout the book, over the past few years, Gibbs and Steen have repeatedly pointed out the methodological and theoretical problems that arise from not disentangling these different facets of metaphor (Gibbs 1998; Steen 2007a, 2007b; Steen and Gibbs 1999). Steen explicitly distinguishes the linguistic and the conceptual systems from their usage and—as mentioned in the introduction to this book—he has argued that metaphor research is pursuing in fact four different cognitive approaches to metaphor and thought ("metaphor in language and thought as a system" and "metaphor in language and thought as use"). Any given investigation of metaphors should be aware of the approach taken in a given study. In his most recent book, Steen (2007b) elaborates and refines the four-feature distinction of system and use, language and thought, pointing out that for researchers of metaphor the distinction between metaphors as symbolic structure and metaphors as behavior plays a critical role.

> When cognitive-linguistically inspired researchers of language investigate metaphor, they typically do so by looking at language as either grammar or usage. Moreover, they have to make a choice in focusing on metaphor in grammar or usage as either language, analyzing linguistic forms, or thought, examining conceptual structures, or both. And finally, they have a further choice in adopting either a sign-oriented, symbolic perspective on metaphor, or a behavior-oriented, social-scientific perspective on the processes and products of metaphor in cognition. When these choices are combined, we end up with a field of research that consists of eight distinct research areas displaying their own object and approach. (Steen 2007b, 25)

Note that Steen reformulates "system" as "grammar" and "use" as "usage," readjusting them to current terminology in cognitive linguistics but also underlining that metaphors are part of the (lexico-) grammar of language and that this grammar always emerges from usage. This elaborated outline of now eight different research areas in cognitive linguistic approaches to metaphor brings in yet another specifically critical new distinction for current research and theory: behavior and symbolic structure. On the level of behavior, we are confronted with psychological processes and products (computation and storing of information); on the level of metaphors as symbolic structures, we are investigating signs and symbolic structures.

In an earlier publication, Steen critically evaluates the lack of differentiation in cognitive linguistics between the perspectives of system (now grammar) and that of use (now usage), and he argues that at least as a methodological heuristic, this distinction is indispensable. Yet he is careful to add that this does not imply an a priori postulation of their ontological status: "As long as it is recalled that these are distinct perspectives on language and thought, not hard-and-fast distinctions between language and thought themselves, it may be useful to differentiate between these approaches as diverging ways of conceptualizing the object of study" (Steen 2007a).

The dynamic view presented in this book constitutes an effort to systematically address the perspective of usage as actual behavior. It has investigated metaphor in language as it is used by actual speakers at a given moment in time. Note that this approach differs from a corpus-linguistic one in that it offers microanalytic, in-depth analyses of metaphors as they are used in speech and text, and it infers online processes from empirical indicators of activated metaphoricity. In this regard, it is interested in uncovering hints as to how metaphors as language may relate to the dynamic activation of metaphoric thinking.

Although I have taken a cognitive perspective on verbal metaphors, I have not presupposed their anchoring in or derivation from conceptual metaphors (i.e., their grounding in conceptual metaphors on Steen's level of "thought as grammar"). This is a different issue, and one that needs empirical documentation—which is what I have offered in the example of the gesture expressing the conceptual metaphor SAD IS DOWN with significant (repeated and slow) downward movements, although this concept was not present in speech. But it is not the primary intention of the book to provide empirical evidence for conceptual metaphors. I think it is at least heuristically necessary to make the distinction between different possible realms of metaphors. Hence, I am also sympathetic to Steen's second distinction, the one between thought and language; I think it is a highly relevant differentiation, insofar as it furthers our aim to empirically investigate the relationship between language and thought. Merely postulating that language *is* thought risks advancing a rather trivial supposition because, of course, all communicative behavior is somehow a product of thought. Providing empirical evidence of how language and thought relate to each other in detail is a highly complex undertaking, as psycholinguistic as well as cognitive anthropological research testifies. This means that both language and thought need to be considered as possibly distinct (on the collective level as well as on the individual level), otherwise they remain theoretical claims and empirically not verifiable. Given the complexity of this issue, it is hardly surprising that the question of how metaphor relates to language and thought has been a highly controversial topic in metaphor research for 25 years (cf. Ortony 1979, 1993a; Katz et al. 1998, Gibbs forthcoming). More methodological and terminological rigor will certainly contribute to enhancing our understanding of how metaphor and thought relate to each other.

What kind of implications does the dynamic view have? As far as I can see, it carries rather far-reaching implications, probably more than I can thoroughly treat in the remaining space here.

Theories of metaphor: To begin with, I would be prepared to take Steen's methodological proposal one step further and suggest that his distinction has consequences for theories of metaphor in that it ultimately demands an integration of all these facets into a unified theory of metaphor. I think, however, that before this is possible, a separate theoretical conceptualization of these different aspects of metaphors is necessary. I hope that the present study has documented the necessity for such separate routes to be taken in order for theoretical and empirical progress to be made. While the "classic" set of dead versus alive metaphors may be relevant on the level of the linguistic system (in Steen's recent approach, grammar: the distinction between novel, entrenched, and historical metaphors), it appears not to be relevant with regard to language in use. On the other hand, the category relevant to use (the dynamic category "sleeping-waking") is not pertinent to the system. It relates to the system only insofar as it draws exclusively upon entrenched and novel metaphors, but their gradability does not directly import on the system as a system. The evaluation of the criteria that inform the established distinction between dead and alive metaphors has revealed that the foremost problem of this classification is what I would like to characterize as terminological "haze." It has most likely evolved out of a specific scholarly orientation toward novel and transparent metaphors in poetic texts (including texts on the artful composing of speeches that have accumulated since antiquity). Without much further reflection, they were taken, as Black says, as the paradigmatic cases. Black was clearly correct with his critique of the uselessness of the dead versus alive distinction—this categorization may only figure as a valuable basis for a theory of metaphor insofar as a critical evaluation of it may lead to important new insights.

Theories of language: The dynamic view advocated in this book does not presuppose one of the currently available linguistic theories. As I have documented in the chapter on mixed metaphors, theoretically competing stances of documenting the semantic structures of metaphorical expressions may provide insights into different aspects of the phenomenon, and they may function as mutually informing and supporting or challenging views upon the same phenomenon. Hence, what I wish to suggest is that no matter which linguistic format of describing language data is applied, adopting a cognitive view onto actual instances of language use may provide new insights into core issues of linguistic theory and the documentation of language. Analyzing language use from the point of view of the cognitive processes involved may offer important additional information, at least insofar as they specifically relate to use. I am thinking, for instance, of deixis (cf. Fricke 2002, 2007), of time (Borgschulte 2007, Núñez and Sweetser 2006), of aspect and aktionsart (cf. Duncan 2002; Müller 2000), of modality (cf. Müller and Speckmann 2002), and of illocutionary force (cf. Kendon 1995, 2004; Müller and Haferland 1997; Ladewig forthcoming; Fatfouta forthcoming; Teßendorf forthcoming); hence, established linguistic concepts, such as indirect speech acts or deixis, may need reformulation in the light of a cognitive view of language use.[1] The case of mixed metaphors illustrates this quite well, I believe. Recall that in contrast to what is common sense in linguistic and conceptual metaphor theories, there is no single dimension of meaning in which mixed metaphors always make sense. Mixed metaphors do not always display semantic inconsistencies regarding their literal meanings or incoherences between source domains. On the other hand, mixed metaphors are not always semantically consistent on the figurative level nor are their target domains always coherently structured. Thus, instead of encountering the expected straightforward explication of the nature of this phenomenon, the close investigation of different cases of mixed metaphors uncovered that it is due to a cognitive process of selection between different possible meaningful elements (including syntax) that are conceptually integrated that the outcome results in meaningful expressions. One consequence of this observation is that the way in which a mixed metaphor may have been meaningful for a given speaker only reflects one out of a range of possible ways of constructing meaning on the basis of the linguistic material that went into a given utterance or sentence. Listeners, readers, and language experts may identify other readings of the same utterance, probably ones that converge with more conventional and normative usages of the respective metaphoric expressions. Apparently, online meaning construction involves a large amount of choice between different elements of meaning that are potentially available. Accordingly, the production of metaphoric language cannot be convincingly described as a mere concatenation of prestored linguistic units into well-formed strings of symbols. Instead, the analysis of mixed metaphors shows that there appear to be normative readings, normative uses of metaphor. But it also shows that these normative uses of conventionalized metaphors still imply an active metaphoricity (otherwise, combining mixed metaphors from different source domains with inconsistent literal meanings would not be problematic). Listeners, readers, and language experts may identify other readings, presumably the ones that converge with the normative and, hence, the more common way of attributing sense to a given metaphor. What is problematic then is that these normative usages inform the theoretical conceptualization of the phenomenon, and, as in the case of mixed metaphors, this may lead to basically false explanations and characterizations. Instead, what appears to take place in mixed metaphors is that speakers and writers depart from these normative uses and their implied salience structures. These salience structures offer a kind of default selection of projection or mapping between domains or spaces. In speaking or writing, this default salience structure may be disregarded and new elements may be selected, may be treated as salient and create new readings. Hence, mixed metaphors are in fact the consequence of a process of cognitive selection that appears to be driven by the orientation of focal attention to pertinent elements of meaning. These observations indicate that adopting a cognitive perspective on actual spontaneous uses of language may offer interesting and potentially challenging cases for current models of language production. As far as I see, the current consensus is that word meanings are retrieved as complete entities—"lemmas"—as for instance in Levelt and colleagues' (Levelt 1989, 1999; Levelt, Roelofs, Meyer 1999) important modular and se-rial model of speech production; but in the mixing of metaphors, various single aspects of lexical and syntactic meaning are retrieved and combined in a creative way that would not be captured by such a serial approach. It appears, therefore, that mixed metaphors would be a highly interesting and revelatory field of study for psycholinguists interested in the production of spoken and written language—probably as interesting as the study of cases of slips of the tongue.

Metaphors—language—thought: I have suggested in this book that meta-phors crucially rest upon a cognitive activity, which is the cognitive process of establishing or activating metaphoricity. I view metaphoricity as being conceived on the utmost level of abstraction as a triadic structure in which an entity A relates two entities B and C such that C is seen in terms of B. The establishment of such a structure is a cognitive process that is in principle modality independent. As I have shown, it may not only materialize in dif-ferent modalities, but it may also cross cut modalities and form multimodal metaphors. Although I have focused on verbal metaphors, I have provided some hints as to further possible modalities through which metaphors may materialize: pictures, gestures, and other nonlinguistic forms of expression that combine to establish such a triadic structure (the sensomotoric roots of primary conceptual metaphors could figure as an example). In this sense, the dynamic view and the refutation of the dead versus alive dichotomy bear upon some of the central controversies regarding the role of metaphors in language and thought. The article "The Fight over Metaphor in Thought and Language" gives a nice overview of what is at stake here (Gibbs 1998). In this article, Gibbs (1998, 88) summarizes the basic issues under discussion (cf. also Gibbs 1999a):

Question 1:

How can we best understand the relationship between metaphoric thought and language use?

Question 2:

To what extent does metaphoric language reflect metaphoric thought?

Gibbs then goes on to systematize possible options regarding the role that metaphoric thought may play in how people use and understand language, and he formulates four hypotheses (Gibbs 1994, 18; 1998, 93–103):

Hypothesis 1: Metaphoric thought plays some role in the historical evolution of what words and expressions mean. (Gibbs 1998, 93)

Hypothesis 2: Metaphoric thought motivates the linguistic meanings that have currency within linguistic communities, or may have some role in speakers'/hearers' presumed understanding of language. (Gibbs 1998, 94)

Hypothesis 3: Metaphoric thought motivates real-life, contemporary speakers' use and understanding of why various words and expressions mean what they do. (Gibbs 1998, 96)

Hypothesis 4: Metaphoric thought functions in people's immediate online use and understanding of linguistic meaning. (Gibbs 1998, 103)

The microanalyses carried out in this book provide support for hypothesis 4. They indicate that metaphoric thought does indeed function in people's immediate online production of so-called dead metaphors. They offer a new kind of empirical support for psycholinguistic and cognitive linguistic research on the question of dead versus alive metaphors, whose results Gibbs (1994) summarizes as follows: "Contrary to the traditional view, that idioms, clichés and proverbs are frozen semantic units or dead metaphors, the evidence from cognitive linguistics and psycholinguistics indicates that many of these conventional expressions reflect metaphoric thought that is very much alive and part of our everyday conceptual systems" (Gibbs 1994, 436). The results upon which Gibbs bases his argument have primarily been gained by inquiring into the comprehension side of metaphoric processing. The arguments offered in this book contribute a new perspective by promoting insights into the online cognitive processes of metaphor production.

Furthermore, these arguments have uncovered that metaphoric thought not only materializes in language but also in words, pictures, and gestures; they also suggest that conceptual metaphors as well as verbal metaphors undergo a selective retrieval of meaning during language production. However, this claim only holds if Gibbs's "metaphoric thought" is interpreted as an expression of what I have termed the modality-independent establishment of metaphoricity. It would not hold if Gibbs's formulation were to conceptualize metaphoric thought in terms of conceptual metaphors only. If this were the case, then one would have to extend the concept of conceptual metaphors to far beyond the scope of the common understanding it has at present. Because, as far as I see, at the moment, CMT does not propose a specific level of linguistic concepts, which most of the examples discussed actually point to. Hence, if there are empirically observable cues indicating the activation of metaphoricity (such as repetition, elaboration, or opposition on the verbal level or depiction of a source domain in a picture or gesture), then they all tend to connect with the specific semantic content (or the rich image) of the verbal metaphor in question and not with a more general level of conceptual metaphors. Thus, however we may model such a separate level, be it in terms of a two-level semantics (Lang 1994) or as a level integrated into internalized cognitive models (Lakoff 1987), somehow empirical indicators of the activation of metaphoricity need to be accounted for. I think, moreover, that this is in fact a highly important issue for CMT, one that has not hitherto received the attention it deserves. I think, furthermore, that this level of rich-image semantics is a least one historical source of the emergence of conceptual metaphors and of systems of conceptual metaphors. I share Weinrich's view that clearly a lot of experiential domains of life are first conceptualized linguistically on the level of rich-image semantics. Thus, at some point in classical times, when people used wax tablets to write on, somebody came to employ the concept or the experience of this cultural technique as a metaphor for describing the abstract phenomenon of memory. Yet this would not be sufficient to give rise to a conceptual metaphor, at least one that transcends the unique and singular metaphorization of experience. In order to develop into a conceptual metaphor on a collective level, language is needed. A linguistic community must not only decide to use this lexeme metaphorically, in which case we would only have an entrenched verbal metaphor, but it must also use this metaphor as an inspiration, as a model for the creation of further related verbal metaphors. Only when we have a cluster of verbal metaphors (and probably supported by evidence from other cultural practices, such as ritual, painting, and dance) can we convincingly assume that something like a conceptual metaphor or, in Weinrich's terms, a mental model has emerged. Hence, the semantics of lexemes does appear to play a fundamental role in the emergence, tradition, and historical change of conceptual metaphors and in the development of systems of conceptual metaphors. It is clearly an area of research that demands more interest and attention than it has received in CMT up to now. To sum up, Gibbs's fourth hypothesis is only supported if metaphoric thought may also be verbal metaphoric thought.

Thought and language—thinking for speaking: It is hardly surprising that the dynamic view advocated in this book is highly sympathetic to Slobin's (1987, 1991, 2000) concept of "thinking for speaking." Slobin intended to overcome the untenably narrow concepts of linguistic relativism by proposing that during the process of speaking people organize their thinking in terms of the categories of their mother tongue, which implies that nonlinguistic cognition and thinking without language may remain unaffected by the structures of language. He did not so much focus on the dynamic organization of thinking processes as he did on cross-cultural differences and their role in language acquisition. But his concept of thinking for speaking has still gained great currency, not only in language acquisition research, but also in linguistic anthropology and in cognitive linguistics in general. I think this concept may be fruitfully extended to the processes observed when metaphors are in use, because it appears that what takes place is indeed an online orientation of metaphoric thinking that is subject to different cognitive processes of activation, which, as we have seen, are implicated in the grading, selection, and creation of meaning. The dynamic perspective provides a wide range of fairly clear supporting evidence in favor of metaphoric thinking playing an active role in speaking and writing.

Language and cognition: Let me end by recalling some important historical precursors and by addressing some of the contemporary work that has not yet been mentioned and that bears important relations to the dynamic view proposed here. First of all, the perspective I have adopted connects to early psychological work on metaphors in particular (Bühler 1982; Stählin 1914; Wundt 1922) and on language in general (Bühler 1982; Wundt 1922). If you wish, these scholars may be regarded in some respects as precursors of cognitive linguistics because they sought to formulate linguistic theories or to provide accounts of language that are in accordance with what was known at the time about cognitive processes and structures. Bühler, for instance, was heavily influenced by gestalt psychology, which nowadays continues to inform cognitive linguistic efforts to identify cognitive principles that govern general and linguistic cognition. An outstanding example is the figure-ground distinction and the processes of foregrounding and backgrounding connected with it; familiarity with these concepts has informed not only Lakoff and Johnson's (1980) concepts of "highlighting" and "hiding" in conceptual metaphors, but also Leonard Talmy's work on the lexicalization patterns of motion verbs and their satellites and his most recent work on the attentional system of language (1978, 1985, 1987, 2003). Note, however, that Talmy, as is common practice in cognitive linguistics, tends to use cognitive principles to explain the structures of the linguistic system. In contrast, Stählin above all intended to describe the online processes of the activation of metaphoricity, which is why he was a great source of inspiration for this book. But Bühler and Wundt did indeed adopt a stance that is similar to the one proposed by cognitive linguists today.

The observations made by taking a perspective of language use from the point of view of cognition are also in line with assumptions of the dynamic nature of consciousness during speaking as proposed by Wallace Chafe (1994). Chafe lucidly examines the continuous flow of consciousness and the very small window of focal attention that he binds to intonation units. The cases of mixed metaphors especially clearly support his concept of a highly selective and constantly moving form of focal attention. These procedural properties of consciousness constitute a challenge to researchers who seek to fathom the process of organizing thinking for speaking that awaits further accounts. The dynamic view proposed here may help to shed some more light onto this facet of the flow of consciousness.

David McNeill and Susan D. Duncan's (McNeill 1992; McNeill and Duncan 2000) work on the imagistic and propositional modes of thought underlying language production has had a large impact on the dynamic view, not only because their concept of the growth point as a minimal idea unit is based on the study of speech and cospeech gesturing, but also because of the intriguing fact that the metaphoric gestures in the examples provided here rely heavily on verbal metaphoricity—which would mean that propositional and imagistic (or maybe more general sensomotoric) forms of thinking closely interact when language is used. If, on the other hand, the gestures' imagery were not to rely on the specific verbal imagery, then it might be rooted in nonlinguistic forms of conceptualization, and this would then contradict McNeill, since he argues that language and gesture form one single system. The close integration of verbal and gestural semantic structure definitely characterizes the interplay between metaphoric language and gesture and hence supports McNeill's assumptions. On the other hand, my observations also show that other pictorial modes of representation can be exploited and combine with verbal language to produce a multimodal metaphor. This kind of interplay points to the possibility that language and imagery (or other sensomotoric conceptualizations) work together closely and form one system rather than claiming that such a semantic symbiosis only holds for gesture. However, recent findings from neurocognitive studies in split-brain patients show that gestures based on actions of the hand (the hand acts; Müller 1998a, 1998b) are generated in the left hemisphere, as language is too (Lausberg et al. 2003; Müller et al. in preparation). In contrast, gestures that embody objects as a whole (the hand represents or embodies; Müller 1998a, 1998b) are generated in the right hemisphere. These findings suggest, however, that the interplay between gesture and language is manifold and awaits further investigation.

Cognition and language use: Taking the perspective of cognition and language use seriously reveals that using language is not the mere instantiation of a linguistic system; rather, this shift in perspective makes it possible to discern that language use is not reducible to a set of recursive rules governing the construction of grammatically correct syntactic units (as Chomskyan linguistics still favors). Rather it must be conceived of as a dynamic online construction of multiply structured units of utterances—multiply structured in terms of syntactic, morphological, semantic, and pragmatic structures and in terms of multiple representational modes that are to be integrated. This integration process is profoundly characterized by creativity. Hence, speakers and writers constantly draw upon an available repertoire of expressive resources that they integrate and shape according to their communicative and interactive affordances. All these aspects have to be processed cognitively, and if one wishes to develop a theory of language that is cognitively realistic, then he or she must account for this complexity of linguistic structure. This is a profound theoretical and methodological issue, and for support I shall return to a classic work on semantics written by Stephen Ullmann:

> To take a philosophical example: Whether the expression "logical form" should be treated in a particular frame as having a metaphorical sense will depend upon the extent to which its user is taken to be conscious of some supposed analogy between arguments and other things (vases, clouds, battles, jokes) that are also said to have "form." Still more will it depend upon whether the writer wishes the analogy to be active in the minds of his readers; and how much his own thought depends upon and is nourished by the supposed analogy. We must not expect the "rules of language" to be of much help in such inquiries. (There is accordingly a sense of "metaphor" that belongs to "pragmatics" rather than to "semantics"— and this sense may be the one most deserving of attention.) (Ullmann 1967, 30)

I regard Ullmann's passage as a more or less explicit indication of the necessity of adopting a pragmatic and a cognitive perspective at least on some facets of semantic inquiry, and it has informed the dynamic view on metaphor offered here. Such a perspective may give rise to new insights and even inspire new views on old problems—that is what I hope to have shown in this book. In full awareness of the multitude of open questions and the many issues that a cognitive approach to metaphors in language use bears upon, I believe that this dynamic view has clearly demonstrated that the ways in which speakers and writers actually employ metaphors is not only a matter of activating certain steps in a speech-production process, which instantiates a collectively established system, but it is also highly revelatory of the very nature of metaphor itself: metaphors operate on the level of a linguistic system and on the level of use, and when they are in use their nature is inherently dynamic. This dynamic property is not, however, reserved for metaphors alone; it is a property of meaning in general. It is in this sense that the dynamic view proposed shares the same guiding spirit of David Mc-Neill's new book, in which he proposes a unified theory of language, speech, gesture, and thought and argues for a dynamic conception of meaning—and more generally—of language, gesture, and thought (McNeill 2006).

By looking at metaphors from a perspective of cognition in language use, we have been able to reject and overcome the traditional dichotomy of dead versus alive metaphors: we have seen that dead metaphors may be activated in speaking and writing and become very much alive indeed. Regarded as elements of a linguistic system they may be dead, entrenched, or novel; as elements used in speech, they oscillate between sleeping and waking, depending on the degrees of activated metaphoricity in given contexts of use.

Finally, however, I share Jackendoff's grasp on the practical impossibility of ever producing an encompassing treatment of any scientific topic: "Life is short, you can't do everything, read everything, make everyone happy with your work. As I. F. Stone put it, 'all you have to contribute is the purification of your own vision, and the addition of that to the sum total of other visions'" (Jackendoff 1996b, 94).

It is in this spirit that the present book has aimed at adding a further piece to the puzzle of explaining metaphor in relation to language and cognition.

Adank, H. 1936. *Essai sur les fondements psychologiques et linguistiques de la métaphore affective*. Genf.

Ammer, K. 1958 *Einführung in die Sprachwissenschaft*, Bd. 1. Halle (Saale).

Aristotle. 1911. *The Poetics of Aristotle. Translated from Greek into English and from Arabic into Latin, with a Revised Text, Introduction, Commentary, Glossary and Onomasticon*. edited by D. S. Margoliouth. London, New York, and Toronto.

Auctor ad Herennium. 1954. *Ad C. Herenium libri IV de ratione dicendi (Rhetorica ad Herenium), edited by* H. Caplan. London and Cambridge, Mass.

Bain, A. 1866. *English Composition and Rhetoric*. London.

Bally, Ch. 1932. *Linguistique générale et linguistique française*. Paris.

Beardsley, M. C. 1958. *Aesthetics. Problems in the Philosophy of Criticism*. New York.

Blair, H. 1783. *Lectures on Rhetoric and belles lettres*. 4 vols. London.

Bouterwek, F. 1815. *Aesthetik*. Zweite, in den Prinzipien berichtigte und völig umgearbeitete Ausgabe, 2. Teil. Göttingen.

Brinkmann, F. 1878. *De Metapher. Studien über den Geist der modernen Sprachen*. Bd. 1: Die Thierbilder der Sprache. Bonn.

Großer Brockhaus. 1955. 16th ed. Wiesbaden.

Brooke Rose, Christine. 1958. *A Grammar of Metaphor*. London.

Cicero. 1950. *De l'orateur*, edited by E. Courbaud.

Coseriu, E. 1956. *La creación metafórica en el lenguaje*. Montevideo.

Croce, B. 1901. *Aesthetik als Wissenschaft vom Ausdruck und allgemeine Sprachwissenschaft. Theorie und Geschichte*, edited by. H. Feist und R. Peters. Tübingen.

Darmesteter, A. 1885. *La vie des mots*. Paris.

Day, A. 1586. *The English Secretorie. Wherein Is Contayned, a Perfect Method, for the Inditing of All Manner of Epistles*. London.

Donatus. 1864. *Ars grammatica = Gramatici Latini ex rec*. Leipzig.

Elster, E. 1879. *Prinzipien der Literaturwissenschaft.* Halle (Saale).

Empson, W. 1952. *The Structure of Complex Words.* London.

Encyclopedia Britannica. 1959. Edited by W. Yust et al. Chicago, London, and Toronto.

Entwistle, W. J. 1953. *Aspects of Language.* London.

Erdmann, K. O. 1901. *Die Bedeutung des Wortes.* Leipzig.

Estrich, R. M., and H. Sperber. 1952. *Three Keys to Language.* s.l.: Rinehart and Com. Inc.

Foss, M. 1949. *Symbol and Metaphor in Human Experience.* Princeton.

Gardiner, A. 1932. *The Theory of Speech and Language.* Oxford.

Gerber, G. 1873–74. *Die Sprache als Kunst.* Bromberg.

Gottschall, R. v. .1882. 2d ed. *Poetik. Die Dichtkunst und ihre Technik. Vom Standpunkt der Neuzeit.* Breslau.

Gray, L. H. 1939. *Foundations of Language.* New York.

Hahn, W. 1879. *Deutsche Poetik.* Berlin.

Hayakawa, S. I. 1949. *Language in Thought and Action.* New York.

Hegel, G. W. F. 1820–29. *Ästhetik,* edited by F. Bassenge. Berlin. (Ost).

Henle, P. 1958. Metaphor. In *Language, Thought, and Culture,* pp. 173–95. Ann Arbor.

Hermogenes. 1913. *Opera,* edited by H. Rabe. Leipzig.

Isidor. 1911. *Hispalensis episcopi etymologiarum sive originum libri XX,* edited by W. M. Lindsay.

Jakobson, R. 1956. Two Aspects of Language and Two Types of Aphasic Disturbances. In *Fundamentals in language,* edited by R. Jakobson and M. Halle. The Hague.

Kainz, F. 1941. *Psychologie der Sprache.* Stuttgart.

Kayser, W., ed. 1961. 3d ed. *Kleines literarisches Lexikon.* Bern and München.

Kleinpaul, E. 1843. *Poetik. Die Lehre von der deutschen Dichtkunst.* Leipzig.

Konrad, H. 1939. *Etude sur la métaphore.* Paris.

Körner, J. 1949. *Einführung in die Poetik.* Frankfurt a.M.

Kronasser, H. 1952. *Handbuch der Semasologie. Kurze Einführung in die Geschichte, Problematik und Terminologie der Bedeutungslehre.* Heidelberg.

Lee, Dorothy D. 1954. Symbolization and Value. In *Symbols and Values: An Initial Study,* edited by L. Bryson et al., pp. 73–85. New York.

Marouzeau, J. 1951. 3d ed. *Lexique de a terminologie linguistique. Français, allemand, anglais, italien.* Paris.

Martini, F. 1957. 2d ed. Poetik. In *Deutsche Philologie im Aufriß,* edited by W. Stammler. Berlin. (West).

Marsais, C. Ch. Seigneur du. 1730. *Traité des tropes ou des différents sens dans lesquels on peut prendre un même mot dans une même langue.* Paris.

Mauthner, F. 1901. *Beiträge zu einer Kritik der Sprache, Bd. 2: Zur Sprachwissenschaft.* Stuttgart.

Meyer R. M. 1906. *Deutsche Stilistik.* München.

Morier, H. 1961. *Dictionnaire de poétique et de rhétorique.* Paris.

Morris, Ch. 1946. *Signs, Language, and Behavior.* New York.

Müller, M. 1863. Metaphor. In *Lectures on the Science of Language,* edited by M. Müller. Second series. London.

Nyrop, K. 1903. *Das Leben der Wörter.* Leipzig.

Ogden, C. K., and I. Richards. 1923. *The Meaning of Meaning. A Study of the Influence of Language upon Thought and of Science of Symbolism.* London.

Paul, H. 1886. *Prinzipien der Sprachgeschichte.* Tübingen.

Paul J. 1804. Vorschule der Aesthetik. In: *J. Pauls sämtliche Werke.* Weimar.

Pei, M. A., and F. Gaynor. 1954. *A Dictionary of Linguistics.* New York.

Pelc, J. 1961. Semantic Functions as Applied to the Analysis of the Concept of Metaphor. In *Poetics. Poetyka,* edited by D. Davie et al. Warschau and The Hague.

Pongs, H. 1927. Das Bild in der Dichtung. Bd. 1: *Versuch einer Morphologie der metaphorischen Formen.* Marburg.

Porzig, W. 1950. *Das Wunder der Sprache. Probleme, Methoden und Ergebnisse der modernen Sprachwissenschaft.* München.

Quintilian, M. Fabi. 1959. *Institutionis oratoriae libri XII,* Edited by L. Rademacher. Leipzig.

Reiners, L. 1949. 2d ed. *Stilkunst. Ein Lehrbuch deutscher Prosa.* München.

Restrepo, F. 1917. *El alma de las palabras. Diseño de semantica general.* Barcelona.

Richards, I. A. 1929. *Practical Criticism. A Study of Literary Judgment.* London.

———. 1936. *The Philosophy of Rhetoric.* New York.

Sandmann, M. 1954. *Subject and Predicat. A Contribution to the Theory of Syntax.* Edinburgh.

Schöne, M. 1947. *Vie et mort des mots.* Paris.

Seidler, H. 1953. *Allgemeine Stilistik.* Göttingen.

———. 1959. *Die Dichtung. Wesen, Form, Dasein.* Stuttgart.

Stageberg, N. C., and W. L. Anderson (1952). *Poetry as Experience.* New York.

Stanford, W. B. 1936. *Greek Metaphor. Studies in Theory and Practice.* Oxford.

Stern, G. 1931. *Meaning and Change of Meaning, with Special Reference to the English Language.* Göteborg.

Ullman, S. 1951. *The Principles of Semantics.* Glasgow and Oxford.

Vendryes, J. 1923. *Le langage. Introduction linguistique à l'histoire.* Paris.

Vianu, T. 1957. *Problemele metaforei si alte studii de stilistca.* Bukarest.

Vossius, Gerardus Joannes. 1630. *Commentariorum rhetoricum, sive oratoriarum institutionum libri sex, ita tertiä hac editione castigati, atque aucti, ut novum opus videri poßint.* Lugduni Batavorum.

Wackernagel, W. 1836–37. *Poetik, Rhetorik und Stilistik. Akademische Vorlesungen,* edited by L. Sieber. Halle (Saale).

Webster's New International Dictionary of the English Language. 1961. 2d ed. Edited by W. A. Neilson. Springfield.

Wellek, R., and A. Warren. 1949. *Theory of Literature.* New York.

Werner, H. 1919. *Die Ursprünge der Metapher.* Leipzig.

Whately, R. 1828. *Elements of Rhetoric, Comprising the Substance of the Article in the Encyclopedia Metropolitana.* London.

Wiegand, J. 1951. *Abriss der lyrischen Tecnik.* Fulda.

Wilpert, G. v. 1959. 2d ed. *Sachwörterbuch der Literatur.* Stuttgart.

Wilson. 1553. *Arte of Rhetorique,* edited by H. Mair. Oxford.

Wundt, W. 1900. *Völkerpsychoogie. Eine Untersuchung der Entwicklung von Sprache, Mythus und Sitte. Bd. 1: Die Sprache.* Leipzig.

Consider the list of authors ordered according to their pertinent disciplines (Lieb 1964, 38–39):

1. Philosophy
   a. Of language: Mauthner (1901), Ogden and Richards (1923), Morris (1946), Hayakawa (1949), Henle (1958).
   b. Of literature (including aesthetics): J. Paul (1804), Bouterwek (1815 ?), Hegel (1820–29), Croce (1901), Pongs (1927), Richards (1936), Konrad (1939), Empson (1952 ?), Beardsley (1958).
   c. *Varia:* Foss (1949).
2. Psychology (of language): Wundt (1900), Werner (1919), Kainz (1941), Estrich-Sperber (1952), Jakobson (1956).
3. Linguistics
   a. General linguistics: M. Müller (1863), Paul (1886), Vendryes (1923), Bally (1932), Gardiner (1932), Gray (1939), Porzig (1950), Marouzeau (dictionary) (1951, 3d ed.), Entwistle (1953), Pei (dictionary) (1954), Ammer (1958).
   b. Semantics: Darmesteter (1885), Erdmann (1901), Nyrop (1903), Restrepo (1917), Stern (1931), Schöne (1947), Ullman (1951), Kronasser (1952).
   c. *Varia:* Brinkmann (1878), Adank (1936 ?), Sandmann (1954), Coseriu (1956), *Webster's New International Dictionary of the English Language* (1961, 2d ed.).
4. Literary criticism
   a. Rhetoric, poetics, stylistics: Artistotle 335–322, Auctor ad Herennium 86–82, Cicero ca. 55–44, Quintilian 95 A.D., Hermogenes ca. 170, Donatus ca. 350, Wilson (1553), Day (1586), Vossius

(1960, 3d ed.), du Marsais (1730), Blair (1783), Whately (1828), Wackernagel (1836–37), Kleinpaul (1843), Bain (1866), Gerber (1873–74), Hahn (1879), Gottschall (1882, 2d ed.) R. M. Meyer (1906), Richards (1929), Körner (1949), Reiners (1949, 2d ed.), Wiegand (1951), Stageberg-Anderson (1952), Seidler (1953), Martini (1957, 2d ed.), Morier (dictionary) (1961).

    b. Literary theory: Elster (1879), (1911), Stanford (1936), Wellek and Warren (1949), v. Wilpert (1959, 2d ed.; dictionary), Seidler (1959), Kayser (dictionary) (1961) (3d ed.; =Seidler), Pelc (1961), Vianu (1961).

    c. *Varia:* Brooke-Rose (1958).

5. Ethnology: Lee (1954).

6. Encyclopedia: Isidor before 636, Großer Brockhaus (1955, 16th ed.), *Encyclopedia Britannica* (1959).

NOTES

INTRODUCTION

1. *Der Tagesspiegel* is the local Berlin newspaper. All translations are by Mary Copple (MC) unless otherwise specified. All diagrams are by CM unless otherwise specified.

2. See Weinrich (1976, 308) for a similar analysis of metaphor: "I suggest taking the sentence as the new basis of a theory of metaphor use: a metaphor is a contradictory predication." Both views are certainly informed by Beardsley's (1962) and Black's (1962) conception. We shall return to the different conceptions regarding the semantic structure of metaphor in chapter 4.

3. "Zur Erzeugung einer *neuen* Metapher ist zumindest ein Satz notwendig. Genauer gesagt ist der metaphorische Prozeß in dem Hauptvorgang zu suchen, dessen Rahmen der Satz ist, nämlich in der Prädikation. Die These ist nun die, daß die Sinnerweiterung, die im Wort vorsichgeht, auf einem sonderbaren, ungewöhnlichen Gebrauch der Prädikation beruht. Die Metapher ist eine 'impertinente Prädikation', also eine solche, die die gewöhnlichen Kriterien der Angemessenheit oder der Pertinenz in der Anwendung der Prädikate verletzt...." (Ricœur 1986, vi; emphasis in the original).

4. "Daß der Wortschatz ein Friedhof ausgelöschter, aufgehobener, 'toter' Metaphern ist, steht fest; dieser Tatbestand bestätigt jedoch nur die These, daß es kein lexikalisches Kriterium für die Frage gibt, ob eine Metapher lebendig ist oder tot. Erst in der Erzeugung eines neuen Satzes, in einem Akt unerhörter Prädizierung entsteht die lebendige Metapher wie ein Funke, der beim Zusammenstoß zweier bisher voneinander entfernter semantischer Felder aufblitzt. In diesem Sinne existiert die Metapher nur in dem Augenblick, in dem das Lesen dem Zusammenstoß der semantischen Felder neues Leben verleiht und die impertinente Prädikation erzeugt" (Ricœur 1986, vi).

5. This line of research will be presented in more detail in chapters 3 and 6.

6. The notion of contextual cues is not to be confused with the pragmatic notion of contextualization cues as developed by Peter Auer (1986, 1992) and John Gumperz (1982, 1990, 1992). Rather, contextual cues are semantic cues that determine the semantics of metaphor in a specific manner. See also Weinrich (1976) and his concept of Kontextdetermination (determination by context).

7. See Lakoff and Johnson's appendix, "The Neural Theory of Language Paradigm," in their 1999 monograph *Philosophy in the Flesh* as well as the afterword in the 2003 edition of their *Metaphors We Live By*.

8. Further reference will be made to pertinent publications. The above-mentioned publications are obviously but the landmark formulations of Lakoff and Johnson's conceptual metaphor theory.

9. This of course is a pertinent facet of language change. See, for instance, Blank (1997), Blank and Koch (1999), Bréal (1899), Closs-Traugott (1985), Dornseiff (1966), Paul (1937), Stern (1931), and Ullman (1967).

10. Cf. also Elisabeth Closs-Traugott, who in her lucid article "'Conventional' and 'Dead' Metaphors" sometimes conflates the historical and the individual aspect of transparency (Closs-Traugott 1985).

11. See Levelt (1999), Rickheit and Strohner (2003), and Schriefers (2003) for reviews of current theories of speech production.

12. Note that differences regarding the nature of the models, for example, more or less modular or connectionist, do no bear upon this question because they share the same basic tenet.

13. The term "conceptual metaphor theory" has become an established form of referring to Lakoff and Johnson's (1980, 1999 and Lakoff 1993, to mention only the most important references) cognitive-linguistic theories of metaphor. In the context of conceptual metaphor theory, it has become common to characterize all other theories of metaphor as traditional. Since proponents of conceptual metaphor theory employ this term in a specific form of rhetoric, I prefer to characterize pertinent theories with respect to their primary focus and not with regard to what are considered traditional or contemporary theories of metaphor. Therefore, in this book, the theories that regard metaphor primarily as a linguistic phenomenon are characterized as linguistic metaphor theory, and the ones that regard it primarily as a conceptual phenomenon are termed conceptual metaphor theory.

14. One of its consequences has been the Pragglejaz metaphor identification group. In this group, metaphor scholars are jointly working on reliable criteria for identifying metaphors. This is a crucial enterprise for an empirically validated reconstruction of conceptual metaphors on the level of the linguistic system (corpus-linguistic analysis). It is also a necessary precondition for designing psycholinguistic experiments and for coding metaphors in discourse. See PragglejazGroup (2007) and Steen (1999, 2002a, 2002b) for details of the identification procedure.

15. I shall return to Steen's (2007b) modified proposal of distinguishing language as a symbolic structure from language as behavior in chapter 7.

16. For a similar critique see Steen (2000).

CHAPTER ONE

1. See Kurz on Aristotle's concept of metaphor (1976, 17): "The analogical schema, that is, the actual position of the parts in the analogy, must be known beforehand in order for the metaphor to be understandable. The metaphor is based on the preverbally specified and known existence of analogical relations."

2. This implication holds despite the fact that Aristotle's theory of understanding as presented in *De Anima* and his conception of sign in *De Interpretatione* does not include language as a form of understanding. Here language is treated separately from the impressions of the soul that are caused by the external world. Language is thought to relate to concepts that result from impressions of the empirical world (cf. Eggs 1984; Lieb 1964, 1981; Mitchell 1986, 1994; Trabant 1989). This does not, however, contradict the view that using language implies certain cognitive processes such as finding analogies between concepts.

3. Lakoff and Johnson take a similar stance in their formulation of conceptual metaphors as "understanding and experiencing one kind of thing in terms of another" (1980, 5). Note, however, that Wittgenstein's concept of seeing-as specifies the processes involved more precisely, and this is why in this book "seeing one thing in terms of another" will be used to describe the cognitive activity underlying metaphor production (and presumably also reception).

4. It is more than a notable aside that this passage figures in Aristotle's treatment of tragedy, which contains a rather long and detailed account of the characteristics of language in general. Hence, although the famous passages on metaphor are included in the *Poetics*, they are not presented as poetic devices but as elements of language as such. Language is a poetic device for the poet, just as stone is for the sculptor. At the end of this chapter, we will return to the fact that Aristotle has been falsely criticized for holding a view of metaphor as a poetic device.

5. Lieb's translation of this passage is based on a close philological study of Aristotle's concept of metaphor; it provides a much closer rendition of the Greek text than Halliwell's translation in Loeb's Classical Library (cf. Lieb 1996).

6. The term "$\mathrm{11rw}$" is an abbreviation of the concept of metaphor of type 1, which is relational and wide.

7. See chapter 4 for a detailed discussion of the different theories of metaphor and their specific variants of the triadic relation.

8. We will return to a closer account of Lakoff and Johnson's conception of conceptual metaphors in general and of the "love is a journey" metaphor specifically in the subsequent chapters 2 and 3.

9. A is the subject matter (the embodiment of a woman); M is the material (clouds); and B is the mental image of a woman (seeing-as).

10. This formulation somewhat alters Aldrich's analysis, which, on the one hand, appears to downgrade the impact of the material of the produced sign when he is speaking about "something arbitrary that is seen in any kind of way," while, on the other hand, he speaks about the embodiment and materialization of the mental image.

11. Lakoff and Johnson (1980, 49) give the following verbal instantiations of the conceptual metaphor LOVE IS A PHYSICAL FORCE: I could feel the *electricity* between us. There were *sparks*. I was *magnetically* drawn to her. The atmosphere around them is always *charged*. There is incredible *energy* in their relationship.

12. The appreciation of metaphors is characteristic of romantic philosophers and poets (cf. also Johnson 1987; Kurz and Pelster 1976).

13. Note that Aristotle's treatment of metaphor in the *Poetics* is integrated into a relatively systematic description of the characteristic traits of language. Aristotle

distinguishes here between the elements of language (from letter and syllable to linguistic categories such as case and sentence) and a repertoire of words (lexicon), which are in turn distinguished in terms of their internal structure (morphology) and their common and uncommon usage (pragmatics). Metaphor and all the other tropes are considered as words with an uncommon usage. Given this larger context, it seems at least not completely mistaken to assume that Aristotle conceived of metaphor not only as a form of poetic language but also as a form of language use in general. (cf. Aristotle 1995).

14. Research in metaphor in the context of applied linguistics is especially sensitive to these issues. See, for instance, Cameron (1999a, 1999b, 2003), Cameron and Low (1999); Deignan (2006), Gibbs (1999b), and Steen (2007a, 2007b).

15. A reaction to this lack of empirical grounding is a biannual conference series on Research and Application of Metaphors (RAaM), which has been providing a forum for research on metaphors in language use since 1996. At the RAaM held in 2006 the International Association for Metaphor Studies was founded, which now offers a home for the community of metaphor scholars interested in "metaphors in the real world." For further information on current trends and activities see www.raam.org.uk.

16. Gerard Steen (2007a, 2007b) critically comments on this lack of distinction and proposes different accounts for the different facets of metaphor. I will return to Steen's criticism and proposal later.

CHAPTER TWO

1. Langer's stance with regard to metaphor as a constructive, cognitive activity is rooted in Ernst Cassirer (1953) and Alfred North Whitehead's (1927) philosophy of symbolic forms.

2. This sensualistic view of the role of metaphor in human understanding and language has a long tradition in the history of European thought. The German philologist Franz Dornseiff (1966, 126), among others, has pointed this out: as advocates of the idea that poetic language is the mother tongue of mankind ("die Poesie als Muttersprache des Menschengeschlechts"), he mentions philosophers such as Haman, Herder, Muratori, Shaftesbury, Vico, and Wood. For instance, Giambattista Vico regards figurative language (metaphor, metonymy, and synecdoche) as the primary, the first language in the process of language evolution (cf. Danesi 1994; Trabant 1994). And Dornseiff writes in a similar vein: "The realm of metaphor is the poetic domain of language . . . metaphoricity is a foundational element of speaking" (Dornseiff 1966, 126, trans. CM).

3. See, for instance, Andrew Ortony's introduction to the seminal volume of collected papers, *Metaphor and Thought* (1979, 2d ed. 1993a), for a similar view.

4. This list provides but a small selection of some of the theories that inform the contemporary controversies. For an overview, see the introductions in Haverkamp (1996, 1998a, 1998b), Ortony (1979, 1993a, 1993b), and Gibbs (forthcoming).

5. A historical aside: Logical positivism was a philosophical movement with roots in Austrian and German philosophy. The Wiener Kreis (Vienna Circle) around the philosopher Moritz Schlick attracted philosophers such as Neurath, Carnap, Gödel, and Popper, among others, and the Berliner Gruppe (Berlin Group) was headed by the logician Hans

Reichenbach. With fascism taking over, most of these scholars emigrated, mostly to England or the United States, where logical positivism became very influential.

6. See Ortony's characterization of the fundamental view of logical positivism: "A basic notion of positivism was that reality could be precisely described through the medium of language in a manner that was clear, unambiguous, and, in principle testable—reality could, and should, be literally describable" (1993b, 1).

7. Ulla Meinecke, "Die Tänzerin" (The Dancer; trans. CM): "Du bist die Tänzerin im Sturm / Du bist ein Kind auf dünnem Eis / Du wirfst mit Liebe nur so um dich / Und immer triffst du mich."

8. Lakoff himself characterized the development of his scientific thinking in a presentation given at a conference on "Mind, Language and Metaphor. Euroconference on Consciousness and the Imagination" held in Kerkrade (the Netherlands) in April 2002.

9. These examples are taken from Lakoff and Johnson (1980, 4, 44–46, 49). As has become common practice in cognitive linguistics, italics indicate the metaphoric parts of the sentences. Italicization in the examples reproduces the emphases in the original.

10. Ten years after Lakoff and Johnson's publication, cognitive linguistics had become a huge and expanding scholarly field incorporating not only research on conceptual metaphor theory (Kövecses 1986, 1988, 1990, 2000a, 2000b, 2002; Lakoff 1987, 1993, 2002; Lakoff and Johnson 1980, 1999; Lakoff and Núñez 2000; Lakoff and Turner 1989; Sweetser 1990) and, more generally, on figurative language (especially metonymy) and thought (cf. Barcelona 2000; Bouvet 2001; Gibbs 1994, 1999b, Goosens et al. 1995; Mittelberg 2003, 2006, forthcoming; Mittelberg and Waugh forthcoming; Panther and Radden 1999; 2003), but also on a wide range of cognitive approaches to language, such as Ronald Langacker's (1987, 1988, 1991, 1998, 1999b) cognitive grammar, Leonard Talmy's (1975, 1985, 1987, 1991, 1994, 2003) work on cognitive typology of motion verbs, on force dynamics, and, recently, on the attentional system of language. Cognitive linguistics also embraces Gilles Fauconnier's (1985, 1997, 1998) theory of mental spaces, Gilles Fauconnier and Mark Turner's (1996, 2002) blending theory, and, most recently, the work on construction grammar' (cf. Croft 2001; Fillmore and Kay 1997; Goldberg 1995, 1996; and Langacker 1987, 1996, 1999a).

11. Note that Lakoff (1993, 207) points out that the names for conceptual metaphors have the status of mnemonics. They do not refer to an assumed propositional structure of conceptual metaphors; on the contrary, conceptual metaphors are conceived of as nonpropositional mappings between a source and a target domain.

12. The relationship between conceptual and verbal metaphors is a topic that we will continue to touch upon throughout the book. Steen and Gibbs, in their introduction to *Metaphor in Cognitive Science*, describe the relationship as follows: "Conventional linguistic metaphors reflect pervasive conceptual metaphors and are perhaps the best source for discovering these metaphoric schemes of thought" (Steen and Gibbs 1999, 1).

13. See Gibbs's (1994) monograph on the poetics of mind for a most detailed overview of the psycholinguistic research on figurative language processing. A more recent overview and discussion are provided in Katz et al. (1998).

14. Consider, for instance, the work of Slobin (1987, 1991) and Slobin and Berman (1994) on cross-cultural language acquisition and the work of Levinson and his Language

and Cognition Group regarding spatial language and cognition in non-Indo-European languages (Gumperz and Levinson 1996 and Levinson 2003 provide overviews and discussion of this recent work).

15. It is with the cognitive and pragmatic turn in the humanities that Anglo-Saxon metaphor scholars have ceased to keep track of scientific developments in Europe, at least insofar as they have not been published in English. The generation of metaphor scholars that preceded this turn (such as, for instance, Black 1962; Brooke-Rose 1958; Richards 1936; Beardsley 1962) maintained the connection with European thinking. Since the 1980s, metaphor research in the Anglo-Saxon world has developed independently of the nonanglophone world. The neglect of Weinrich's work is one of the consequences. See Olaf Jäkel (1999) for a similar argument.

16. For empirical support in favor of conceptual metaphor theory's fundamental claims, see Gibbs (1993a, 1994, 1998); for an overview of the critical points in the psycholinguistic discussion of the relationship between figurative language and figurative thought, see Katz (1998); for explicit criticism, see Murphy (1996, 1997). For reconstructions of systems of conceptual metaphors, see Baldauf (1997); Liebert (1992) for conceptual metaphor systems in contemporary German; Buchholtz (1993, 1996) for verbal and conceptual metaphors in psychoanalytic discourse; Kövecses (1986, 1988, 1990, 2000a, 2000b) for emotions; and Lakoff (2002) for moral systems in American politics. For a summary of systematic theoretical evidence (polysemy, inference, novel metaphors, semantic change), see Lakoff (1993). For semantic change as evidence, see Sweetser (1990); for novel metaphors as evidence, see Lakoff and Turner (1989).

17. See Katz (1998) for a similar distinction in his review *Figurative Language and Thought*.

18. Among them are Blumenberg (1960), Bühler (1982), Henle (1958), Stählin (1914), Ricœur (1986), and Wundt (1922) (to name just a few). This seems to be the right moment to make a "rhetorical" statement regarding the impossibility of honestly accounting for all the approaches to metaphor in the way they deserve. This would easily fill an entire book, of course. The bibliographies of Bosque (1984), Shibles (1971), van Noppen (1985), van Noppen and Hols (1990), and Nuessel (1991) are vivid testimony of this situation. Interestingly, there is no textbook on metaphor that seeks to document the different approaches (older but still pertinent exceptions are provided by Kurz (1982) and Kurz and Pelster (1976). The introduction to metaphor by Kövecses (2002) is an introduction to the study of metaphor from the perspective of conceptual metaphor theory and hence does not provide an overview of the field of metaphor theories or research. The classic volumes (Anglo-Saxon as well as German) are edited volumes, which bring important contributions to metaphor theory to the attention of a wider audience (cf. Haverkamp 1996, 1998a, 1998b; Johnson 1981; Ortony 1993a; Shibles 1972). Exceptions are Lieb's (1964) reconstruction of the historical concept of metaphor, and Gibbs's (forthcoming) *The Cambridge Handbook of Metaphor and Thought*.

19. See Gibbs's various publications in support of the view that not only metaphor is pervasive in thought and language but also other tropes, such as metonymy, oxymoron, and irony, are also broadly used figurative modes of speaking (cf. Gibbs 1993a, 1993b, 1994 for a summary of earlier work). Gibbs sees these uses of figurative language as indicators of the inherently figurative structures of our mind (cf. Gibbs 1994).

20. Gibbs (1994) gives a most detailed overview of this wide field of experimental psycholinguistic research. A more recent documentation of the diverging lines in psycholinguistic research on figurative language is given in the joint monograph by Katz et al. (1998) *Figurative Language and Thought.*

CHAPTER THREE

1. There are two fundamental commitments of cognitive linguistics: first, to formulate general cognitive principles to explain linguistic phenomena; and second, to show that these principles are psychologically real. Lakoff formulated these hitherto implicit cognitive commitments in his contribution to the first issue of the then newly founded journal *Cognitive Linguistics*: "The cognitive commitment is a commitment to make one's account of human language accord with what is generally known about the mind and the brain, from other disciplines as well as our own [i.e., linguistics—CM]" (Lakoff 1990, 40). The second commitment is a generalization commitment: "The generalization commitment is a commitment to characterizing the general principles governing all aspects of human language" (Lakoff 1990, 40).

2. Steen's (2007a, 2007b) proposal of four or eight different cognitive approaches for researching metaphor in applied linguistics (or language) seeks to disentangle these facets systematically. I shall come back to Steen's proposal in the concluding chapter of the book.

3. See Forceville's (2005) analysis "Visual Representations of the Idealized Cognitive Model of Anger in the Asterix Album La Zizanie."

4. This is an elaboration of Lakoff and Kövecses' concept of "basic-level metaphors" (1987, 218).

5. Grady, Taub, and Morgan (1996) actually introduce the terms "primitive" and "compound" metaphors. Their terminology highlights the hierarchical and compositional structure of these two forms of conceptual metaphor. My use of "primary" and "complex" metaphors follows later publications by Grady and others (cf. Lakoff and Johnson 1999; Kövecses 2002) in which they are replaced by the terms "primary" and "complex" metaphors.

6. Johnson relates his concept of image-schema to the Kantian concept of schema (cf. Johnson 1987, 24, 152–57). See also Lakoff (1990) on the relation of abstract reason and image schemas.

7. Kövecses (2002) introduces the notion of "simple metaphors" to account for this type of metaphor, and he gives an overview of different forms conceptual metaphors.

8. Note, however, that this is a form of metonymy and can hence only be regarded as metaphor in a wider sense.

9. This relates to the issue of cross-metaphorical coherence (cf. chapter 5).

10. This analysis might appear obvious, but it should be emphasized that this is a fundamental semiotic process in which hand movements exploit the semantics inherent in everyday bodily activities. For this kind of semiosis, compare Calbris (2003), Mittelberg 2006; Mittelberg and Waugh forthcoming, Müller and Haferland (1997), Müller (1998, 2004, in preparation), Posner (2003), and Streeck (1994).

11. This issue is discussed in more detail in chapter 4 of this book.

12. We will return to this in the context of a review of the different variants of the dead versus alive distinction in chapter 6.

13. For an overview of research in lexical fields see Schmidt (1973). Weinrich, furthermore, mentions Paul Claudel's notion of *champ de figures* as a source of his concept of image field. For a critical evaluation and an actualization of word field theory, see Fricke (1996).

14. Sweetser's (1990) proposal of conceptual metaphors inducing the direction of linguistic change points in a similar direction.

15. For a detailed overview of metaphor and gesture, see Cienki and Müller (forthcoming a); for a recent survey of the field see Cienki (forthcoming) and Cienki and Müller (forthcoming b).

16. See Müller (1998a) for a detailed account of these categories of gestures.

17. My observations regarding gestural and verbal expressions of motion events indicate that there are similar forms of variation in literal speech and gesture (cf. Müller 1998a).

18. Aldrich uses the term "visual metaphor," which I replace here with the term "pictorial metaphor."

CHAPTER FOUR

1. For similar views, see Bühler (1982 = [1936]) and Wundt (1922).

2. Cf. also Kyratzis (in preparation).

3. Lieb reconstructs the extensions of the historical concepts of metaphor. Note, furthermore, that I am using the term "sense" here in a nontechnical manner, not in the Fregean terms of "sense and reference."

4. See also chapter 1.

5. Lieb's translation is based on a close philological study of Aristotle's concept of metaphor; it provides a much closer rendition of the Greek text than Halliwell's translation in Loeb's Classical Library (cf. Lieb 1967 [1996]).

6. Concentrating on the four basic versions is in line with Lieb's argument that the Aristotelian concept of metaphor in a wider sense (11rw) is fundamental in that the other ones can be traced back to the concept of metaphor as developed in the first part of Aristotle's classical account of metaphor already quoted above.

7. The first example is taken from a song by Stevie Wonder (lyrics and music by Stevie Wonder, 1972); the second one is taken in this form from Lieb (1996) and originates from Homer's *Iliad*: Holding this shield before him, Ajax son of Telamon, came up close to Hector and menaced him, saying, "Hector, you shall now learn, man to man, what kind of champions the Danaans have among them even besides *lion-hearted Achilles* cleaver of the ranks of men. He now abides at the ships in anger with Agamemnon shepherd of his people, but there are many of us who are well able to face you; therefore begin the fight" (*The Iliad*, book VII). Black (1993) complains about the boring insistence with which the problem of metaphor has been discussed for 2000 years on the basis of this very example taken from Homer, which, I might add, is exceptionally simple. Thus, my intentions here are to connect with the tradition and to overcome it with an example from contemporary English.

8. Lieb subsumes "similarity" (Merkmalsgleichheit) and "analogy" (Analogie) under the term "resemblance" (Ähnlichkeit). I will use "analogy" as a general term here (instead of Lieb's term "resemblance").

9. Note that this analysis departs from Lieb's assumption that although the types (2rw) and (2rn) are logical subsets of the types (1rw) and (1rn), they are not included in type 1. Discursively expressed, this means that Lieb holds that the substitution and the comparison theories are based on dyadic rather than triadic structures. I do not share his assumption and hold instead that both of these concepts of metaphor also presuppose a third relatum, and this is a linguistic sign. It is the linguistic sign that either substitutes a literal expression or that stimulates the comparison. Hence this view presupposes a triadic structure as much as the two Aristotelian ones.

10. Ricœur (1986, 20–31) traces it back to Aristotle, but Quintilian is the first to explicitly formulate it (cf. Lieb 1964, 57–59).

11. At least not by scholars of style, literary criticism, and rhetoric. Right from the start, historical linguists of course recognized the overwhelming presence of "dead" metaphors in language and their important role in language change.

12. Surprisingly, Beardsley's (1962) related proposal has not received comparable attention.

13. For an overview of the discussion, see Katz (1998).

14. For a critical evaluation of Searle's account see Closs-Traugott (1985).

15. The conceptual metaphor LOVE IS A JOURNEY would then be motivated by a larger scale metaphor such as LIFE IS A JOURNEY. How this is experientially grounded remains unclear.

16. Different linguistic forms of the names for conceptual metaphors have been used. For the most part, they have the structure TARGET-DOMAIN IS SOURCE-DOMAIN or TARGET-DOMAIN AS SOURCE-DOMAIN. Therefore, we may encounter terminological variations such as LOVE IS A JOURNEY (Lakoff and Johnson 1980, 44) and LOVE-AS-JOURNEY (Lakoff 1993, 207).

CHAPTER FIVE

1. This example is taken from a *BBC News* 1987 broadcast and was uttered by the president of the Farmers' Union.

2. Without having access to the context of the utterance, it is not clear which of two possible figurative readings of the idiomatic expression "to be in the pipeline" was intended: instead of just referring to the actual distribution of the butter stocks, the president could also be referring to the ongoing discussion of the overproduction of butter in the EU. The first reading appears to be more plausible, at least out of context. Furthermore, the idea of an ongoing discussion of the overproduction of butter would most likely also include the issue of distributing the butter stocks.

3. For instance, in newspapers (the *New Yorker*), in the German political journal *Der Spiegel* (*Hohlspiegel*), and in popular books on style; cf., for instance, Schneider (1999).

4. See, for instance, Wolfgang Kayser (Kayser 1976, 43) in his classical introduction to literary theory:

The transition from metaphor to catachresis is smooth, where the latter is understood to be the use of an inappropriate expression. This use can be thoroughly incorrect (he plucked potatoes; he drank soup), but it can also serve particular intentions and then approach the metaphor: loud tears, a withered light. An intensification of the catachresis produces the oxymoron, the connection of two images that actually exclude each other. In the Petrarchism of the 16th and 17th centuries, but also beforehand in the "flowery" poetry of the Middle Ages, time and time again, one comes across expressions such as the bitter sweetness (love), her sweet bitterness, the living death, the dead life, the dark sun. Oxymorons are not uncommon in Shakespearean texts where, incidentally, they function somewhat differently from the way they do in Petrarchism:

Beautiful tyrant, fiend angelical! (*Romeo and Juliet*)
His humble ambition, proud humility,
His jarring concord, and his discord dulcet,
His faith, his sweet disaster . . . (*All's Well That Ends Well*).

5. Here is the quote: "An image break easily occurs when somebody uses common images in a formulaic manner, without really visualizing them" (Reiners 1976, 333).

6. Note that Lakoff uses consciousness here presumably in the sense of conscious awareness. Throughout this book the term "consciousness" is used as a cover term for the entire architecture and processes of human consciousness.

7. Cienki and Swan (2001) provide a detailed discussion of the problems related to cross-metaphorical coherence in spoken language.

8. Italics marking the metaphors follow Lakoff and Johnson's notation.

9. See Steen's (1999) article "From Linguistic to Conceptual Metaphor in Five Steps," in which he critically assesses the lack of methodological rigor in the identification of conceptual metaphors. Steen documents the need for closer lexical level analysis in the process of conceptual metaphor identification (cf. also PragglejazGroup 2007; Steen 2002a, 2002b, 2007b).

10. For an analysis of cross-metaphorical coherence in conceptual metaphors, see Cienki and Swan (n.d.).

11. For an excellent survey of this work see Gibbs (1994), and for a more recent discussion of the state of the art see Katz, Cacciari, Gibbs, and Turner (1998).

12. Note that I am using "idiom" in the following as a general term to refer to metaphorical phraseological units. I do not refer to the wide range of different "fixed forms" that also belong to the category of idioms, such as sayings, proverbs, binominals, or formulaic expressions. For a pertinent classification of phraseological units of German, see Burger, Buhofer, and Sialm (1982, 30–31). For a cognitive linguistic analysis of German idioms, see Dobrovol'skij (1995, 1997). On the vitality of metaphors in German idioms, see Burger (1998, 2004).

13. Hadumod Bußmann (1990, 2d. ed.) Lexikon der Sprachwissenschaft, 371.

14. See, for instance, Braak (1969). It is one of those endlessly repeated examples in German linguistic reference literature (comparable to "Green ideas sleep furiously" or "The cat is on the mat" in the Anglo-Saxon world).

15. I am very grateful to Wallace Chafe for assistance in finding the adequate literal and the idiomatic translations of the examples provided in this chapter.

16. The term "literally" is used in this context to characterize the source domain, image field, or secondary subject of a verbal metaphor. Hence, it does not implicitly seek to introduce the distinction between a literal and a figurative meaning. Rather, I regard them as two facets of a verbal metaphor.

17. This is, of course, the very nature of conditional clauses in German (cf. Eisenberg 1986) as well as in English " . . . conditional clauses state the dependence of one circumstance or set of circumstances on another" (Quirk and Greenbaum 1973, 323–324; see also Sweetser 1996).

18. Note that this analysis contrasts in some respects with the analysis provided by Grady, Oakley, and Coulson (1999) because they claim that the inference of incompetence is due to the incongruity of the butcher's means with the surgeon's ends. This analysis misses some relevant aspects: first, the goal of the butcher's work seems to be more the preparation of a dead animal for consumption than the killing of animals. Instead, the killing of an animal is—if it is performed by the butcher at all—only the first step in this procedure, not the ultimate goal of butchery; second, even the means of the butcher contradict the means employed by a surgeon (the means of a butcher is cutting off parts; the means of a surgeon is putting together parts); and third, the goals of both professions also appear to contradict each other (the goal of a butcher is preparing for consumption; the goal of a surgeon is healing). Therefore, the inference of incompetence seems to be more adequately explained in terms of an interaction between both the means and the end of their respective work.

19. For a condensed account of the basic principles of conceptual blending, see Fauconnier and Turner (2002, 47–50) and Grady, Oakley, and Coulson (1999, 107).

20. This analysis is in line with Cienki and Swan's view on salience and blending: "The particular elements of the inputs which will actually be blended are determined by their salience within the context in which they are being invoked" (Cienki and Swan n.d., 7). Context triggers different projections into the conceptual blend, and this determines which concepts are salient and which are not.

21. Cienki and Swan (n.d.) have found a similar formal blend in their material.

CHAPTER SIX

1. Recent exceptions to this trend can be found in metaphor studies that analyze metaphors in literary as well as in ordinary language texts (Cameron 1999a, 1999b, 2003; Deignan 2005; Goatly 1997).

2. The issue of the vitality (Lebendigkeit) of metaphors has received interest in two fields with different focuses in different countries. It has been under scrutiny and debated since the 1980s in Anglo-American psycholinguistics, specifically in the context of figurative language processing but also in relation to indirect speech acts; Gibbs (1993b, 1994) and Katz et al. (1998) offer critical evaluations and an overview of the discussions; Ortony (1993a) contains some classical papers by psycholinguists involved in this debate (Gentner and Jeziorski 1993; Gibbs 1993a; Glucksberg and Keysar 1993; Paivio and Walsh 1993; Winner and Gardner 1993; see also Stock, Slack, and Ortony 1993). Cacciari and Tabossi

(1993) offer a selection of papers with regard to idiom processing. More recent publications are Berghoff (2005), Colston and Katz (2005), Gibbs (1999c), Glucksberg (2001), and Keysar et al. (2000). The vitality of metaphors in idioms is a long-standing and established topic of European phraseology. Cf. Burger (1996, 1998, 1999, 2004); Burger, Buhofer, and Sialm (1982); Dobrovol'skij (1995, 2003); Häcki-Buhofer 2003; Häcki-Buhofer and Burger (1992, 1994).

3. I am relying here on Kluge (1975).

4. It is interesting, although probably not really surprising, that this aspect of verbal metaphors was especially present in earlier psychological treatments of language, such as those of Wilhelm Wundt (1922), Karl Bühler (1982), and Friedrich Kainz (1972). In contrast, the eminent historical linguist Hermann Paul did not use it as criterion. He simply speaks of metaphors that have attained the level of common usage ("usuell"). And even when he talks about conceptual aspects of metaphors, he remains focused on the collective level of a language community, which documents a specific focus of interest on a certain facet of the world in its commonly used metaphors: "[B]y looking at all the metaphors that had become common usage in a language, one recognizes which interests were particularly powerful in the language community" (Paul 1937, 95; first published 1886).

5. Entrenchment connects to the conceptualization parameter, a well-known feature in processes of grammaticalization (cf. Closs-Traugott 1985). The concept of entrenchment is an important and fundamental trait of conceptual metaphor theory, and I shall return to it later in this section.

6. See Schlegel's account of poetic metaphors in chapter 1.

7. Clearly, the dead (historical) ones in Lakoff's terms are also conventionalized, and therefore the distinction between historical and conventional metaphors appears somewhat misleading.

8. These questions are at the core of psycholinguistic research into metaphor processing, more specifically the processing of idioms and indirect speech acts (Gibbs 1993b; Glucksberg 2001; Keysar and Bly 1995; Keysar, Glucksberg, and Horton 2000). Gibbs (1994) and Katz et al. (1998) offer critical overviews and discussions of this debate. See also Kyratzis (2003) for a detailed account of this controversy.

9. See Gibbs (1994a, 119): "The results of the extensive empirical investigations reviewed in this chapter do not support many of the hypotheses suggested by linguists, philosophers, and literary theorists who specifically contend that figurative language is special and always demands extra work to be interpreted. Instead, the psycholinguistic research indicates that people can understand many instances of figurative expression effortlessly, without the explicit recognition that such language is special or reflective of deviant thought."

10. With applied linguistics' growing interest in metaphor, this has begun to change. See Deignan (2005)—inspired by Goatly (1997) and Lakoff (1987)—for a recent classification that addresses vitality and conventionalization and distinguishes four categories of metaphor: innovative, conventionalized, dead, and historical.

11. Other accounts of dynamic aspects of metaphors are Cameron (1999a, 1999b, 2002), Deignan (2005), Stöckl (2004), and Hanks (2006). Note that these authors do not have a shared understanding of dynamicity. Whereas for Cameron and Deignan the dynamics is a matter of degree in metaphorically motivated linguistic expressions (Deignan

2005, 39), for Hanks, dynamic metaphors are ad hoc coinages that contrast with conventional metaphors; Stöckl in turn addresses issues regarding the pictorial revitalization of conventionalized verbal metaphors.

12. Note that related concepts have been suggested by Cameron and Steen. Cameron (1999b) puts forward the concept of "process metaphor" in her work on metaphors in spoken discourse; Steen (1992) proposes "psychological metaphors" in his work on the perception of metaphors in literature. It is noteworthy that these concepts crop up when scholars are trying to come to grips with an empirically based analysis of metaphors (as opposed to discussing the same kind of "invented" examples as was the custom in metaphor theory for many years).

13. Cameron (1999b, 109) defines the necessary conditions for process metaphors as follows: "A stretch of language in its discourse context is said to be a process metaphor if a discourse participant perceives an incongruity between two domains referring to the same topic and, in processing, resolves the perceived conceptual incongruity, so that some meaning is transferred across domains."

14. "Tiefschläge

Unter die Gürtellinie des politischen Gegners gingen wohl einige der Redebeiträge vom vergangenen Aschermittwoch.

Verbale Attacken gehören zur Politik. Das haben die letzten Tage wieder gezeigt. Aber die Reden vom Aschermittwoch werfen auch diese Frage auf: Wo beginnt eigentlich die Beleidigung?"

CHAPTER SEVEN

1. For a new proposal of a theory of local deixis in German that systematically integrates deictic gestures, see Ellen Fricke (2002, 2007).

REFERENCES

Abraham, Werner. 1998. *Linguistik der uneigentlichen Rede. Linguistische Analysen an den Rändern der Sprache*. Tübingen: Stauffenburg Verlag.

Aldrich, Virgil C. 1996. Visuelle Metapher. In *Theorie der Metapher*, edited by Anselm Haverkamp, pp. 142–59. Darmstadt: Wissenschaftliche Buchgesellschaft (first published in 1968).

Aquinas, Thomas. Summa II.

Arens, Hans. 1967. *Sprachwissenschaft. Der Gang ihrer Entwicklung von der Antike bis zur Gegenwart*. Frankfurt: Athenäum Fischer Verlag.

Aristotle. 1995. *Poetik*. Translated by Stephen Halliwell. Loeb Classical Library. Cambridge, MA, and London: Harvard University Press.

Auer, Peter. 1986. Kontextualisierung. *Studium Linguistik* 19:22–47.

———. 1992. Introduction: John Gumperz approach to contextualization. In *The contextualization of language*, edited by Peter Auer and Aldo di Luzio, pp. 1–37. Amsterdam: John Benjamins.

Augustine. *Confessions*.

Baldauf, Christa. 1997. *Metapher und Kognition: Grundlagen einer neuen Theorie der Alltagsmetapher*. Frankfurt: Peter Lang.

Barcelona, Antonio, ed. 2000. *Metaphor and Metonymy at the Cross-Roads*. Berlin and New York: Mouton de Gruyter.

Barfield, Owen. 1962. Poetic Diction and Legal Fiction. In *The Importance of Language*, edited by Max Black, pp. 51–71. Englewood Cliffs, NJ: Prentice-Hall.

Barsalou, Larry. 1987. The Instability of Graded Structure: Implications for the Nature of Concepts. In *Concepts and Conceptual Development: Ecological and Intellectual Factors*, edited by Ulric Neisser. Cambridge: Cambridge University Press.

Bartsch, Renate. 2002. *Consciousness Emerging. The Dynamics of Perception, Imagination, Action, Memory, Thought, and Language*. Amsterdam: John Benjamins.

Beardsley, Monroe C. 1962. The Metaphorical Twist. *Philosophy and Phenomenological Research* 22(3):293–307.

Bergson, Henri. 1946. *Matière et Mémoire*. Paris.

Bertau, Marie-Cécile. 1996. *Sprachspiel Metapher. Denkweisen und kommunikative Funktion einer rhetorischen Figur*. Opladen: Westdeutscher Verlag.

Black, Max. 1962. *Models and Metaphors. Studies in Language and Philosophy*. Ithaca, NY: Cornell University Press.

———. 1993. More about Metaphor. In *Metaphor and Thought*, edited by Andrew Ortony, pp. 19–41. 2d ed. Cambridge: Cambridge University Press.

Blank, Andreas. 1997. *Prinzipien des lexikalischen Bedeutungswandels am Beispiel der romanischen Sprachen*. Tübingen: Niemeyer.

Blank, Andreas, and Peter Koch, eds. 1999. *Historical Semantics and Cognition*. Berlin: Mouton de Gruyter.

Blumenberg, Hans. 1960. *Paradigmen zu einer Metaphorologie*. Archiv für Begriffsgeschichte 6. Bonn: Bouvier.

Borgschulte, Gudrun. 2007. Verbal and Gestural Localization of Time in German Discourse. Talk given at the Third International Conference of the International Society for Gesture Studies, "Integrating Gestures," which was held on June 12–21, 2007, in Evanston, IL.

Bosque, Ignazio. 1984. Bibliografía sobra la metáfora. *Revista de Literatura* 46: 173–94.

Bouvet, Danielle. 2001. *La dimension corporelle de la parole. Les marques posturo-mimo-gestuelles de la parole, leurs aspects métonymiques et métaphoriques, et leur rôle au cours d'un récit*. Paris: Peeters.

Braak, Ivo. 1969. *Poetik in Stichworten*. Kiel: Hirt (reprint 1974).

Bréal, Michel. 1899. *Essai de sémantique*. Paris: Hachette.

Bressem, Jana. Forthcoming. Recurrent Form Features in Co-speech Gestures. In *Recurrence in Coverbal Gestures—Investigating Form and Function*, edited by Jana Bressem and Silva Ladewig. Amsterdam and Philadelphia: John Benjamins.

Brinkmann, Friedrich. 1878. *Die Metaphern. Studien über den Geist der modernen Sprachen. Bd. 1: Die Thierbilder der Sprache*. Bonn: Adolph Marcus.

Brooke-Rose, Christine. 1958. *A grammar of Metaphor*. London: Secker and Warburg.

Brünner, Gisela. 1987. Metaphern für Sprache und Kommunikation in Alltag und Wissenschaft. *Diskussion Deutsch* 94: 100–19.

Buchholtz, Michael B., ed. 1993. *Metaphernanalyse*. Göttingen: Vandenhoeck and Ruprecht.

———. 1996. *Metaphern der "Kur". Eine qualitative Studie zum psychotherapeutischen Prozeß*. Opladen: Westdeutscher Verlag.

Bühler, Karl. 1982. *Sprachtheorie. Die Darstellungsfunktion der Sprache*. Stuttgart: Fischer (first published 1936).

Burger, Harald. 1996. Phraseologie und Metaphorik. In volume 2 of *Lexical Structures and Language Use*, edited by Ernst Weigand, and Franz Hundsnurscher, pp. 167–178. Beiträge zur Dialogforschung 10. Tübingen.

———. 1998. Idiom and Metaphor—Their Relation in Theory and Text. In *Europhras '97*, edited by Peter Durco, pp. 30–36. Bratislava.

———. 1999. Problembereiche einer historischen Phraseologie. In *Europhras '95. Europäische Phraseologie im Vergleich: Gemeinsames Erbe und kulturelle Vielfalt*, edited by Wolfgang Eisenmann, pp. 79–108. Bochum.

———. 2004. Aspekte der "Lebendigkeit" des Idioms. In *Verschränkung der Kulturen. Der Sprach- und Literaturaustausch zwischen Skandinavien und den deutschsprachigen Ländern*, edited by Oskar Bandle et al., pp 3–22. Festschrift Hans-Peter Naumann. Tübingen.

Burger, Harald, Annelies Buhofer, and Ambros Sialm. 1982. *Handbuch der Phraseologie*. Berlin: De Gruyter.

Cacciari, Cristina and Patrizia Tabossi, eds. 1993. *Idioms, Processing Structure and Interpretation*. Hillsdale, NJ: Lawrence Erlbaum.

Calbris, Geneviève. 1985. Espace-Temps: Expression gestuelle du temps. *Semiotica* 55 (1/2): 43–73.

———. 1990. *The Semiotics of French Gestures*. Bloomington, IN: Indiana University Press.

———. 2003. From Cutting an Object to a Clear Cut Analysis: Gesture as the Representation of a Preconceptual Schema Linking Concrete Actions to Abstract Notions. *Gesture* 3 (1): 19–46.

Cameron, Lynne. 1999a. Operationalising "Metaphor" for Applied Linguistic Research. In *Researching and Applying Metaphor*, edited by Lynne Cameron and Graham Low, pp. 3–28. Cambridge: Cambridge University Press.

———. 1999b. Identifying and Describing Metaphor in Spoken Discourse Data. In *Researching and Applying Metaphor*, edited by Lynne Cameron and Graham Low, pp. 105–32. Cambridge: Cambridge University Press.

———. 2003. *Metaphor in Educational Discourse*. London and New York: Continuum.

———. 2007. A Discourse Dynamics Framework for Metaphor. The Open University. http://creet.open.ac.uk/projects/metaphoranalysis/theories.cfm?paper=ddfm.

Cameron, Lynne, and Low, Graham, eds. 1999. *Researching and Applying Metaphor*. Cambridge: Cambridge University Press.

Cann, Ronnie. 1993. *Formal Semantics. An Introduction*. Cambridge: Cambridge University Press.

Cassell's Dictionary. 1987. New York: Macmillan.

Cassirer, Ernst. 1953. *Philosophie der symbolischen Formen (I). Die Sprache*. Darmstadt: Wissenschaftliche Buchgesellschaft.

Chafe, Wallace. 1994. *Discourse, Consciousness, and Time. The Flow and Displacement of Conscious Experience in Speaking and Writing*. Chicago and London: University of Chicago Press.

———. 1996. How Consciousness Shapes Language. *Pragmatics and Cognition* 4 (1): 55–64.

Cienki, Alan. 1997. Motion in the Metaphorical Spaces of Morality and Reasoning as Expressed in Language and Gesture. *International Journal of Communication. A Review of Cognition, Culture and Communication* 7 (1/2): 85–98.

————. 1998. Metaphoric Gestures and Some of Their Relations to Verbal Metaphorical Expressions. In *Discourse and Cognition: Bridging the Gap*, edited by Jan-Pierre Koenig, pp. 189–204. Stanford, CA: Center for the Study of Language and Information.

————. 2000. The Production of Metaphoric Gestures: Evidence for On-line Cognitive Processing of Metaphoric Mappings. Unpublished manuscript.

————. 2003. Overview of, and Potential for, Research on Metaphor and Gesture. Introduction to the Theme Session of Metaphor and Gesture. ICLC 2003. Unpublished manuscript.

————. Forthcoming. Why Study Metaphor and Gesture. In *Metaphor and Gesture*, edited by Alan Cienki and Cornelia Müller. Amsterdam and Philadelphia: John Benjamins.

Cienki, Alan, and Cornelia Müller. Forthcoming a. Metaphor, Gesture and Thought. In *Cambridge Handbook of Metaphor and Thought*, edited by Raymond W. Gibbs. Cambridge: Cambridge University Press.

————., eds. Forthcoming b. *Metaphor and Gesture.* Amsterdam and Philadelphia: John Benjamins.

Cienki, Alan, and Deanne W. Swan. 2001. Metaphors, Coherence, and Blending. Unpublished manuscript.

Closs-Traugott, Elisabeth. 1985. "Conventional" and "Dead" Metaphors Revisited. In *The Ubiquity of Metaphor. Metaphor in Language and Thought*, edited by Wolf Paprotté and René Dirven, pp. 17–56. Amsterdam: Benjamins.

Coenen, Hans Georg. 2002. *Analogie und Metapher. Grundlegung einer Theorie der bildlichen Rede.* Berlin and New York: de Gruyter.

Cohen, Ted. 1975. Figurative Speech and Figurative Acts. *Journal of Philosophy* 72: 669–82.

Cohen, L. Jonathan. 1993. The Semantics of Metaphor. In *Metaphor and Thought*, edited by Andrew Ortony, pp. 58–70. Cambridge: Cambridge University Press.

Colston, Herbert, and Albert Katz. 2005. *Figurative Language Comprehension Social and Cultural Influences.* Hillsdale, NJ: Lawrence Erlbaum.

Croft, William. 2001. *Radical Construction Grammar: Syntactic Theory in Typological Perspective.* Oxford: Oxford University Press.

Danesi, Marcel. 1994. The Strategic Interaction View of Language: Robert J. Di Pietro's Vichian Paradigm for Theoretical and Applied Linguistics. In *Georgetown Roundtable on Language and Linguistics 1993: Strategic Interaction and Language Acquisition: Theory Practice, and Research*, edited by James E. Alatis, pp. 480–91. Washington, DC: Georgetown University Press.

Davidson, Donald. 1967. Truth and Meaning. *Synthese* 17: 304–23.

————. 1975. Semantics for Natural languages. In *The Logic of Grammar*, edited by Donald Davidson and G. Harman. Encino, CA: Dickenson.

————. 1978. What Metaphors Mean. *Critical Inquiry* 5: 31–47.

Deacon, Terrence W. 1997. *The Symbolic Species. The Co-evolution of Language and the Brain.* New York: Norton.

Deignan, Alice. 2005. *Metaphor and Corpus Linguistics*. Amsterdam and Philadelphia: John Benjamins.

Diderot. Lettre sur les sourds et muets. 1875. In *Œuvres complètes*, edited by Assézat. Vol. 1. Paris 1875.

Dobrovol'skij, Dmitirij. 1995. *Kognitive Aspekte der Idiom-Semantik. Studien zum Thesaurus deutscher Idiome*. Tübingen.

———. 1997. Idiome in kognitiver Perspektive: zur Begriffsbestimmung. In *Ethische Konzepte und mentale Kulturen I*, edited by Mariann Skog-Söderved, pp. 16–57. Umea.

Dornseiff, Franz. 1966. *Bezeichnungswandel unseres Wortschatzes*. Lahr: Moritz Schaumburg Verlag.

Duncan, Susan D. 2002. Gesture, Verb Aspect, and the Nature of Iconic Imagery in Natural Discourse. *Gesture* 2 (2): 183–206.

Durand, Jacques. 1987. Rhetorical Figures in the Advertising Image. In *Marketing and Semiotics: New Directions in the Study of Signs for Sale*, edited by J. Umiker-Sebeok, pp. 295–318. Berlin: Mouton/de Gruyter.

Eco, Umberto. 1984. *Semiotics and the Philosophy of Language*. Bloomington, IN: Indiana University Press.

Edelmann, Gerald M., and Giulio Tononi. 2000. *A Universe of Consciousness. How Matter Becomes Imagination*. New York: Basic Books.

Eggs, Ekkehart. 1984. *Die Rhetorik des Aristoteles. Ein Beitrag zur Theorie der Alltagsargumentation und Syntax von komplexen Sätzen im Französischen*. Frankfurt, Bern, and New York: Lang.

Eisenberg, Peter. 1986. *Grundriß der deutschen Grammatik*. Stuttgart: Metzler.

Farthing, G. William. 1992. *The Psychology of Consciousness*. Upper Saddle River, NJ: Prentice Hall.

Fatfouta, Firdaous. In preparation. Forms of the Tunesian Ring Gesture. In *Recurrence in Coverbal Gestures—Investigating Form and Function*, edited by Jana Bressem and Silva Ladewig. Amsterdam and Philadelphia: John Benjamins.

Fauconnier, Gilles. 1985. *Mental Spaces. Aspects of Meaning Construction in Natural Languages*. Cambridge, MA: Cambridge University Press.

———. 1997. *Mappings in Thought and Language*. Cambridge: Cambridge University Press.

———. 1998. Mental Spaces, Language Modalities, and Conceptual Integration. In *The New Psychology of Language*, edited by Michael Tomasello, pp. 251–79. Mahwah, NJ: Erlbaum.

Fauconnier, Gilles, and Mark Turner. 1996. Blending as a Central Process of Grammar. In *Conceptual Structure, Discourse and Language*, edited by Adele Goldberg, pp. 113–30. Stanford: Center for the Study of Language and Information.

———. 2002. *The Way We Think. Conceptual Blending and the Mind's Hidden Complexities*. New York: Basic Books.

Fillmore Charles J., and Paul Kay. 1997. *Construction Grammar*. Unpublished manuscript. www.icsi.berkeley.edu/~kay/bcg/ConGram.html.

Flanagan, Owen. 1998. Consciousness. In *A Companion to Cognitive Science*, edited by William Bechtel and George Graham. Malden, MA: Blackwell.

Forceville, Charles. 1996. *Pictorial Metaphor in Advertising*. London and New York: Routledge.

———. 1999. The Metaphor Colin Is a Child in Ian McEwan's Harold Pinter's, and Paul Schrader's The Comfort of Strangers. In *Metaphor and Symbol* 14(3): 179–98.

———. 2000. Compasses, Beauty Queens and Other PCs: Pictorial Metaphors in Computer Advertisements. *Hermes, Journal of Linguistics* 24: 31–55.

———. 2002. The Identification of Target and Source in Pictorial Metaphors. *Journal of Pragmatics* 34: 1–14.

———. 2005. Visual Representations of the Idealized Cognitive Model of Anger in the Asterix Album La Zizanie. *Journal of Pragmatics* 37(1): 69–88.

Frey, Gerhard. 1980. *Theorie des Bewußtseins*. Freiburg: Verlag Karl Alber.

Fricke, Ellen. 1996. *Die Verben des Riechens im Deutschen und Englischen. Eine kontrastive semantische Analyse*. KIT-Report 136. Berlin: Technische Universität Berlin.

———. 2002. Origo, Pointing, and Speech. The Impact of Co-speech Gestures on Linguistic Deixis Theory. *Gesture* 2(2): 207–26.

———. 2007. *Origo, Geste und Raum. Lokaldeixis im Deutschen*. Berlin, New York: De Gruyter.

Friedrich, Hugo. 1968. Die Metapher (Bochumer Disk). *Poetica* 2: 100–30.

Gentner, Dedre, and Michael Jeziorski. 1993. The Shift from Metaphor to Analogy in Western Science. In *Metaphor and Thought*, edited by Andrew Ortony, pp. 474–80. 2d ed. Cambridge: Cambridge University Press.

Gibbs, Raymond W., Jr. 1993a. Process and Products in Making Sense of Tropes. In *Metaphor and Thought*, edited by Andrew Ortony, pp. 252–76. 2d ed. Cambridge: Cambridge University Press.

———. 1993b. Why Idioms Are Not Dead Metaphors. In *Idioms, Processing Structure and Interpretation*, edited by Cristina Cacciari and P. Tabossi, pp. 57–77. Hillsdale, NJ: Lawrence Erlbaum.

———. 1994. *The Poetics of Mind. Figurative Thought, Language, and Understanding*. Cambridge: Cambridge University Press.

———. 1998. The Fight over Metaphor in Thought and Language. In *Figurative Language and Thought*, edited by Albert N. Katz, Cristina Cacciari, Raymond W. Gibbs, Jr., and Mark Turner, pp. 119–57. New York and Oxford: Oxford University Press.

———. 1999a. Researching Metaphor. In *Researching and Applying Metaphor*, edited by Lynn Cameron and G. Low, pp. 29–47. Cambridge: Cambridge University Press.

———. 1999b. Speaking and Thinking with Metonymy. In *Metonymy in Language and Thought*, edited by K.-U. Panther and G. Radden, pp. 61–76. Amsterdam/Philadelphia: John Benjamins.

———. 1999c. Intentions in the Experience of Meaning. Cambridge: Cambridge University Press.

———., ed. Forthcoming. *The Cambridge Handbook of Metaphor and Thought.* Cambridge: Cambridge University Press.

Gibbs, Raymond W., Jr., and H. Colston. 1995. The Cognitive Psychological Reality of Image Schema and Their Transformations. *Cognitive Linguistics* 6:347–78.

Gibbs, Raymond W., Jr., and Gerard J. Steen, eds. 1999. *Metaphor in Cognitive Linguistics.* Amsterdam and Philadelphia: John Benjamins.

Gilot, Francoise, and Carlton Lake. 1964. *Life with Picasso.* New York: McGraw-Hill.

Giora, Rachel 2003. *On Our Mind: Salience, Context, and Figurative Language.* New York: Oxford University Press.

———., ed. 2007. *Metaphor Processing.* Special issue of *Brian and Language* 100. Oxford: Academic Press.

Glucksberg, Sam. 2001. *Understanding Figurative Language: From Metaphors to Idioms.* Oxford and New York: Oxford University Press.

Glucksberg, Sam, and Boaz Keysar. 1990. Understanding Metaphorical Comparisons: Beyond Similarity. *Psychological Review* 97: 3–18.

———. 1993. How Metaphors Work. In *Metaphor and Thought,* edited by Andrew Ortony, pp. 401–24. 2d ed. Cambridge: Cambridge University Press.

Goatly, Andrew. 1997. *The Language of Metaphor.* London: Routledge.

Goldberg, Adele E. 1995. *Constructions.* Chicago: University of Chicago Press.

———., ed. 1996. *Conceptual Structure, Discourse and Language.* Stanford, CA: Center for the Study of Language and Information.

Goodman, Nelson. 1981. Metaphor as Moonlighting. In *Philosophical Perspectives on Metaphor,* edited by Mark Johnson, pp. 221–27. Minneapolis: University of Minnesota Press.

Goossens, L., P. Pauwels, B. Rudzka-Ostyn, A.-S. Simon-Vandenbergen, and J. Vanparys, eds. 1995. *By Word of Mouth: Metaphor, Metonymy and Linguistic Action in a Cognitive Perspective.* Amsterdam and Philadelphia: John Benjamins.

Grady, Joseph. 1997. Foundations of Meaning: Primary Metaphors and Primary Scenes. University of California, Berkeley, Ph.D. diss.

———. 1999. A Typology of Motivation for Conceptual Metaphor: Correlation vs. Resemblance. In *Metaphor in Cognitive Linguistics,* edited by Raymond W. Gibbs, Jr., and Gerard J. Steen, pp. 79–100. Amsterdam and Philadelphia: John Benjamins.

Grady, Joseph, Todd Oakley, and Seana Coulson. 1999. Blending and Metaphor. In *Metaphor in Cognitive Linguistics,* edited by Raymond W. Gibbs, Jr., and Gerard J. Steen, pp. 101–24. Amsterdam and Philadelphia: John Benjamins.

Grady, Joseph, Sarah Taub, and Pamela Morgan. 1996. Primitive and Compound Metaphors. In *Conceptual Structure, Discourse and Language,* edited by Adele E. Goldberg, pp. 177–87. Stanford, CA: Center for the Study of Language and Information.

Grice, H. P. 1975. Logic and Conversation. In *Syntax and Semantics 3: Speech Acts*, edited by P. Cole and J. L. Morgan, pp. 41–58. New York: Academic Press.

Gumperz, John J. 1982. *Discourse Strategies*. Studies in Interactional Sociolinguistics. Cambridge: Cambridge University Press.

———. 1990. Contextualization and Understanding. In *Rethinking Context*, edited by A. Duranti and Charles Goodwin. New York: Cambridge University Press.

———. 1992. Contextualization Revisited. In *The Contextualization of Language*, edited by Peter Auer and Aldo Di Luzio, pp. 39–53. Amsterdam: John Benjamins.

Gumperz, John J., and Stephen C. Levinson, eds. 1996. *Rethinking Linguistic Relativity*. Cambridge: Cambridge University Press.

Häcki-Buhofer Annelies. 2003. Psycholinguistik der lexikalischen Lebendigkeit: Phraseologismenkenntnis in verschiedenen Lebensaltern am Beispiel einiger schweizerdeutscher Phraseologismen. In *Spracherwerb und Lebensalter*, edited by Annelies Häcki Buhofer, pp. 279–92. Tübingen und Basel.

Häcki-Buhofer Annelies, and Harald Burger. 1992. Gehören Redewendungen zum heutigen Deutsch? *Fremdsprachen lehren und lernen* 21:11–32.

———. 1994. Phraseologismen im Urteil von Sprecherinnen und Sprechern. In *Europhras 92. Tendenzen der Phraseologieforschung, Studien zur Phraseologie und Parömiologie 1*, edited byBarbara Sandig, pp. 1–33. Bochum.

Hanks, Patrick. 2006. Metaphoricity Is Gradable. In *Corpus-Based Approaches to Metaphor and Metonymy*, edited by Anatol Stefanowitsch and Stefan Th. Giries, pp. 17–35. Berlin/New York: Mouton de Gruyter.

Hausmann, Carl R. 1989. *Metaphor and Art*. Cambridge: Cambridge University Press.

Haverkamp, Anselm, ed. 1983. *Theorie der Metapher*. Darmstadt: Wissenschaftliche Buchgesellschaft. Reprint 1996.

———. 1998a. Einleitung. In *Die paradoxe Metapher*, edited by Anselm Haverkamp, pp. 7–25. Frankfurt a.M.: Suhrkamp.

———., ed. 1998b. *Die paradoxe Metapher*. Frankfurt a.M.: Suhrkamp.

Heckhausen, Heinz. 1968. Die Metapher. In *Diskussion zu: Die Metapher*, edited by R. Harweg, H. Heckhausen, C. Heselhaus, U. Suerbaum, H. Weinrich, et al. *Poetica* 2: 100–30.

Henle, Paul. 1958. *Language, Thought, and Culture*. Ann Arbor: University of Michigan Press.

Humboldt, Wilhelm von. 1839. *Über die Kawi-Sprache auf der Insel Java, nebst einer Einleitung über die Verschiedenheit des menschlichen Sprachbaues*. Hrsg. J.K.E. Buschmann. Mit e. Vorw. v. Alexander von Humboldt. Berlin: Druckerei der Königlichen Preußischen Akademie der Wissenschaften.

———. 1985. *Über die Sprache. Ausgewählte Schriften*, selected and edited by Jürgen Trabant. München: DTV.

Jackendoff, Ray. 1992. *Languages of the Mind*. Cambridge: MIT Press.

———. 1996a. How Language Helps Us Think. *Pragmatics and Cognition* 4 (1): 1–34.

———. 1996b. Conceptual Semantics and Cognitive Semantics. *Cognitive Linguistics* 7: 93–129.

Jäkel, Olaf. 1999. Kant, Blumenberg, Weinrich: Some Forgotten Contributions to a Cognitive Theory of Metaphor. In *Metaphor in Cognitive Linguistics*, edited by Raymond Gibbs and Gerard Steen, pp. 9–27. Amsterdam, Philadelphia: John Benjamins.

Jastrow, Joseph. 1900. *Fact and Fable in Psychology*. New York: Houghton Mifflin.

Jaynes, Julian. 1976. *The Origin of Consciousness in the Breakdown of the Bicameral Mind*. Boston: Houghton Mifflin Co.

Johns, Bethany. 1984. Visual Metaphor: Lost and Found. *Semiotica* 52 (3/4): 291–333.

Johnson, Mark. 1981. *Philosophical Perspectives on Metaphor*. Minneapolis: University of Minnesota.

———. 1987. *The Body in the Mind. The Bodily Basis of Meaning, Imagination, and Reason*. Chicago and London: University of Chicago Press.

Kainz, Friedrich. 1972. *Über die Sprachverführung des Denkens*. Berlin: Duncker and Humblot.

Katz, Albert N. 1998. Figurative Language and Figurative Thought: A review. In *Figurative Language and Thought*, edited by Albert N. Katz, Cristina Cacciari, Raymond W. Gibbs, Jr., and Mark Turner, pp. 3–43. New York and Oxford: Oxford University Press.

Katz, Albert N., Cristina Cacciari, Raymond W. Gibbs, Jr., and Mark Turner. 1998. *Figurative Language and Thought*. New York and Oxford: Oxford University Press.

Kayser, Wolfgang. 1976. *Das sprachliche Kunstwerk. Eine Einführung in die Literaturwissenschaft*. 17th ed. Bern and Munich: Francke.

Kendon, Adam. 1995. Gesture as Illocutionary and Discourse Structure Markers in Southern Italian Conversation. *Journal of Pragmatics* 23: 247–79.

———. 2004. *Gesture: Visible Action as Utterance*. Cambridge: Cambridge University Press.

Kennedy, John. 1982. Metaphor in Pictures. *Perception* 11: 589–605.

Keysar, Boaz, and B. Bly. 1995. Intuitions of the Transparency of Idioms: Can You Keep a Secret by Spilling the Beans? *Journal of Memory and Language* 34: 89–109.

Keysar, Boaz, Y. Shen, S. Glucksberg, and W. S. Horton. 2000. Conventional Language: How Metaphorical Is It? *Journal of Memory and Language* 43: 576–93.

Kluge, Friedrich. 1975. *Etymologisches Wörterbuch*. Berlin: De Gruyter (first published in 1883).

Köhler, Wolfgang. 1947. *Gestalt Psychology. An Introduction to New Concepts in Modern Psychology*. New York: Liveright.

Köller, Wilhelm. 1975. *Semiotik und Metapher. Untersuchungen zur grammatischen Struktur und kommunikativen Funktion von Metaphern*. Stuttgart: J.B. Metzlersche Verlagsbuchhandlung.

———. 1986. Dimensionen des Metaphernproblems. *Zeitschrift für Semiotik* 4: 379–410.

Kövecses, Zoltán. 1986. *Metaphors of Anger, Pride, and Love: A Lexical Approach to the Study of Concepts.* Amsterdam and Philadelphia: John Benjamins.

———. 1988. *The Language of Love: The Semantics of Passion in Conversational English.* Lewisburg: Bucknell University Press.

———. 1990. *Emotion Concepts.* New York: Springer.

———. 2000a. *Metaphor and Emotion: Language, Culture and Body in Human Feeling.* Cambridge: Cambridge University Press.

———. 2000b. The Scope of Metaphor. In *Metaphor and Metonymy at the Crossroads,* edited byAntonio Barcelona, pp. 79–92. Berlin and New York: Mouton de Gruyter.

———. 2002. *Metaphor. A Practical Introduction.* Oxford: Oxford University Press.

Kubczak, Hartmut. 1978. *Die Metapher. Beiträge zur Interpretation und semantischen Struktur der Metapher auf der Basis einer referentialen Bedeutungsdefinition.* Heidelberg: Carl Winter.

Kurz, Gerhard. 1976. Theorie. In *Metapher. Theorie und Unterrichtsmodell,* edited by Gerhard Kurz and Theodor Pelster, pp. 7–98. Düsseldorf: Schwann.

———. 1982. *Metapher, Allegorie, Symbol.* Göttingen: Vandenhoeck and Ruprecht.

Kurz, Gerhard, and Theodor Pelster. 1976. *Metapher. Theorie und Unterrichtsmodell.* Düsseldorf: Schwann.

Kyratzis, Sakis. 2003. A New Metaphor for Metaphor. Evidence for a Single Dynamic Metaphorical Category. Unpublished manuscript.

Ladewig, Silva. In preparation. The Crank Gesture—Systematic Variation of Form and Context. In *Recurrence in Coverbal Gestures—Investigating Form and Function,* edited by Jana Bressem and Silva Ladewig. Amsterdam and Philadelphia: John Benjamins.

Lakoff, George. 1970. *Linguistics and Natural Logic.* Dordrecht: D. Reidel.

———. 1987. *Women, Fire, and Dangerous Things: What Categories Reveal about the Mind.* Chicago: University of Chicago Press.

———. 1990. The Invariance Hypothesis: Is Abstract Reason Based on Image-Schemas? *Cognitive Linguistics* 1: 39–74.

———. 1993. The Contemporary Theory of Metaphor. In *Metaphor and Thought,* edited by Andrew Ortony, pp. 202–51. Cambridge: Cambridge University Press.

———. 1996. The Metaphor System for Morality. In *Conceptual Structure, Discourse and Language,* edited by Adele E. Goldberg, pp. 249–66. Stanford, CA: Center for the Study of Language and Information.

———. 2002. *Moral Politics. How Liberals and Conservatives Think.* Chicago and London: University of Chicago Press (first published in 1996).

———. 2003. Afterword. In *Metaphors We Live By,* edited by George Lakoff and Mark Johnson, pp. 243–76. Chicago and London: Chicago University Press.

Lakoff, George, and Mark Johnson. 1980. *Metaphors We Live By.* Chicago and London: Chicago University Press.

———. 1999. *Philosophy in the Flesh.* New York: Basic Books.

Lakoff, George, and Zoltán Kövecses. 1987. The Cognitive Model of Anger Inherent in American English. In *Cultural Models in Language and Thought,* edited by Dorothy Holland and Naomi Quinn, pp. 195–221. Cambridge: Cambridge University Press.

Lakoff, George, and Rafael Núñez. 2000. *Where Mathematics Comes From. How the Embodied Mind Brings Mathematics into Being.* New York: Basic Books.

Lakoff, George, and Mark Turner. 1989. *More than Cool Reason. A Field Guide to Poetic Metaphors.* Chicago: Chicago University Press.

Lang, Ewald. 1994. Semantische vs. konzeptuelle Struktur: Unterscheidung und Überschneidung. In *Kognitive Semantik/Cognitive Semantics. Ergebnisse, Probleme, Perspektiven,* edited by Monika Schwarz, pp. 26–40. Tübingen: Narr.

Langacker, Ronald W. 1987. *Foundations of Cognitive Grammar.* Stanford: Stanford University Press.

———. 1988. An Overview of Cognitive Grammar. In *Topics in Cognitive Linguistics,* edited by Brygida Rudzja-Ostyn, pp. 3–48. Amsterdam /Philadelphia: John Benjamins.

———. 1991. *Concept, Image and Symbol. The Cognitive Basis of Grammar.* Berlin: De Gruyter.

———. 1996. A Constraint on Progressive Generics. In *Conceptual Structure, Discourse and Language,* edited by Adele E. Goldberg, pp. 249–66. Stanford, CA: Center for the Study of Language and Information.

———. 1998. Conceptualization, Symbolization, and Grammar. In *The New Psychology of Language: Cognitive and Functional Approaches to Language Structure,* edited by Michael Tomasello, pp. 1–39. Mahwah, NJ, and London: Erlbaum.

———. 1999a. *Grammar and Conceptualization.* Berlin and New York: Mouton de Gruyter.

———. 1999b. Assessing the Cognitive Linguistic Enterprise. In *Cognitive Linguistics: Foundations, Scope, and Methodology,* edited by Theo Janssen and Gisela Redeker, pp. 13–59. Berlin and New York: Mouton de Gruyter.

Langer, Susanne K. 1957. Philosophy in a New Key. A Study in the Symbolism of Reason, Rite, and Art. Cambridge, MA: Harvard University Press.

Lausberg Hedda, R. F. Cruz, S. Kita, E. Zaidel, and A. Ptito. 2003. Pantomime to Visual Presentation of Objects: Left Hand Dyspraxia in Patients with Complete Callosotomy. *Brain* 126: 343–60.

Lausberg, Heinrich. 1960. *Handbuch der literarischen Rhetorik. Eine Grundlegung der Literaturwissenschaft.* München: Max Hueber.

Levelt, Willem J. M. 1989. *Speaking. From Intention to Articulation.* Cambridge, MA: MIT Press.

———. 1999. Models of speech production. Review. *Trends in Cognitive Sciences* 3(6): 223–232.

Levelt, Willem J. M., Ardi Roelofs, and Antje S. Meyer. 1999. A Theory of Lexical Access in Speech Production. *Behavioral and Brain Sciences* 22: 1–75.

Levinson, Stephen C. 2003. *Space in Language and Cognition. Explorations in Cognitive Diversity.* Cambridge: Cambridge University Press.

Lieb, Hans Heinrich. 1964. Der Umfang des historischen Metaphernbegriffs. Unpublished diss., Köln.

———. 1983. Was bezeichnet der herkömmliche Begriff "Metapher"? In *Theorie der Metapher*, edited by Anselm Haverkamp, pp. 340–55. Darmstadt: Wissenschaftliche Buchgesellschaft. Reprint 1996.

———. 1981. Das "semiotische Dreieck" bei Ogden und Richards: Eine Neuformulierung des Zeichenmodells von Aristoteles. In *Logos semantikos. Studia linguistica in honorem Eugenio Coseriu 1921–1981*, edited by Jürgen Trabant, pp. 137–56. Vol. 1. *Geschichte der Sprachphilosophie und der Sprachwissenschaft*. Berlin: De Gruyter.

Liebert, Wolf Andreas. 1992. *Metaphernbereiche der deutschen Alltagssprache. Kognitive Linguistik und die Perspektiven einer Kognitiven Lexikographie.* Frankfurt a.M.: Peter Lang.

Lucy, John A. 1992a. *Language Diversity and Thought. A Reformulation of the Linguistic Relativity Hypothesis.* Cambridge: Cambridge University Press.

———. 1992b. *Grammatical Categories and Cognition. A Case Study of the Linguistic Relativity Hypothesis.* Cambridge: Cambridge University Press.

Lyons, John. 1977. *Semantics.* Vols. 1 and 2. Cambridge: Cambridge University Press.

de Man, Paul. 1978. The Epistemology of Metaphor. *Critical Inquiry* 5: 12–30.

Martin, Wallace. 1993. Metaphor. In *The New Princeton Encyclopedia of Poetry and Poetics*, edited by Alex Preminger and T.V.F. Brogan, pp. 760–66. Princeton: Princeton University Press.

McArthur, Tom, ed. 1992. *The Oxford Companion to the English Language.* Oxford: Oxford University Press.

McGlone, M. 1996. Conceptual Metaphors and Figurative Language Interpretation: Food for Thought? *Journal of Memory and Language* 35: 544–65.

McNeill, David. 1992. *Hand and Mind: What Gestures Reveal about Thought.* Chicago: University of Chicago Press.

———. 2006. *Gesture and Thought.* Chicago: University of Chicago Press.

McNeill, David, and Susan D. Duncan. 2000. Growth-Points in Thinking-for-Speaking. In *Language and Gesture*, edited by David McNeill. Cambridge: Cambridge University Press.

Meier, Hugo. 1963. *Die Metapher. Versuch einer zusammenfassenden Betrachtung ihrer linguistischen Merkmale.* Winterthur: Verlag P. G. Keller.

Metzger, Wolfgang. 1954. *Gesetze des Sehens.* Frankfurt a.M.: Kramer-Verlag.

Metzinger, Thomas, ed. 1996. *Bewußtsein. Beiträge aus der Gegenwartsphilosophie.* Paderborn: Schöningh.

Miller, George A. 1993. Images and Models, Similes and Metaphors. In *Metaphor and Thought*, edited by Andrew Ortony, pp. 357–400. 2d ed. Cambridge: Cambridge University Press.

Mitchell, W. J. Thomas. 1986. *Iconology: Image, Text, Ideology.* Chicago and London: University of Chicago Press.

———. 1994. *Picture Theory. Essays on Verbal and Visual Representation.* Chicago and London: University of Chicago Press.

Mithen, Steven. 1996. *The Prehistory of the Mind. The Cognitive Origins of Art, Religion and Science.* London: Thames and Hudson.

Mittelberg, Irene 2003. Making Grammar Visible: The Use of Metaphoric Gestures to Represent Grammatical Categories and Structures. In Proceedings of the First Congress of the International Society for Gesture Studies: Gesture—The Living Medium. University of Texas at Austin. http://www.utexas.edu/coc/cms/ International_House_of_Gestures/Conferences/Proceedings/Contributions.

———. 2006. *Metaphor and Metonymy in Language and Gesture: Discourse Evidence for Multimodal Models of Grammar.* Ph.D. diss., Cornell University.

———. Forthcoming. Peircean Semiotics Meets Conceptual Metaphor: Analyses of Gestural Representations of Grammar. In *Metaphor and Gesture,* edited by Cornelia Müller and Alan Cienki. Amsterdam and New York: John Benjamins.

Mittelberg, Irene, and Linda R. Waugh. Forthcoming. Multimodal Figures of Thought: A Cognitive-Semiotic Approach to Metaphor and Metonymy in Co-speech Gesture. In *Multimodal Metaphor,* edited by Charles Forceville and Eduardo Urios-Aparisi. Berlin/New York: Mouton de Gruyter.

Mooij, Jan Johann Albinn. 1976. *A Study of Metaphor. On the Nature of Metaphorical Expressions, with Special Reference to Their Reference.* Amsterdam, New York, and Oxford: North Holland Publishing Company.

Morris, Desmond. 1977. *Manwatching.* London: Jonathan Cape.

———. 1994. *Bodytalk: The Meaning of Human Gesture.* New York: Crown Trade.

Morris, Desmond, Peter Collett, Peter Marsh, and Mary O'Shaughnessy. 1979. *Gestures: Their Origins and Distribution.* London: Jonathan Cape.

Müller, Cornelia. 1998a. *Redebegleitende Gesten. Kulturgeschichte—Theorie—Sprachvergleich.* Berlin: Berlin Verlag Arno Spitz.

———. 1998b. Iconicity and gesture. In *Oralité et Gestualité: Communication Multimodale, Interaction,* edited by Serge Santi et al., pp. 321–28. Montréal, Paris: L'Harmattan.

———. 2000. Zeit als Raum. Eine kognitiv-semantische Mikroanalyse des sprachlichen und gestischen Ausdrucks von Aktionsarten. In *Botschaften verstehen. Kommunikationstheorie und Zeichenpraxis. Festschrift für Helmut Richter,* edited by Ernest W. B. Hess-Lüttich and H. Walter Schmitz, pp. 211–28. Frankfurt a.M.: Peter Lang.

———. 2003. Gestik als Lebenszeichen "toter Metaphern". Tote, schlafende und wache Metaphern. *Zeitschrift für Semiotik* 1–2: 61–72.

———. 2004. The Palm Up Open Hand. A Case of a Gesture Family? In *The Semantics and Pragmatics of Everyday Gestures. The Berlin conference,* edited by Cornelia Müller and Roland Posner, pp. 233–56. Berlin: Weidler Buchverlag.

————. 2007. A Dynamic View on Gesture, Language and Thought. In *Gesture and the Dynamic Dimension of Language. Essays in Honor of David McNeill*, edited by Susan D. Duncan, Justine Cassell and E. Levy, pp. 109–16. Amsterdam and Philadelphia: John Benjamins.

————. Forthcoming. What Gesture Reveals about the Nature of Metaphor. In *Metaphor and Gesture*, edited by Alan Cienki and Cornelia Müller. Amsterdam and Philadelphia: John Benjamins.

————. In preparation. Modes of Representation as Semiotic Devices in Gestures and Signs (of Signed Languages). *Gesture.*

Müller, Cornelia, and Alan Cienki. Forthcoming. When Speech and Gesture Come Together. Forms of Multimodal Metaphor in the Use of Spoken Language. In *Multimodal Metaphor*, edited by Charles Forceville and Eduardo Urios-Aparisi.

Müller, Cornelia, and Harald Haferland. 1997. Gefesselte Hände. Zur Semiose performativer Gesten. *Mitteilungen des Germanistenverbandes* 3:29–53.

Müller, Cornelia, Hedda Lausberg, Katja Liebal, and Ellen Fricke. In preparation. Gestural Modes of Representation or How Hands Turn into Gestures: Semiotic Structures, Neurological Foundations, and Evolutionary Implications.

Müller, Cornelia, and Gerald Speckman 2002. Gestos con una valoración negativa en la conversación cubana. *DeSignis 3*, pp. 91–103. Buenos Aires: Gedisa.

Murphy, G. L. 1996. On Metaphoric Representation. *Cognition* 60: 173–204.

————. 1997. Reasons to Doubt the Present Evidence for Metaphoric Representation. *Cognition* 62: 99–108.

Neumann, Ragnhild. 2004. The Conventionalization of the Ring Gesture in German Discourse. In *The Semantics and Pragmatics of Everyday Gestures. Proceedings of the Berlin Conference April 1998* edited by Cornelia Müller and Roland Posner. Berlin: Weidler Buchverlag.

Nuessel, Frank. 1991. Metaphor and Cognition: A Survey of Recent Publications. *Journal of Literary Semantics* 20: 37–52.

Núñez, Rafael, and Eve Sweetser. 2006. With the Future behind Them: Convergent Evidence from Aymara Language and Gesture in the Crosslinguistic Comparison of Spatial Construals of Time. *Cognitive Science* 30: 1–40.

Oksaar, Els. 1988. *Fachsprachliche Dimensionen.* Tübingen: Narr.

Ornstein, Robert E. 1977. *The Psychology of Consciousness.* New York: Harcourt Brace Jovanovich.

Ortony, Andrew, ed. 1979. *Metaphor and Thought.* 1st ed. Cambridge: Cambridge University Press.

————. 1988. Are Emotion Metaphors Conceptual or Lexical? *Cognition and Emotion* 2: 95–103.

————., ed. 1993a. *Metaphor and Thought.* 2d ed. Cambridge: Cambridge University Press.

————. 1993b. Metaphor, Language, and Thought. In *Metaphor and Thought*, edited by Andrew Ortony, pp. 1–16. 2d ed. Cambridge: Cambridge University Press.

Paivio, Allan, and Mary Walsh. 1993. Psychological Processes in Metaphor Comprehension and Memory. In *Metaphor and Thought*, edited by Andrew Ortony, pp. 307–28. 2d ed. Cambridge: Cambridge University Press.

Panther, Klaus-Uwe, and Günter Radden, eds. 1999. *Metonymy in Language and Thought*. Amsterdam and Philadelphia: John Benjamins.

Panther, Klaus-Uwe, and Linda L. Thornburg, eds. 2003. *Metonymy and Pragmatic Inferencing*. Amsterdam/Philadelphia: John Benjamins.

Pauen, Michael, and Gerhard Roth, eds. 2001. *Neurowissenschaften und Philosophie*. München: Wilhelm Fink Verlag.

Paul, Hermann. 1937. *Prinzipien der Sprachgeschichte*. Halle: Niemeyer (first published in 1886).

Pöppel, Ernst 2000. *Grenzen des Bewußtseins. Wie kommen wir zur Zeit, und wie entsteht Wirklichkeit?* Frankfurt a.M.: Insel Verlag.

Posner, Roland 2003. Everyday Gestures as a Result of Ritualization. In *Gestures. Meaning and Use*, edited by Monica Rector, Isabella Poggi, and Nadine Trigo, pp. 217–29. Porto: Universidade Fernando Pessoa.

PragglejazGroup. 2007. MIP: A Method for Identifying Metaphorically Used Words in Discourse. *Metaphor and Symbol* 22: 1–39.

Pylkkänen, Paavo, and Tere Vadén, eds. 2001. *Dimensions of Conscious Experience*. Amsterdam: John Benjamins.

Quinn, Naomi. 1999a. Research on Shared Task Solutions. In *A Cognitive Theory of Cultural Meaning*, edited by Claudia Strauss and Naomi Quinn, pp. 137–88. Cambridge: Cambridge University Press.

———. 1999b. Research on the Psychodynamics of Shared Understandings. (Ch 7). In Claudia Strauss and Naomi Quinn, eds. *A Cognitive Theory of Cultural Meaning*, edited by Claudia Strauss and Naomi Quinn, pp. 189–209. Cambridge: Cambridge University Press.

Quirk, Randolph, and Sidney Greenbaum. 1973. A University Grammar of English. London: Longman.

Reddy, Michael J. 1993. The Conduit Metaphor: A Case of a Frame Conflict in Our Language about Language. In *Metaphor and Thought*, edited by Andrew Ortony, pp. 164–201. 2d ed. Cambridge: Cambridge University Press.

Reiners, Ludwig. 1976. *Stilkunst. Ein Lehrbuch deutscher Prosa*. München: Beck.

Richards, Ivor Armstrong. 1936. *The Philosophy of Rhetoric*. New York: Oxford University Press.

Rickheit, Gert, and Hans Strohner 2003. Modelle der Sprachproduktion. In *Sprachproduktion (Enzyklopädie der Psychologie)*, edited by Theo Herrmann and Joachim Grabowski, pp. 265–86. Göttingen and Bern and Toronto and Seattle: Hogrefe.

Ricœur, Paul. 1986. *Die lebendige Metapher*. München: Wilhelm Fink.

Röhrich, Lutz. 1994. *Lexikon der sprichwörtlichen Redensarten*, Bd. 4. Freiburg and Basel and Wien: Herder.

Röhrich, Lutz, and Wolfgang Mieder. 1977. *Sprichwort*. Stuttgart: Metzler.

Rose, S. 1993. *The Making of Memory*. London: Transworld.

Sadock, Jerrold M. 1993. Figurative Speech and Linguistics. In *Metaphor and Thought*, edited by Andrew Ortony, pp. 42–57. 2d ed. Cambridge: Cambridge University Press.

Sapir, Edward. 1949. *Selected Writings of Edward Sapir in Language, Culture, and Personality*, edited by D. G. Mandelbaum. Berkley and Los Angeles: University of California Press.

Schank, Roger. 1982. *Dynamic Memory*. Cambridge: Cambridge University Press.

Schlegel, August Wilhelm. 1963. *Die Kunstlehre. Kritische Schriften und Briefe*, edited by E. Lohner. Stuttgart: Kohlhammer.

Schmidt, Lothar, ed. 1973. *Wortfeldforschung. Zur Geschichte und Theorie des sprachlichen Feldes*. Darmstadt: Wissenschaftliche Buchgesellschaft.

Schneider, Wolf. 1999. *Deutsch für Kenner. Die neue Stilkunde*. Hamburg: Piper (first published in 1996).

Schön, Donald A. 1993. Generative Metaphor: A Perspective on Problem-Setting in Social Policy. In *Metaphor and Thought*, edited by Andrew Ortony, pp. 137–73. 2d ed. Cambridge: Cambridge University Press.

Schriefers, Herbert 2003. Methodologische Probleme. In *Sprachproduktion (Enzyklopädie der Psychologie)*, edited by Theo Herrmann and Joachim Grabowski, pp. 3–26. Göttingen and Bern and Toronto and Seattle: Hogrefe.

Searle, John R. 1993. Metaphor. In *Metaphor and Thought*, edited by Andrew Ortony, pp. 83–111. 2d ed. Cambridge: Cambridge University Press.

Shibles, Warren. 1971. *Metaphor: An Annotated Bibliography and History*. Whitewater: Language Press.

———. 1972. *Essays on Metaphor*. Whitewater: Language Press.

Shore, Brad. 1996. *Culture in Mind: Meaning Construction and Cultural Cognition*. New York: Oxford University Press.

Slobin, Dan I. 1987. Thinking for Speaking. *Proceedings of the Thirteenth Annual Meeting of the Berkeley Linguistics Society*, 435–45.

———. 1991. Learning to Think for Speaking: Native Language, Cognition, and Rhetorical style. *Pragmatics* 1: 1–25.

———. 2000. Verbalized Events: A Dynamic Approach to Linguistic Relativity and Determinism. In *Evidence for linguistic relativity*, edited by Susanne Niemeier and René Dirven, pp. 107–38. Amsterdam: John Benjamins.

Slobin, Dan I., and Ruth A. Berman. 1994. *Relating Events in Narrative. A Crosslinguistic Developmental Study*. Hillsdale, NJ: Lawrence Erlbaum.

Sperber, Dan, and Deirdre Wilson. 1986. *Relevance. Communication and Cognition*. Oxford, UK, and Cambridge, MA: Blackwell.

Stählin, Wilhelm. 1914. *Zur Psychologie und Statistik der Metaphern. Eine methodologische Untersuchung*. Leipzig and Berlin: Verlag Wilhelm Engelmann.

Steen, Gerard J. 1994. *Understanding Metaphor in Literatire: An Empirical Approach*. London: Longman.

———. 1999. From Linguistic to Conceptual Metaphor in Five Steps. In *Metaphor in cognitive linguistics*, edited by Raymond W. Gibbs, Jr. and Gerard J. Steen, pp. 57–77. Amsterdam and Philadelphia: John Benjamins.

———. 2000. Metaphor and Language and Literature: A Cognitive Perspective. [Review article]. *Language and Literature* 9 (3): 261–77.

———. 2002a. Towards a Procedure for Metaphor Identification. *Language and Literature* 11 (1): 17–33.

———. 2002b. Identifying Metaphor in Language: A Cognitive Approach. *Style* 36 (3): 386–407.

———. 2006. Metaphor in Applied Linguistics: Four Cognitive Approaches. *Documentação de Estudos em Lingüística Teórica e Aplicada—D.E.L.T.A.* 22, (1): 21–44.

———. 2007a. Metaphor in Language and Thought: How Do We Map the Field? In *Converging and Diverging Tendencies in Cognitive Linguistics*, edited by Mario Brdar and Milena Zic Fuchs.

———. 2007b. *Finding Metaphor in Grammar and Usage: A Methodological Analysis of Theory and Research*. Amsterdam and Philadelphia: John Benjamins.

Steen, Gerard J., and Raymond W. Gibbs, Jr. 1999. Introduction. In *Metaphor in Cognitive Linguistics*, edited by Raymond W. Gibbs, Jr. and Gerard J. Steen, pp. 1–8. Amsterdam and Philadelphia: John Benjamins.

Stefanowitsch, Anatol, and Gries Stefan Th., eds. 2006. *Corpus-based Approaches to Metaphor and Metonymy*. Berlin and New York: Mouton De Gruyter.

Stern, Gustaf. 1931. *Meaning and Change of Meaning with Special Reference to the English Language*. Bloomington: Indiana University Press.

Sternberg, Robert J., Roger Tourangeau, and Georgia Nigro. 1993. Metaphor, Induction, and Social Policy: The Convergence of Macroscopic and Microsopic Views. In *Metaphor and Thought*, edited by Andrew Ortony, pp. 277–303. 2d ed. Cambridge: Cambridge University Press.

Stibbe, A. 1996. Metaphor and Alternative Conceptions of Illness. Unpublished Ph.D. diss. Lancaster University.

Sticht, Thomas G. 1993. Educational Uses of Metaphor. In *Metaphor and Thought*, edited by Andrew Ortony, pp. 621–32. 2d ed. Cambridge: Cambridge University Press.

Stock, O., J. Slack, and Andrew Ortony. 1993. Building Castles in the Air: Some Computational and Theoretical Issues in Idiom Comprehension. In *Idioms: Processing, Structure, and Interpretation*, edited by Cristina Cacciari and P. Tabossi. Hillsdale, NJ: Lawrence Erlbaum.

Stöckl, Hartmut. 2004. *Die Sprache im Bild—Das Bild in der Sprache. Zur Verknüpfung von Sprache und Bild im massenmedialen Text. Konzepte—Theorien—Analysemethoden*. Berlin and New York: De Gruyter.

Störel, Thomas. 1997. *Metaphorik im Fach. Bildfelder in der musikwissenschaftlichen Kommunikation*. Tübingen: Günter Narr.

Streeck, Jürgen. 1988. The Significance of Gesture: How It Is Achieved. *Papers in Pragmatics* 2: 60–83.

———. 1993. Gesture as Communication 1: Its Coordination with Gaze and Speech. *Communication Monographs* 60 (4): 275–99.

———. 1994. "Speech-Handling": The Metaphorical Representation of Speech in Gestures. A Cross-Cultural Study. Austin, TX. Unpublished manuscript.

Sweetser, Eve. 1990. *From Etymology to Pragmatics. Metaphorical and Cultural Aspects of Semantic Structure.* Cambridge: Cambridge University Press.

———. 1996. Mental Spaces and the Grammar of Conditional Constructions. In *Spaces, Worlds, and Grammar,* edited by Gilles Fauconnier and Eve Sweetser, pp. 318–33. Chicago and London: University of Chicago Press.

———. 1999. Regular Metaphoricity in Gesture: Bodily-Based Models of Speech Interaction. In CD-ROM *Proceedings of the 16th International Congress of Linguists,* held in Paris in July 1997.

Tag, Susanne. In preparation. Combinational Patterns in Coverbal Gesture Complexes. In *Recurrence in Coverbal Gestures—Investigating Form and Function,* edited by Jana Bressem and Silva Ladewig. Amsterdam and Philadelphia: John Benjamins.

Talmy, Leonard. 1975. Semantics and Syntax of Motion. In *Syntax and Semantics,* edited by John P. Kimball, pp. 181–238. Vol. 4. New York: Academic Press.

———. 1978. Figure and Ground in Complex Sentences. In *Universals of Human Language,* edited by Joseph Greenberg, Charles Ferguson, and Edith Moravcsik, pp. 625–49. Vol. 4. Stanford: Stanford University Press.

———. 1985. Lexicalization Patterns: Semantic Structure in Lexical Forms. In *Grammatical Categories and the Lexicon, Vol. III. Language Typology and Syntactic Description,* edited by Timothy Shopen, pp. 57–149. Cambridge: Cambridge University Press.

———. 1987. Lexicalization Patterns: Typologies and Universals. *Cognitive Science Program Report* 47: 1–9. Berkeley: University of California.

———. 1991. Path to Realization: A Typology of Event Conflation. *Proceedings of the 17th Annual Meeting of the Berkeley Linguistics Society,* pp. 1–40. Berkeley: University of California.

———. 1994. How Grammar Structures Concepts. Unpublished manuscript.

———. 2003. *The Attentional System of Language.* Cambridge: MIT Press.

Tarski, Alfred. 1935. Der Wahrheitsbegriff in den formalisierten Sprachen. *Studia Philosophica* 1, 261–405 (English translation in Tarski 1956).

Tessendorf, Sedinha. In preparation. Research in Recurrent Coverbal Gestures: The Case of the Spanish "Brushing Aside Gesture." *Recurrence in Coverbal Gestures—Investigating Form and Function,* edited by Jana Bressem and Silva Ladewig. Amsterdam and Philadelphia: John Benjamins.

Trabant, Jürgen. 1985a. Nachwort. In *Über die Sprache. Ausgewählte Schriften,* edited by Wilhelm von Humboldt, pp. 159–74. München: DTV.

———. 1985b. Zur Textauswahl. In *Über die Sprache. Ausgewählte Schriften*, edited by Wilhelm von Humboldt, pp. 175–77. München: DTV.

———. 1989. *Zeichen des Menschen. Elemente der Semiotik.* Frankfurt a.m.: Fischer.

———. 1994. *Neue Wissenschaft von alten Zeichen: Vicos Sematologie.* Frankfurt a.m.: Suhrkamp.

Trier, Jost. 1931. Über Wort- und Begriffsfelder. In *Der deutsche Wortschatz im Sinnbezirk des Verstandes. Die Geschichte eines sprachlichen Feldes*, edited by Jost Trier. Bd. I: Von den Anfängen bis zum Beginn des 13. Jhd. Heidelberg: Carl Winter (republished in Lothar Schmidt, ed., 1973, *Wortfeldforschung. Zur Geschichte und Theorie des sprachlichen Feldes*, pp. 1–38, Darmstadt: Wissenschaftliche Buchgesellschaft).

———. 1934a. Deutsche Bedeutungsforschung. In *Germanische Philologie. Ergebnisse und Aufgaben, Festschrift für Otto Behaghel*, edited by Alfred Goetze, Wilhelm Horn, and Freidrich Maurer. Heidelberg: Carl Winter (republished in Lothar Schmidt, ed., 1973, *Wortfeldforschung. Zur Geschichte und Theorie des sprachlichen Feldes*, pp. 116–29, Darmstadt: Wissenschaftliche Buchgesellschaft).

———. 1934b. Das sprachliche Feld. Eine Auseinandersetzung. *Neue Jahrbücher für Wissenschaft und Jugendbildung* 10, 428–49 (republished in Lothar Schmidt, ed., 1973, *Wortfeldforschung. Zur Geschichte und Theorie des sprachlichen Feldes*, pp. 129–62, Darmstadt: Wissenschaftliche Buchgesellschaft).

———. 1938. Über die Erforschung des menschenkundlichen Wortschatzes. In *Actes du Ive congrès international de linguistes* (Kopenhagen 1936) (pp. 92—98. Kopenhagen: Munksgaard (republished in Lothar Schmidt, ed., 1973, *Wortfeldforschung. Zur Geschichte und Theorie des sprachlichen Feldes*, pp. 185–92, Darmstadt: Wissenschaftliche Buchgesellschaft).

———. 1968. Altes und neues vom sprachlichen Feld. In Duden-Beiträge zur Fragen der Rechtschreibung, der Grammatik und des Stils, Heft 34 (pp. 9–20). Mannheim and Zürich: Dudenverlag des Bibliographischen Instituts. (republished in Lothar Schmidt, ed., 1973, *Wortfeldforschung. Zur Geschichte und Theorie des sprachlichen Feldes*, pp. 453–64, Darmstadt: Wissenschaftliche Buchgesellschaft).

Turner, Mark, and Gilles Fauconnier. 1995. Conceptual Integration and Formal Expression. *Journal of Metaphor and Symbolic Activity* 10 (3): 183–204.

Ueding, Gert, ed. 1998. *Historisches Wörterbuch der Rhetorik.* Tübingen: Niemeyer.

Ullmann, Stephen. 1967. *Semantics. An introduction to the science of meaning.* Oxford: Blackwell (first published in 1962).

van Noppen, Jean-Pierre. 1985. *Metaphor: A Bibliography of post-1970 Publications.* Amsterdam and Philadelphia: John Benjamins.

van Noppen, Jean-Pierre, and Edith Hols. 1990. *Metaphor II: A Classified Bibliography of Publications, 1985–1990.* Amsterdam and Philadelphia: John Benjamins.

van Dijk, Teun. 1975. Formal Semantics of Metaphorical Discourse. *Poetics* 4: 173–98.

Weinrich, Harald. 1958. Münze und Wort. Untersuchungen an einem Bildfeld. In *Romanica: Festschrift für Gerhard Rohlfs*, pp. 508–21. Halle: Max Niemeyer.

———. 1963. Semantik der kühnen Metapher. *Deutsche Vierteljahresschrift für Literaturwissenschaft und Geistesgeschichte* 37: 325–44.

———. 1964. Typen der Gedächtnismetaphorik. *Archiv für Begriffsgeschichte* 9: 96–104.

———. 1967. Semantik der Metapher. *Folia Linguistica* 1: 3–17.

———. 1976. *Sprache in Texten.* Stuttgart: Ernst Klett Verlag.

———. 1982. *Textgrammatik der französischen Sprache.* Stuttgart: Klett.

Wertheimer, Max. 1923. Untersuchungen zur Lehre von der Gestalt II. *Psychologische Forschung* 4: 301–50.

White, Roger M. 1996. *The Structure of Metaphor: The Way the Language of Metaphor Works.* Oxford: Blackwell.

Whitehead, Alfred N. 1927. *Symbolism. Its meaning and Effects.* New York: Fordham University Press.

Whittock, Trevor. 1990. *Metaphor and Film.* Cambridge: Cambridge University Press.

Whorf, Benjamin Lee. 1956. *Language, Thought, and Reality.* Massachusetts: MIT Press.

Winner, Ellen, and Howard Gardner. 1993. Metaphor and Irony: Two Levels of Understanding. In *Metaphor and Thought*, edited by Andrew Ortony, pp. 425–43. 2d ed. Cambridge: Cambridge University Press.

Wittgenstein, Ludwig. 1958. *Philosophical Investigations.* Translated by G. E. M. Anscombe. Oxford: Oxford University Press.

———. 1953. *Philosophische Untersuchungen.* In *Werkausgabe*, edited by Ludwig Wittgenstein, pp. 225–618. Bd. 1. Frankfurt a.M.: Suhrkamp (reprint 1984).

Wollheim, Richard. 1987. Painting, Metaphor, and the Body: Titian, Bellini, De Kooning, etc. In *Painting as an Art*, edited by Richard Wollheim, pp. 305–57). Princeton, NJ: Princeton University Press.

Wundt, Wilhelm. 1922. *Völkerpsychologie. Eine Untersuchung der Entwicklungsgesetze von Sprache, Mythus und Sitte. Bd. 2: Die Sprache.* Leipzig: Alfred Kröner Verlag.

Wustmann, Gustav. 1943. *Sprachdummheiten.* Berlin: De Gruyter (first published in 1893).

NAME INDEX

SUBJECT INDEX